Racial Competition and
Class Solidarity

Contents

Acknowledgments

This is a truly collaborative project. In addition to substantive contributions from all four co-authors, we have benefited from the guidance and support of numerous colleagues at Emory University, Floyd State College, Skidmore College, University of New Hampshire, and other institutions. For critique of and help with specific parts of this project, we are grateful to Dan Cornfield, Jennifer Delton, Michael Goldfield, Larry Griffin, Douglas Heckathorn, Herbert Hill, Jeffrey Leiter, Rory McVeigh, Joya Misra, Vinnie Roscigno, Mason Stokes, and Kathryn Ward. Thanks to Judy Margo for her research assistance. We are especially appreciative of all the encouragement and insight offered by our colleague and friend Edgar Kiser.

For their help with various phases of our research, we wish to also thank Frank Zabrosky of the University of Pittsburgh's Archives of Industrial Society, Ray Boryczka of the Walter P. Reuther Library at Wayne State University, Linda Shopes and Linda Ries of the Pennsylvania Historical Museum Commission, the staff of the Southern Labor Archives at George State University, and the staff of the Lucy Scribner Library of Skidmore College.

CHAPTER 1

Introduction

Race has a special power in American history. Racial divisions are woven deeply into the nation's social fabric, and egalitarian ideals have never been sufficient to ensure their eradication. For black Americans, the Civil War brought slavery to an end only to usher in an era of Jim Crow laws, pervasive racism, lynching, and rigid codes of racial etiquette. When World War I sparked the Great Migration and thousands of blacks moved from field to factory, racial inequality was recast in an urban, industrial context. For the Chinese, a wave of hostility crested in 1882 and induced Congress to end the nation's tradition of open immigration. The Chinese Exclusion Act was the first of many immigration restrictions targeting citizens of Asian countries, and the internment of Japanese Americans during World War II represented an extension of these discriminatory policies. These and other examples demonstrate how the architecture of racial inequality was reconstituted rather than dismantled in the decades following the Civil War. Although the forms of racial injustice embodied in law and custom varied regionally and evolved over time, it took nearly a century before the most egregious manifestations of discrimination—in voting, education, public accommodations, and employment—became the focus of concerted federal action.

Class conflict has been pervasive since the nation's founding. In countless instances it has intersected and even infused the processes of racial inequality and conflict alluded to above. As workers battled collectively to secure decent wages, safe working conditions, and even the right to unionize, the contours of their struggle were frequently etched

1

in racial terms. Eligibility for union membership often stopped at the color line, which was particularly true in the nineteenth century, during the Progressive Era, and into the 1930s. As the labor movement gained ground during the New Deal years and beyond, its membership policies became increasingly progressive, but in practice, unions continued to reinforce white privilege. Given the historical salience of race and class prior to the Civil Rights Movement, when were people able to pursue common objectives across racial lines? How did different groups balance the frequently competing imperatives of class and racial identity? What factors promoted interracial cooperation, and what are the implications for improving race relations in the future?

This book examines how race influenced the trajectory of the American labor movement between the 1850s and the 1950s, a period that witnessed profound changes in work, labor markets, and politics. Cycles of discrimination, hostility, and distrust shaped race relations among U.S. workers. Even as workers confronted employers demanding better wages and working conditions, racial antagonism often divided workers' interests and loyalties. There were, however, rare moments during which cooperation and coordinated action replaced racial animus. Despite palpable legacies of racial conflict and discrimination, workers were occasionally able to forge interracial coalitions, often as class conflict escalated. Though they were generally limited or fleeting, there is much to be learned from instances of solidarity. This book considers how and why those moments emerged.

GENERAL THEORETICAL QUESTIONS

A unified theory of race relations should explain both conflict and solidarity, the Janus faces of racial interaction. But the lure of drama in history and the analytical separation of topics in sociology have compartmentalized theorizing about these countervailing processes. Interracial conflict, particularly between black and white workers, has long been a source of working-class division, but its impact and prevalence has obscured instances of interracial solidarity in historical research. Because racial divisions have been significant for the failure of particular strikes, sociological analyses have also been overly focused on racial conflict. As a result, theories of ethnic and racial antagonism fail to explain why and when workers overcome an environment of racism to achieve stable, interracial unionism.

General theories of racial competition, including the split labor market variant that informs our analysis, reflect this conceptual underdevelopment (Bonacich 1972; Wilson 1978; Marks 1981; Boswell 1986). The split labor market approach analyzes how workers' wages, resources, and motives are linked to ethnicity and race (we focus exclusively on race). As racial groups' labor market positions become more divergent, the potential for competition and conflict increases. The theory has helped to explain how and why workers' labor market positions may be influenced by race, and in turn, how these differences affect the dynamics of job competition and union organizing (see Bonacich 1975, 1976; Bonacich and Cheng 1984; Hilton 1979; Christiansen 1979; Makabe 1981; Boswell 1986; Peled and Shafir 1987). However, split labor market research has focused on minority strikebreaking and subsequent racial antagonism, and sojourning migration was central to the explanation.[1] Seldom have split labor market studies concentrated on solidarity (Brown and Boswell 1995), and few studies have compared cases (Boswell and Jorjani 1988) to assess the factors that contribute to strikebreaking versus solidarity.

Given the accumulation of separate case studies, a comparative approach to split labor markets is long overdue. This study examines solidarity versus strikebreaking by comparing cases of union organizing drives in particular industries. Because our goal is not merely to demonstrate the theory but to expand and refine it, we address a number of specific issues and questions about the theory in the next chapter. We do not argue that class and race may *only* intersect in labor market configurations. Split labor market theory takes a preexisting level of racism as an historical given. For all our cases, noneconomic factors as well as labor market considerations influenced interracial dynamics among workers (see Frederickson 2002). However, we also duly note where, and under what conditions, workers have been active agents in the construction of racism, rather than solely focusing on the results of white worker "privilege" (Roediger 1991, p. 10, 1994). As Sugrue (1996, p. 393) suggests, we seek to identify the reasons white workers draw on racist ideologies in one situation and pursue interracial solidarity in another. Our goal is to explain why and when racism may appear to be a rational response to competition and conflict. We do not discount the ideological or cultural salience of "felt" racism. Racial attitudes are resilient and may transcend processes of urbanization, bureaucratization, industrialization, or political mobilization (Allen 1994; Hill 1968, 1996,

1998; Goldfield 1997; Lamont 2000). At the same time, however, our work considers class formation and class struggle to be mechanisms through which racial competition and racism are created, regenerated, and maintained (Greenberg 1980; Saxton 1990).

We acknowledge that the experience and meaning of "solidarity" are not necessarily simple or straightforward. Workers may join interracial unions without ever feeling solidarity across racial lines, much less becoming integrated in their families and friendships. Rank and file workers often hold racist beliefs, yet still decide to support interracial organizing and integrated unions because it is in their interests. And, union organizations may actively support interracial solidarity, even if their members do not. We would argue that interracial unions are necessary for class solidarity; they break cycles of racial competition and conflict. By evening labor costs and thus narrowing the racial split in the labor market, interracial alliances offer an alternative to competition.

Split labor market theory focuses specifically on minority motives and the degree to which political resources (e.g., rights of citizenship and electoral representation) and economic resources (e.g., wages and living expenses) converge in the labor market. A divergence in political and economic resources between racial groups increases the likelihood of minority strikebreaking; sojourners or other highly mobile minorities will be especially difficult to organize. Does the logic of competition apply in the converse? As articulated by Bonacich and others, the unstated assumption of past research is that the absence of a split labor market explains interracial solidarity. This assumption results in part from the primacy of sojourning migration in the theory. Bonacich (1972, 1975, 1976), Wilson (1978), and others fail to consider instances when minority strikebreaking took place without sojourning. Is it the case, then, that interracial solidarity is most likely when few minority workers are sojourners? Or, is sojourning secondary to other factors? Past research has not explored whether other factors are necessary for interracial union solidarity aside from an absence of sojourning. In addition, the effects of sojourning migration (or its equivalent) need to be untangled from other important political and ideological factors that condition labor relations. For instance, repression by the militia raises the costs of labor activity, legislation can empower workers by granting them new rights, employer benevolence may increase workers' loyalty, and racially progressive union policies can be important for bridging racial divisions. We examine the impact of state repression and legislation on union efficacy and the institutionalization of racial ideologies in the form of employer paternalism and union policies.

We explain these factors in detail in the next chapter, but here we should mention several additional questions that we will address in the course of the book. First, when do dominant workers and unions actively discriminate against racial minorities? Racial prejudice and individual acts of discrimination were common, but large-scale racial conflict came in waves, with only scattered events interceding. Explaining when racial antagonism flares has been a standard focus of split labor market analysis, which, we will see, applies here as well, but what factors led dominant unions to pursue strategies of interracial solidarity? We examine the circumstances that led union leaders to institutionalize strategies of interracial organizing in specific cases. Unlike craft unions that can limit membership to skilled workers, industrial unions attempted to organize the entire work force, including less skilled labor that could be replaced by excluded minorities. Industrial unions typically included statements affirming nondiscrimination, yet they often did little to counter discrimination and some faced strikebreaking by minorities. In spite of the obvious benefits, labor leaders repeatedly encountered difficulty in forging interracial coalitions. The exceptions were often radical, short-lived unions, such as the Industrial Workers of the World or the National Miners Union. Consistent success, we will find, came from tactical innovations in organizing, driven by past failures, and copied from defunct radical unions. What they literally called a "formula" of proto-affirmative action proved necessary (although not sufficient) for success. This formula remains a guide for organizing today.

We must ask not only when do white workers pursue racial inclusion, but also when do minority workers look past white racism to join in class solidarity? If the "formula" was not sufficient, why did it fail? Many of the same variables that encourage white workers to support unions also condition the extent of allegiance among racial minorities. We will also identify particular sources of minority participation, such as labor costs, stable residence in a community, and relations with employers. And in a final twist, while our theories assume that minority solidarity with dominant workers would enhance the prospects of union victory, we must explain the case of postwar southern textiles, where an inclusive union met with defeat.

A final question is, When do employers discriminate? Racial competition theories posit a relatively passive role for employers, who will hire the cheapest workers possible (holding skill constant) to minimize labor costs. In this view, employers do not discriminate or consciously maintain a reserve army of minority labor. Employers may be racist, but those who discriminate would have to pay higher wages and have fewer workers to choose from, especially during a strike. Past versions of the theory consider discrimination in the workplace solely as the outgrowth of intra-class struggles between dominant and minority labor. However, it is clear that in some of our cases employers did actively engage in discriminatory policies. In the later chapters, we address how and when employers discriminated and how they avoided the costs of their racism.

JUSTIFICATION OF CASES

"If the new Committee for Industrial Organization follows the pattern of the United Mine Workers of America—and there seems no reason to doubt that it will—in the matter of the color line in labor, then Negro workers ought to flock to the CIO unhesitatingly, for the UMW are known far and wide for their absolute equality, regardless of color" (*Crisis* 1936, quoted in Foner and Lewis 1981, p. 339). In the 1930s, leaders of the United Mine Workers of America (UMW) and the Congress of Industrial Organizations (CIO) took a number of unprecedented steps to recruit black workers. In so doing, they earned this extraordinary endorsement in the NAACP's publication *Crisis*. A series of political and economic factors converged that made such a strategy plausible and effective. Having learned from successes and failures in other organizing drives, industrial union leaders understood the special circumstances of the 1930s.

"The President wants you to join the union!" In 1933 John L. Lewis urged mineworkers through the narrow window of political opportunity provided by the Roosevelt administration's ambivalent backing of industrial labor. In the case of bituminous coal mining, the New Deal's support went beyond the symbolic encouragement that the National Industrial Recovery Act signified to workers in most industries. At the same time, black out-migration from the South abated during the Depression, which helped to stabilize the workforce, and more significantly, aligned interests among black and white mineworkers who increasingly shared dissatisfaction with their treatment at the hands of coal operators.

As the circumstances changed, the UMW, led by Lewis, adopted bold new organizing strategies that were specifically oriented toward the recruitment of black mineworkers. For more than a decade the use of black strikebreakers had consistently undermined organizing efforts and reproduced interracial worker antagonism. Thus, the UMW's new tactics, which were borrowed from the more radical but marginal National Miners Union, signified a turning point in the industrial union movement. As "the last hired, first fired," black mineworkers harbored no particular loyalty to coal operators, but a decade of empty rhetoric and racist hostility on the part of white-dominated unions had generated distrust on that front as well.

The crucial tactical innovation was the integration of black unionists into the leadership structure of local unions. According to the "miners' formula," a forerunner to affirmative action, the unions systematically used black organizers and union executives to convince black workers of their sincerity (Nyden 1977). After a long organizing drive through-out the summer of 1933, the UMW won recognition and favorable contracts in the fall of that year, and thereby provided the inspiration and strategic template for interracial organizing campaigns of industrial workers throughout the decade. Confronting similarly difficult chal-lenges and unlikely odds, steel and auto workers subsequently employed variants of the strategy and met with comparable success.

Each of these cases is part of a larger narrative linked to the history of the Congress of Industrial Organizations. CIO unions in all three industries overcame both white racism and black strikebreaking to forge a stable interracial solidarity based on the common interests of workers. This narrative encompasses six union drives, two each in the coal, steel, and auto industries. The first drive for each union was defeated in part because of racial division. The second drive was won in equal proportion because the union institutionalized its rhetoric about racial equality in the miners' formula (Foner 1974, p. 218; Brueggemann and Boswell 1998). The formula worked. However ex-aggerated the NAACP's favorable assessment of the CIO in 1936, those original industrial unions remain today among the country's most in-tegrated institutions and most powerful advocates for racial equality and common class interests.

Powerful and ruthless employers, indifferent or hostile government, deep-seated interracial antagonism, and material vulnerability among workers in the coal, steel, and auto industries made these successes extraordinary. These cases stand in stark contrast to the more typical instances of interracial hostility that characterize much of American labor history. In 1869, for example, some four hundred white silver miners in Comstock, Nevada, attacked Chinese workers and ran them out of the district. The miners, all men and all white, feared that the mine owners would hire the Chinese workers, who would soon be laid off from the nearly complete railway. In an area of the country where just about everybody was from some place else, they considered the Chinese permanent foreigners. And in a time when unions were rare, racist antagonism against the Chinese united the miners like nothing before. The white miners knew that Chinese wages were one-third their own. They also knew that those low wages were worth a fortune in China, where most of the sojourning Chinese would soon return. Miners, however, were hard to replace and they were fierce about sticking together. No Chinese worked underground in Comstock (Lingenfelter 1974, pp. 114–16).

"The Great Steel Strike" of 1919 produced similar results but under different circumstances. As had been the case decades earlier with Chinese workers on the West Coast, this is a story of minority migrants, this time poor southern blacks seeking a better life, pitted against dominant unions trying to prevent a decline in their wages. But in this strike, strategies of both exclusion and integration failed. Although some union locals actively encouraged black membership, most discriminated. Northern industrial labor markets were swelled by returning American soldiers and thousands of blacks who sought refuge from the poverty and racial oppression of the South. In this context, most blacks allied themselves with employers rather than support a strike led by the craft-oriented and generally conservative American Federation of Labor (AFL). The widespread use of black strikebreakers from the South helped defeat the union, and ongoing racial antagonism weakened the labor movement for more than a decade.

Move forward in history to 1948 and we find a dramatically different set of actions and results: minorities support the union while white workers defect; the union preaches integration and the employers practice discrimination. While all involved were citizens and none were sojourning migrants, none of this prevented one of the biggest defeats in U.S. labor history. The union in that case was the CIO itself, which launched "Operation Dixie," the biggest drive to date, to organize the textiles and other industries of the modernizing "New South." The minorities were poor southern blacks who "blessed the CIO" for what it could bring. The dominant workers were poor southern whites who blessed their employers for what they had (Griffith 1988; Goldfield 1994).

Although they comprised different sets of historical circumstances, the cases of Comstock, the Great Steel Strike, and Operation Dixie are similar in their outcomes, all of which provide a striking contrast to the more unusual CIO drives of the 1930s. The historical rarity of cases that parallel the progressivism of the New Deal–era industrial drives partly accounts for the neglect of interracial solidarity in theories dealing with race and collective action. However, the comparison of multiple cases is the key to understanding the range of labor outcomes that obtained prior to the Civil Rights Movement. The success of the early CIO efforts reflects the effectiveness of specifically defined affirmative action programs in combination with other favorable conditions. Yet because CIO unions subsequently failed to breach racist paternalism in the South, mass unionization remained weak in a region that grew proportionally in terms of jobs, population, and political influence. How best to realize interracial solidarity is still a burning question for the U.S. labor movement and for American society.

Each of these organizing drives deals with a pivotal episode in the history of race and labor relations. We use these cases to test deductive propositions and to construct inductive generalizations for a competition theory of racial conflict and class solidarity.

SCOPE CONDITIONS

In subsequent chapters, we examine the patterns of race relations that accompanied nine individual labor organizing drives and associated strikes from 1869 to 1952 in U.S. history. The cases are bracketed, more or less, by the Civil War and the Civil Rights Movement, each of which brought a qualitative shift in race relations. The choice of scope conditions is always theoretically significant. Our choice is relevant for two theoretical reasons, one historical and the other analytical.

Historically, the social structure, political environment, and "taken-for-granted" ideological presumptions of actors start to shift noticeably at the margins of our time period. Delineating the period between such shifts allows for a guileless comparability of cases. Within this time frame, "all else equal" is a relatively unchallenged and reasonable assumption, though some will always assail a scope as too wide. Wilson's (1978) influential book on race relations describes our period as one where split labor market dynamics are the dominant determinants of race relations, in contrast to caste and class dynamics before and after. For labor relations, the usual turning points are 1881, with the rise of the AFL, and the 1950s, which witnessed the AFL-CIO merger. Relative stability and then decline follow (Goldfield 1987; Foner 1988; Rayback 1966). We are perhaps entering a new period as the current AFL-CIO leadership is trying to revitalize the labor movement, drawing in some ways on lessons of interracial organizing learned during the earlier period. Our relatively early starting point introduces the risk that our first case may not be fully comparable to the others, as mass production had yet to become commonplace. However, we feel that this risk is acceptable given the industrial nature of mining by the 1860s, and, we think, outweighed by the benefits of including the Chinese case.

Each case was selected for its historic impact on the labor movement and race relations. These were pivotal cases, we find, because they provided models that many others followed. We limit the comparison to large and lasting industrial unions so as to focus on racial distinctions that are not heavily confounded with skill differences. Industrial unions were the most powerful and lasting in mining, and we draw three cases from that industry. Discrimination against Chinese immigrants in the western states between 1850–82 reveals the impact of international sojourning migration on racial competition during the origins of the U.S. labor movement. The surge of racial violence by miners in the late 1860s kept Chinese workers out of the underground mines throughout the West. It also contributed to the passage of the 1882 Exclusion Act, which prohibited further Chinese immigration. In addition, such violence aided the resurgence of the pro-exclusion Democratic Party among the white working class (Saxton 1990).

The Great Steel strike of 1919 was one of the largest and most important of a series of post–World War I class conflicts that employers broke by importing black strikebreakers. It was coincident with race riots and other conflicts that established the tenor of race relations in northern industrial centers. The failure of the 1919 steel strike was symbolic of the decline in organized labor that would occur during the 1920s, a decline largely attributable to the political power of employers and owners as well as internal divisions in the ranks of labor. Due to the large-scale migration of rural, southern blacks to the industrial cities of the North, this period initiated a new phase of race relations within the labor movement. Prior to that time, with some exceptions such as the Chinese in California, racial conflict was not woven into the dynamics of labor organizing as blacks were largely confined to southern agriculture.

Perhaps the most obvious cases to include for this study are the mass production organizing drives of the CIO in the 1930s and early 1940s (see Goldfield 1998). After the AFL failed to build an industrial union in the steel industry, the United Mine Workers became the progenitor of the CIO. That the CIO managed to organize across racial lines on a massive scale made possible a union movement that could take advantage of the New Deal and which could muster the resources to support it. As example and as advocate, the CIO unions sparked and fueled nearly every major move toward racial integration thereafter (despite burning less brightly during the early Civil Rights Movement, Draper 1994; Hill 1996).[2]

In the South, industrialization incorporated black labor alongside whites in some cases, notably timber, longshoremen, or coal. There was even successful unionization of blacks and whites by the UMW (and earlier by the Knights of Labor). But textiles, the South's largest industry from 1865 through the 1960s, employed a highly segregated workforce. Whites held the vast majority of operative positions. Blacks, if hired at all, held menial positions and served as an obvious and threatening "reserve army" (McLaurin 1978; Rachleff 1984). This is the industry that counted the most when interracial unionization failed during Operation Dixie, our last case.

The failure of the CIO's Operation Dixie to overcome racial division in the postwar South's dominant industry diminished those gains. The case of Operation Dixie extends our analysis past the end of World War II, into the early 1950s. It illustrates the extent to which labor failed to consolidate the gains made during the New Deal era into lasting and pervasive industrial mobilization. Thus, the failure of Operation Dixie limited future union expansion and greatly contributed to a relative decline that subsequent amelioration of race relations in the South has not reversed (Goldfield 1994). The case also underscores the particular difficulties faced by labor organizers fighting the southern institution of racist paternalism maintained by employers. Especially interesting is that minority workers were more favorably disposed to labor organizing than their white counterparts, who more often sided with their employers.

Of course, there were many other major events in labor history in which race did not play a central part. Haymarket and Homestead come to mind, as do Pullman, Patterson, and, more recently, PATCO (Gordon 1964, 1978, 1981; Dunbar 1981; Clawson and Clawson 1999). Also left out are short-lived radical unions that achieved interracial solidarity, such as the Industrial Workers of the World, which failed to institutionalize their sometimes spectacular union drives or strikes. Why they failed is a different story than the one we tell here. We also do not examine white ethnic divisions. By focusing on race we largely jump over the period of 1880–1914 when labor relations were heavily shaped by the immense immigration of South and East Europeans, about which there have been numerous excellent studies (Piore 1979; Gutman 1976). After World War I, race, more than white ethnic differences or skill distinctions, was the major division within the working class that impeded industrial union organizing (Northrup 1944). European immigration had fallen off during the war and became tightly regulated thereafter, while deskilling and mechanization had displaced craft labor in mass production. Of course, examples abound of racial conflict outside the labor market, and there are numerous cases where citizens forged interracial solidarity outside of labor unions, especially during the heyday of the Civil Rights Movement. A linear history of race and labor relations could also enumerate many more cases similar to the ones we present here and connect them with intervening narrative. We sacrifice a continuous flow of history in select-ing cases, but we contend that the racial conflicts and interracial solidari-ties examined here epitomize the types of struggles commonly found.

Understanding the historical events surrounding race and labor is the focus of the narrative chapters. We use these narratives for the purposes of building a general theory of racial competition. Analytically, we sought to include critical comparisons, where outcomes differ but determinants are similar in all but one major instance, and crucial tests, where the theory's precepts so obviously apply that explanatory failure would constitute refutation of the model (Eckstein 1979). Despite the historical brackets described above, the period is expansive enough to include exceptions to theoretical expectations and to consider reason-able alternatives. It is also a period where the possibilities are more open and more visible than they would be later. National unions, employers, and other actors had greater leniency to publicly express racist beliefs prior to the successes of the Civil Rights Movement. The conditions and institutions that fostered interracial solidarity—which constitute one of our major foci—were also in formation. The possibilities for alternatives, such as radical class coalitions or racist fascism, even though unrealized, were also greater during this era than after World War II. This is not to say that more sweeping temporal and/or cross-national comparisons are inappropriate; on the contrary, they will be necessary to further develop the generality of the theory. For this project, however, the scope allows us to obtain our twin goals: narrative explanations of how pivotal events unfolded and comparative analysis of common processes in diverse cases.

Split labor market theory is applicable in each case of industrial organizing as clear racial differences exist in the price of labor, political resources, or motives, independent from skill or other personal attributes. Racism is nearly ubiquitous, although for each case its social origins and intensity may differ. Racial ideologies are thus part of the available "tool kit" with which actors made sense of the world during this period (Swidler 1986). Also available were ideologies and examples of equality and interracial solidarity. Though racist beliefs were common in all cases, as we explain in the next chapter, how actors responded was conditioned by both the short-term rationality of market competition and the long-term institutionalization of race relations. While each case has unique conditions and institutions, in the conclusions we compare the following common variants: the levels of union success, the degree of working-class interracial solidarity, the forms of competition and conflict, the role of the state and local government repression, union policies of minority inclusion or exclusion, and levels of employer discrimination and/or paternalism. This comparison affords an opportunity to explore the factors that give rise to divergent outcomes across a number of instances of the split labor market.

Notably, the Chinese case offers particular insight into the enactment of anti-immigration legislation, the role of the state, and the reproduction of split labor markets. It also provides a contrast with the remaining cases, which focus on black-white conflict. The post–World War I racial conflicts in northern industrial cities precipitated new conceptions of race relations as an urban issue among workers and serve as the "crucial tests" of racial competition theories. The unstated assumption that solidarity follows from an absence of a split labor market is investigated by way of the CIO organizing drives of the 1930s. The contrary results found in Operation Dixie provide an ideal crucial comparison for testing the usefulness of the theory.

We limit the analysis to determinants of race and labor relations in industrial unions, mainly but not exclusively to black–white relations. This excludes white ethnic (including Hispanic) conflict, gender stratification, craft union racism, and community relations. While split labor market theory may be important for any of these issues, they fall outside the scope of our inquiry and represent qualitatively different processes of discrimination. Additionally, we do not provide analyses of labor conflict involving Japanese, Native American, or other minority groups that represented a very small percentage of the labor force during the period in question. The exclusion of white ethnic variation may be the most troubling limitation to some, and we do not intend to imply that this is an unimportant consideration. But as Lieberson's (1980) authoritative study documents, the mobility patterns of blacks (and Chinese in our period)[3] differ qualitatively from those of white ethnics. The qualitative difference justifies analytical separation.

ANALYTIC STRATEGY

This book examines a number of historically important cases that reveal the crosscutting effects of race and class on worker interests, mobilization, and the efficacy of the organized labor movement. Our goal is to explain when racial competition produces strikebreaking and when workers can overcome racial divisions through interracial class solidarity. The "analytic narratives" (Bates, Greif, Levi, Rosenthal, and Weingast 1998) in the following chapters underscore the salience of race relations for understanding the history of the labor movement in the United States. At the same time, race relations cannot adequately be studied without considering processes of class conflict and intra-class competition that may reinforce racial identity. Because the trajectories of race relations and the labor movement are historically linked, neither can be appropriately understood in isolation. Producing a comprehensive model and method of analysis is necessary for achieving our goal.

To help us analyze union organizing in split labor markets, we use Heckathorn's (1988, 1989, 1990a, 1990b) game theory models of collective action to simulate labor organizing (chapter 2). The model starts with the simple premise that unions reward strikers and punish strikebreakers, at least those it can monitor. Sanctions are applied and rewards gained by both the individual worker and the worker's group as a whole. Thus, all workers have an interest in encouraging the coopera-

tion of others (even more so than their interest in their own cooperation), which they achieve through their interpersonal connections. These
connections contribute mightily to the effectiveness of the strike. Game
theory often stops at the point of simulation, but we want to know
how well the model applies empirically. This means comparing the
narratives to see whether the predicted sequence of events occurs, and
if so, under what conditions. By characterizing each strike in terms of
the organizing sequence that it resembles, we can combine the game
theory model with systematic case comparisons.

Starting with Skocpol's (1980) comparison of social revolutions,
applications of formal comparative methods have become increasingly
common and increasingly sophisticated. Ragin's (1987) development of
QCA was a leap forward, principally because it provided a replicable
methodology grounded in explicit logical principals. Its application
requires analysts to confront contrary evidence, dismissed exceptions,
and flawed assumptions; QCA makes explicit what researchers have to
emphasize, dismiss, and assume in order to arrive at a particular interpretation. While QCA is useful as a comparative strategy, it relies on
case simplification and thus does not provide the historical texture
found in our narrative chapters, which are condensed from larger studies. Our approach is to present detailed case histories that can be
analyzed in a comparative fashion with the goal of delineating those
factors that account for minority strikebreaking and the varying levels
of class solidarity associated with union organizing drives. Our use of
QCA helps make our approach replicable, systematic, and explicit.
However, because many of our conclusions will be obvious from the
case histories themselves, and because readers primarily interested in
the case histories may find the mechanics of QCA somewhat tedious,
we have relegated our formal analyses to an appendix.

ORGANIZATION OF THE BOOK

In the next chapter, we trace the development and review the precepts
of racial competition and split labor market theories. Following the
review, we use game theory principles to expand upon the theory's
basic premises and derive models of working-class solidarity versus
strikebreaking. Chapter 3 supplements the prior theoretical discussion
by analyzing split labor markets in terms of the larger world economy.
We argue that the uneven pattern of global economic development is

associated with three distinct types of labor migration, each of which has implications for the reproduction of split labor markets, and hence, racial antagonism. Specifically, we review the sojourning immigration of Chinese into the United States in the nineteenth century and discuss significance of the Great Migration, which began to bring large numbers of black agricultural workers into northern cities circa 1916.

Chapters 4 through 7 present the case studies in chronological order, beginning with the Comstock miners' discrimination against Chinese workers in the nineteenth century in chapter 4, the 1919 steel strike in chapter 5, six organizing drives that became the heart of the CIO during the Great Depression in Chapter 6, and the postwar case of Operation Dixie in chapter 7. Each of these historical chapters provides a narrative sequence for the specific period. While we devote particular attention to the theoretical factors outlined in chapter 2, these narrative chapters contain all the major ingredients that our sources deemed historically relevant.

Comparing cases and testing theory in historical sociology differs in purpose from traditional social history, which seeks to offer novel interpretations of events. Social history necessarily draws on primary sources, while comparing cases requires an authoritative source or convergence among multiple sources. Critical case studies fall somewhere in between depending on how much past research has established the relevant facts. For instance, the narrative of the 1919 steel strike is well known, less so for the case of Chinese miners, while we offer a novel interpretation from primary sources of that less known case of Operation Dixie.

In chapter 8, we consider the results of our work for the development of racial competition theory and for understanding race and class relations in general. Our conclusions are informed by our case comparison, and for interested readers, we provide the technical details of our methodology in an appendix to the book. Our cases show that racial competition and conflict frequently become acute during labor organizing drives and strikes. More difficult to explain are the sources of employer discrimination and interracial solidarity, especially when the latter emerges despite racial competition. Utilizing our case comparison, we seek to further develop a theoretical framework and an appropriate methodology for the study of these phenomena. Our goal is the development of general theory, which we think is the ultimate but surely not singular purpose of comparative historical sociology (see Kiser and Hechter 1991, 1998). With this goal in mind, we conclude with a discussion of our empirical results and our revisions to the original split labor market approach.

CHAPTER 2

Theories of Racial Competition and Organizing Solidarity

Racial competition theories have a long history and the general idea predates modern social science. In Figure 2.1 we offer a partial etiology of competition theories, or more precisely, of the antecedents to the present work. Inherently, such a schematic is fraught with offenses as it inevitably leaves out important contributors and connotes a descendant that supposed progenitors may rightfully deny. Having made that apology, we attempt to place this study in context.

Both Marx and Weber address racial competition and conflict in ways that foreshadow current discussions, although neither offered an explicit theory. Becker and Blalock perhaps deserve that recognition. Becker's (1957) economic analysis of discrimination argued that, all else equal, wage differences depend on employers' willingness to incur a cost for being associated with employees having certain preferred racial characteristics. Where workers are equally productive, higher dominant wages reflect the price employers will pay to maintain the association. Becker's analysis suggests that barring state intervention, market competition should eventually weed out employers who pay for a racial preference (and thus erode racial wage disparities in the process). Blalock (1967) brought social psychological theories together with elements from several areas within the social sciences to construct a series of ninety-seven propositions that apply to minority group relations. Although he focused on black–white relations and used limited historical data, his propositions influenced subsequent research and linked varied theories of race relations.

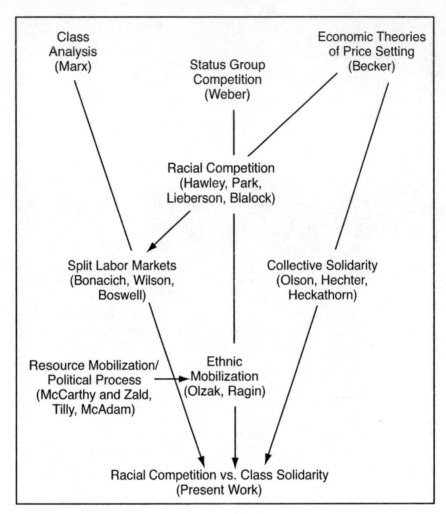

Figure 2.1 Partial Etiology of Competition Theories of Race Relations

The central development, at least for our purposes, is split labor market theory. The seminal contribution is Bonacich's (1972) work, which combined class and race dynamics to explain racial antagonism. Wilson (1978) used the approach successfully and Boswell's (1986) work extended and developed the theory in a more analytical direction, which we continue here. In the same vein, we draw on theories of resources mobilization and political process (Tilly 1978; McAdam 1999), collective action (Olson 1965), and Heckathorn's (1990a, 1991) game theory models to incorporate class solidarity.

A split labor market exists where labor costs differ between racial groups, holding constant their efficiency and productivity.[1] The cost differential typically originates with variations in regional or national economies that result from uneven capitalist development, which produces differences in wages and expenses. Uneven development shapes migration patterns, which historically has meant that migrants from poorer areas have served as cheap labor in more developed regions (we discuss migration patterns in chapter 3).

Labor costs include, but are not limited to, wage differentials, and refer to the cost to the employer of sustaining a given work force. The weaker a group of workers in terms of political and economic resources, the lower the labor cost associated with that group (Bonacich 1972, pp. 549–50).[2] Labor cost differences create two competing working-class groups that identify each other by race: cheap (minority) labor and higher priced (dominant) labor. Rural migrants, immigrants, and sojourners have historically become cheap labor. Other factors constant (especially average productivity, skill, and turnover rates), employers will replace high-cost dominant labor with cheap minority labor (Bonacich 1972, p. 550). The threat of replacement transfers *class conflict* between workers and employers to *racial competition* in the labor market (Bonacich 1972; Boswell 1986).

The migration of low-cost minority labor may drive down prevailing wage scales and threaten labor organizations. In response, dominant labor will attempt to prevent competition at the lower wage. One strategy, perhaps the most obvious to individual workers, is to exclude minority employment (especially immigrants) or to segregate them from most desirable jobs. Segregation confines minority labor to lower-status and lower-paying positions (Bonacich 1972, pp. 555–58). Formal or informal rules may legitimate segregation and allocate jobs according to experience, skill level, or seniority that is disproportionately held by dominant labor. The alternate strategy is class solidarity.

Class solidarity requires interracial union organizing to prevent wage undercutting and provide collective benefits to the working class as a whole (Bonacich 1975, 1979; Marks 1981; Brueggemann and Boswell 1998). This presumes the existence of a potent and credible organization, a presumption we investigate in the next section. Even with a strong, interracial union, a solidarity strategy requires that both cheap and higher priced labor give primacy to long-term, class-based interests. This is less likely when labor markets are split (Bonacich 1979, p. 34). Minority workers may have little motivation to support class solidarity, despite the union's strategy. If they are recent migrants, they often have fewer options or support networks, less information about local strikes or conditions, and a greater need for immediate wages. Additionally, racial networks and obligations may clash with union solidarity, and racist ideologies may skew and distort information (Boswell 1986).

If minority workers are sojourners, migrants who intend soon to return to the place of origin (Siu 1952), then only short-term benefits are of interest. Strikebreaking becomes more attractive (immediate, higher income) and striking more costly (lack of resources and greater vulnerability to repression). Sojourners gain no long-term benefits from union organization, strikes, or investments in human capital. Given a convenient exit, they endure harsh working conditions and are less interested in collective voice. Their intent is to quickly save (or remit) money to purchase land, start a business, get married, or otherwise become established in their lower-cost homeland (Siu 1952; Bonacich 1972, p. 551). If wages rise, then their job commitment may actually diminish as they will more quickly achieve their objective (Berg 1961; Bonacich 1972; Boswell and Jorjani 1988). In heavy industry, sojourners tend to be young single males who are the most mobile and least enmeshed in local networks (Bonacich 1972, p. 550; Bonacich and Cheng 1984, p. 27).

Despite intentions, sojourners often fail to return to their homeland for a variety of reasons. They continue to split the labor market, however, until their temporary orientation ends. If they stay in one region, their orientation to a specific job may be short-term. Even if they stay at a specific job, they have the option of returning. In short, sojourners' orientation to a job or locale is only economic and lacks the same degree of commitment that holds for long-term residents. As such, sojourners are the quintessential source of split labor markets. However, as we discuss below, the focus on sojourning in split labor market research has limited the historical applicability of the theory. All recent migrants (and especially single young males) share sojourning characteristics to the extent that they are poor but mobile.

Dominant workers react to the undercutting potential of cheaper minority labor with racial antagonism because of economic deprivation, not because of false consciousness or traditional mistrust. To be sure, racist prejudice or stereotyping leads dominant workers to perceive a greater racial difference in wages than actually exists. However, the perception of differences originates from differences in motivations and circumstances that correlate with race. Any union will attempt to limit employment to its members and will foster antagonism against strikebreakers. Faced with displacement or wage cuts, union workers will attempt to exclude replacements. This only becomes a *racial* conflict where strikebreakers (or other "cheap labor") are of a different racial group (Bonacich 1972, 1975, 1976, 1979; Wilson 1978).

Since Bonacich's introduction of split labor market theory, a series of studies have applied it to instances of racial conflict. The research has served to test the theory and has also produced a set of factors that have been inductively added to expand, refine, or resolve problems. In the process, researchers have modified the theory and expanded its scope through a haphazard form of "analytical induction."[3] While each case study may contribute an inductive theoretical refinement, cumulatively it remains unclear whether conclusions apply generally across multiple cases.[4] Let us briefly summarize some of those added factors. Wilson (1978), Marks (1981), and others add that employers may actively promote racial divisions rather than remain passive.[5] When employers pursue this strategy, and how they maintain profitability, is unexplained. Boswell (1986) explains the reproduction of racial splits in the labor market by adding the recursive effect of racist ideology, market crowding, and state enforcement. Peled and Shafir (1987) emphasize how dominant labor fails to maintain its position without state support, while Burawoy's (1981) criticism is that the theory's market focus ignores state-sponsored racism and state reinforcement of dominant worker racism. Hodson (1995) demonstrates that racial heterogeneity by itself does not necessarily generate racial divisions, but the analysis does not consider migration or other resource differences. Racial heterogeneity alone does not tell us anything about union solidarity.

These factors have been affixed to the theoretical framework to enhance particular explanations or solve case-specific anomalies. Some of these factors are the central focus of other perspectives, such as issues of solidarity, which are missing from the split labor market inventory. The more relevant ones we discus here are Olzak's closely related competition model, theories of employer discrimination, and collective action and political process theories. We follow our review of this literature with a formal game theoretic model to incorporate each of the political and ideological factors that condition labor market relations.

ETHNIC MOBILIZATION: OLZAK'S CONTRIBUTION TO RACIAL
COMPETITION THEORY

The general racial and ethnic competition perspective introduced by
Hawley (1945) and Park (1950) and subsequently developed by Lieberson
(1961), Blalock (1967), Hannan (1979), and Banton (1980) has generated two major research agendas: the split labor market studies described above and Olzak's (1992) competition theory of ethnic
mobilization.[6] The shared premise is that immigration and industrialization lead to increased interaction and competition between ethnic groups.
Worker movement from economically depressed areas to regions with
greater opportunities threatens prevailing wage scales and floods labor
markets with cheaper labor. Members of incoming migrant populations
may be subjected to violence and discrimination when they threaten
the job security of dominant workers. The level of ethnic mobilization
and the degree of conflict depends on the size of the incoming population and the rate of influx. Competition worsens during economic
recessions so that ethnic conflict is highest when both immigration and
unemployment are high (Olzak 1992, pp. 32–37).

Olzak (1992, p. 37) considers split labor market theory a variant
of the more general competition approach, a perspective we share. Her
work focuses more on the resource mobilization of ethnic communities, rather than the resource differential between ethnic groups in the
labor market. Demonstrating racial labor cost differentials is difficult,
which Olzak (1992, pp. 114–16) considers a limitation of split labor
market theory. To avoid this problem, she focuses on "more general
indicators of competition: economic prosperity and economic well-
being" (Olzak 1992, p. 115). The problem we have with general indicators is that they do not tell us if the resource difference between
dominant and minority workers has changed, only that competition has
intensified. Thus, most of the variation in the split in the labor market
comes from *sojourner and recent migration*, factors that are not central to
Olzak's agenda.

In a criticism that applies to all racial competition theory, Belanger
and Pinard (1991) argue that the theory assumes (but does not show)
a direct connection between competition and conflict. They contend
that competition produces conflict only where individuals perceive
competition as unfair. Where interdependence or mutual benefit characterizes competition, however, conflict is less likely to erupt (1991,

p. 449). Conflict will be widespread and intense where it is a group (rather than individual) dynamic and where it involves collective goals (not just individual ones) (1991, p. 450).

Olzak subsequently addresses the issue of competition-conflict linkages (1992, pp. 29–31, 114–15). She recognizes that while evidence of direct competition is limited, potential competition can prompt ethnic mobilization and conflict before direct competition occurs (see also Saxton 1971). Historically, patterns of union and political mobilization reflect proactive efforts to prevent competition. The theory need not establish proof of direct competition, since the *threat* of competition has had a similar impact on ethnic relations (Bonacich 1979, pp. 25–30 makes a similar point, as does Boswell 1986).[7] Neither perspective, however, considers the significance of individual versus collective goals, an issue to which we return below.

EMPLOYER RACISM

"Divide and conquer" or "divide and rule" is a thesis that has taken various forms, the basic thrust of which is that employers gain from racial strife while both dominant and minority workers lose (see Wilson 1978; Roemer 1979; Bonacich 1979, pp. 37–41; Reich 1981). Racial conflict and discrimination benefit capital by maintaining working-class divisions that inhibit unionization, solidarity, and mobilization. These divisions allow lower overall wages to prevail (Roemer 1979, pp. 695, 703; Reich 1981). Employers do not lose profits to indulge an irrational "taste for discrimination," but benefit where discrimination and internal class divisions keep workers docile and nonunion (Roemer 1979, p. 703). In one systematic comparison, for instance, Reich (1981) found that cities with the greatest difference in white versus black wages also had the *lowest* wages for both blacks and whites. Capitalist market forces do not work to eliminate racial inequality over the long term, as posited by neoclassical economic theory (Roemer 1979, p. 695). A perfectly competitive capitalist economy reproduces (as opposed to eliminates) racial inequality because it benefits individual capitalists (Roemer 1979, p. 703; Reich 1981).

In contrast to Becker's (1957) neoclassical model, the divide and conquer approach holds that the institutions of capitalist society reproduce working-class racism and discrimination. Racial inequality persists despite its apparent irrationality because it serves employers' interests.

Employer strategies to undermine unions include the importation of minority strikebreakers, the imposition of yellow dog contracts, and blacklisting (Foner 1974; Freeman and Medoff 1984). The selective importation of black strikebreakers, which we will examine in detail, was a successful tactic before World War II for inflaming racism and dividing labor (Spero and Harris 1969, pp. 128–46; Bonacich 1976; Wilson 1978; Gordon, Edwards, and Reich 1982, pp. 152–53).

The active tactics of capitalists in divide and conquer arguments contrast with their passive role in split labor market theory (Bonacich 1972, p. 557), where racism emanates from dominant labor. Bonacich (1979, pp. 38–39) notes that many neo-Marxist formulations "explain" a phenomenon (such as racial inequality) by showing that it serves the interests of capital. This "Marxist functionalism" is problematic because it is "based on the reasoning that the end-state determines the processes which lead to it" (1979, p. 39). This type of logic makes it difficult to see how market competition has encouraged dominant workers to oppress minorities in deliberate ways. Without clear evidence of employer discrimination, one cannot assume they instigate divisions and conflict simply because they may benefit from it. In the case narratives, we investigate whether employers instigate racial conflict, and if so under what conditions.

A related explanation of employer discrimination can be found in instances of *paternalism*. Employers in company towns who were paternalistic offered workers protection and provided it in ways that went beyond wages. The tradeoff for protection is loyalty and subservience. Paternalistic exchange relies on the dependence and vulnerability of workers coupled with employers' "benevolent" domination (see Jackman 1994). Where paternalism breeds loyalty, it can obviously impede unionization efforts (see Brueggemann 2000; Brown 2000). This takes on a racial dimension when paternal relations are confined to workers of a single race or when a racial group benefits disproportionately from paternalistic protections. In such a scenario, a variant of the divide and conquer argument, one racial group is "bought off" by capital. Economic rewards or other privileges prevent this segment from engaging in class struggle and represent another means of instilling working-class divisions. Employer paternalism, although briefly addressed by Bonacich (1975, p. 611; 1976, p. 38; 1979, p. 40), is not integrated into the theory or addressed in previous empirical studies.

A clear example of racist paternalism existed in southern textile mill towns from the late nineteenth to the mid-twentieth century (McLaurin 1971; Simpson 1981; Zingraff and Schulman 1984). Such towns often amounted to huge paternalistic systems, from which blacks were excluded. Many started as "company towns," where the employer owned or funded virtually every social institution, including medical services, police protection, garden plots, churches, schools, libraries, hospitals, athletic clubs, rifle clubs, literary clubs, stores, and housing (McLaurin 1971, pp. 28–39; Simpson 1981, p. 383). Access to the various services and resources depended on loyalty to the employer.

Just as community-embedded paternalism fosters an ideology of subordination, it also contributes to institutions that facilitate these ends (Zingraff and Schulman 1984, p. 100). Herring notes that "their paternalism was a complex social structure that worked against unionism. The structure was self-perpetuating. It generated a culture that supported it. It prevented the growth of indigenous worker-controlled social structures that might form the basis of organized opposition" (1949, pp. 114–17; also see Simpson 1981, p. 384). There was, in effect, no conceptual or structural mechanism within the context of a paternalistic relationship for improving economic and political conditions. "Worker-controlled social structures capable of generating an autonomous working class consciousness and culture simply did not exist in the mill village" (Boyte, quoted in Zingraff and Schulman 1984, p. 100).

Thus, before a paternalistic relationship develops, there is a material reality reflected in the economic vulnerability of workers that leads to their dependence on employers. Then, as the protective and loyalty interaction develops, it is institutionalized in various spheres of the community that encompass a degree of security and identity for the subordinated workers. Paternalism is personalized. The genuine concern of an employer who pays the hospital bills of a worker's sick child is matched by an equally genuine outrage at the ungrateful union organizer demanding health insurance. Employers interact with and know employees as members of the community. As workers often embrace this relationship like a family, it can become "sacred" and unquestioned, at least for as long as the community remains stable (McLaurin 1971; Simpson 1981). Regarding paternalism in southern textile towns, Zingraff and Schulman (1984, p. 100) state that workers assume subordinate positions in both mill and community. They adopt an ideology that legitimates

their subordination by obscuring the material relationship in employment and making it more difficult to see alternative possibilities (Zingraff
and Schulman 1984, p. 100). One result is that they will tolerate poorer
working conditions, lower wages, and limited upward mobility.

Note however, that the conscious acceptance of subservience and
loyalty by workers can be turned against employers who renege on their
obligations and who treat their workers as only employees (Simpson
1981; McLaurin 1971). Implicit, and sometimes explicit, is that disloyalty
is punished. Walkouts or strikes are the ultimate punishment workers
could invoke against a disloyal employer, while an employer's ultimate
punishment is dismissal. The latter was made credible in southern mills
by the existence of an available pool of low wage labor in the form of
excluded blacks. Threatening to employ blacks was something a paternalistic southern employer could rarely mention without undermining the
"proof" of their benevolence toward their white workers. Yet the potential threat, and the reality of blacks in worse circumstances, remained.

Most research on racial paternalism focuses on white southerners.
But most interesting for our cases was employer paternalism in the
North during the 1930s (Cayton and Mitchell 1939). Paternalism in
the North was not confined to blacks, although they were sometimes
given more consideration and it held a greater appeal to them. Low
wages, few employment opportunities, and racially biased seniority
policies all contributed to the ongoing economic vulnerability of black
workers in the North. The economic insecurity of black migrants coupled
with racism from white workers and their unions made a paternalistic
relationship with the employer particularly appealing.

If we extend the logic of split labor market theory, paternalism
motivates recent migrants to tolerate undesirable work conditions and
refuse to invest in improving those conditions (Bonacich 1972, p. 550).
In effect, paternalism makes recent migrants similar to sojourners in
terms of motives. The difference is that paternalism spawns loyalty and
subordination, while sojourners consider their circumstances temporary.
Workers in paternalistic relations may consider their subjugation legitimate as long as their loyalty is reciprocated. Employers make a paternalistic commitment to employees by providing individual services besides
wages. Services such as company housing, credit at the company store,
or personal loans may be no different in total compensation than in
non-company towns (although probably less than comparable union
wages). What makes paternalism profitable is that the "services" are

dependent upon loyalty. This raises the costs of labor conflict for workers, including quitting, which increases the power of managers or employers to exploit workers.[8] In this sense, paternalism is a personalized form of welfare capitalism. The distinction is that loyalty develops through personal, individual relations rather than (or besides) impersonal policies, and thus carries a strong emotional content of reciprocal commitment. Workers in paternalistic relations remain in their situation for some period, loyal and subservient. On the other hand, sojourners usually get no such commitment from employers and do not remain in the current situation very long.

In the short term, the behavior of such groups is the same. Both tolerate undesirable work conditions and avoid union organizing. Working conditions for sojourners are often considerably worse, because workers under paternalism receive some "welfare" services, even if such services contribute to the institutionalization of their subordination. In regard to wages, economic mobility, and political influence, the circumstances of sojourning and paternalism are more similar. Both paternalistic and temporary orientations are motives that reduce the costs of subordinated labor. Paternalism takes on a racist character when services are offered to one racial group (a common southern phenomenon) or when paternalistic services are offered to all but only generate loyalty among a minority group that lacks alternate resources (an occasional northern phenomenon).

UNION ORGANIZATION AND THEORIES OF COLLECTIVE BEHAVIOR

The analysis of theories of collective behavior moves the focus of our discussion from racial conflict within the working class to relations between workers and union organizations. In a seminal work, Olson (1965) suggests that what unions offer and what motivates workers to join are collective goods. That is, the conditions, goals, or benefits that a union strives to achieve are directed toward workers as a collective entity. "Unions are for *collective* bargaining" (1965, p. 75). Olson applies a rational choice theory in which the basic principle is that individuals make decisions based on costs and benefits. A central assumption is that each person has a set of preferences or priorities, and faces limited options for realizing those preferences and pursuing the related goals. A second important assumption is that resources are scarce and that individuals weigh options against one another in light of this scarcity. As a result, they attach subjective probabilities to the options based on the likelihood of realizing their goals; options are assessed in terms of their probabilities and relative costs and benefits.[9]

Following Olson (1965), studies of collective behavior have garnered the most influence in sociology where they have been concerned with collective preferences, structural options, and organizational behavior. Germane to this study is Hechter's (1990) formulation that the level of group solidarity results from the dependence of members on the group organization (see also Taylor 1987). This includes material dependence, but also dependence on the supply of information about resources and alternatives. Race and class solidarity may be considered alternate sources of solidarity (although not necessarily so). The question is, to what extent does an actor receive resources from each group source?

Other important determinants of group solidarity include the establishment of controls for monitoring and sanctioning members, the likelihood of compliance, and the extensiveness of group obligations (Hechter 1990; Heckathorn 1990a). Some degree of coercion is essential for addressing the free-rider problem (Olson 1965, p. 96). That is, without selective incentives for joining, some workers will enjoy the benefits of an effective union effort without incurring any of the costs. Also important is the demand for "jointly-produced goods" (Hechter 1990, p. 151), which cannot be attained efficiently through individual action, and "public goods" or "collective goods," the attainment of which requires collective behavior (Olson 1965). The desire for such public goods factors into individual decisions, even when these desires contradict individual preferences (Muller and Opp 1986).

People must choose among structurally shaped options. The state and other institutions that structure the relationship between individuals and groups affect the options individuals perceive as viable (Elster 1985; Przeworski 1985). For instance, union power increases when state legislation enhances the returns for individual workers who join the union. Legislation favorable to labor in the 1930s and 1940s, for instance, contributed to unions demanding and obtaining recognition that fostered increasing union growth (Olson 1965, p. 82). Similarly, if the state has a history of punishment or violent reaction to union activity, the costs are great and labor activism is less likely.

Economic conditions are comparably important. In a tight labor market, the risks of workers joining a union or participating in a strike are lower because alternate jobs are much more likely to be available as compared with conditions in a slack labor market (Cornfield 1985). Olson (1965, p. 82) explains that there is a perceived tradeoff between higher wages and full employment, so that demands for higher wages are much more likely to take place in a tight labor market. Union membership grows during tight markets, when organized labor has more political leverage and can more easily establish compulsory union membership (Olson 1965, p. 82; Cornfield 1986, p. 1115). The ability of the union to monitor and sanction rises as well. In a slack market, there is more competition between workers, and racial cleavages may emerge as whites are threatened by minority workers.

SOCIAL MOVEMENTS

Related to theories of collective behavior are "resource mobilization" and "political process" theories of social movements, which offer insights on issues of racial competition and class solidarity (see McCarthy and Zald 1977; Tilly 1978; McAdam 1983, 1999; McAdam, McCarthy, and Zald 1988).[10] A central focus of this approach is the organizational and external circumstances that shape costs and opportunities that account for individual rationality. McAdam (1999, pp. 43–48) argues that an organization embodying some current of a social movement must have internal strength derived from a certain degree of "organizational readiness." This includes strong leadership and coherent membership. For a union, its demonstrated viability and efficacy contribute to its appeal among risk-averse workers. Past strike success provides perhaps the best evidence that future success is possible and worth the risk. State actions are also important, and not just in terms of direct repression. Whenever government policies undermine union efficacy, individual workers will be less inclined to join.

A social movement organization must also encompass "structures of solidary incentives," which refer to the "myriad interpersonal rewards that provide the motive force for participation in these groups. It is the salience of these rewards that helps explain why recruitment through established organizations is generally so efficient" (McAdam 1999, p. 45). Note the similarity to Hechter's (1990) arguments, but with a greater stress here on interpersonal relationships (see also Heckathorn 1990a). A tight network of personal relationships may substitute for the monitoring and the sanctions offered by a formal organization (and vice versa, those outside a network of personal connections would be the ones most likely to free-ride). As potential participants contemplate action such networks are particularly important, especially in the context of conflicting alternatives.

Concerning interracial organizing, the same logic is applicable but the "solidary incentives" are necessarily more complex when there are "cross-cutting solidarities" (e.g., race) (McAdam 1999). The question is not just whether a union is racially inclusive, but how such principles of inclusion are manifest in the organization. Has the union *institutionalized* racial inclusion in visibly credible ways? For instance, are blacks represented among the union leaders and organizers? Are there tangible rewards for minority labor? Will the union oppose discrimination, including within its ranks? Union inclusion must overcome the racially charged mechanisms of control used by employers that undermine interracial solidarity.

DISCUSSION

From our overview of the literature, three issues emerge as problematic for split labor market theory. The first is the primacy of sojourning migration. Because strikebreaking occurred with the migration of Asians to the West or of southern blacks to the North, Bonacich (1972, 1975, 1976), Wilson (1978), and others failed to consider whether minority strikebreaking took place without sojourning. The focus on sojourning migration has tended to obscure other factors that could account for split labor market dynamics. Conversely, given the right conditions, recent migrant minority workers might abandon their temporary orientation toward industrial employment and participate in collective action. Union strategies would play an important role in incorporating recent migrant workers into the labor movement.

A second key issue is an unstated assumption that the absence of a split labor market explains interracial solidarity. Historical analyses have pointed to minority strikebreaking as a key cause of strike failure and subsequent racial antagonism. However, industry-wide analyses did not focus on particular cases of interracial solidarity, precluding a comparative analysis of strikebreaking versus solidarity. While some studies place greater emphasis on the state and ideology, the centrality of sojourning reinforces the original focus. Split labor market studies do not concentrate on solidarity and rarely compare cases. To explain when split labor markets produce strikebreaking and when workers can overcome the split, we need to expand the theory to include analyses of solidarity.

Third, political and ideological conditions emerge in the literature as mediating explanations for labor market behavior. Several studies focus on the state, especially its role in conducting or allowing repression. Marxists emphasize employer discrimination (paternalism in our case) and political process theory includes questions of organizational readiness (specifically, racial inclusion practices). We first build a formal model of class solidarity versus racial competition, then return to these issues. We contend that politics and ideology condition labor relations, thus they can be incorporated into the model without violating its basic assumptions. That is, rather than just adding any factors that might matter, we ask how each affects the split in the labor market and the capacity of unions to overcome that split.

The main contribution of recent work in collective behavior theory lies in the insight it offers into the motivations of individuals and the capacity of organizations to monitor and sanction behavior. These arguments explicate the risks and gains of collective action in terms of the perceived choices, shaped by structures such as the state and economic conditions. One important formulation is game theory, which we use in the next section to create computer-simulated models of union organizing under split labor market conditions.

A GAME THEORETIC MODEL OF SOLIDARITY VERSUS STRIKEBREAKING

Our goal in this section is to fuse a micro-level orientation to individual rational action with the racially divided constitution of group preferences provided by split labor market theory. To this, we also add the state and institutional foci found in competing theories. We seek to develop a theory-driven model of collective action that is capable of empirical refutation or support. A first step is to identify the costs, benefits, and risks that confront workers in a strike situation.

Costs, Benefits, and Risks

Strikebreaking versus union solidarity provides a classic dilemma in studies of collective action (Olson 1965). The choice depends on workers' estimates of the costs, benefits, and risks, along with the probability of success and the possibility of free-riding. Strikebreaking provides the immediate benefit of employment at the cost of interpersonal and union sanctioning (possibly including violence). Strikebreakers risk union sanctions and interpersonal conflict (sometimes violent) if the strike succeeds, and lower wages, worse working conditions, and enhanced management control if the strike fails.[11] Conversely, solidarity provides a higher benefit if the strike succeeds and if the costs of striking can be recouped, but strikers risk job loss and other costs if the strike fails.

Assessments of costs, benefits, and risks are perhaps more numerous and ambiguous than most participants can fully calculate. Even if a worker decides to strike, the actions of a single individual have little effect. Because unions pursue collective goods, the possibility of free-riding may provide little motivation for any individual to strike. In this sense, strikebreaking versus solidarity offers a difficult choice between individual, short-term goals that are at odds with long-term, collective goals. Individuals face a union that has already decided to organize the plant, and to strike if necessary. Unions have the time and resources to calculate costs and benefits, even if individuals do not (Stinchcombe 1990). The calculations of unions may be wrong, but their decisions should correspond to structural conditions. To win, they must overcome conflicting individual interests by monitoring and sanctioning compliance and otherwise ensuring the solidarity of collective obligation. Success also depends on numerous factors, such as union solidarity, company solidarity, resources, market conditions, state support or repression, and crosscutting (non-class) racial and other interests.

While we could discuss other factors, our concern is with racial conflict that divides class solidarity. Costs, benefits, and risks are correlated with race in a split labor market, according to the theory's postulates. It may be rational for white workers to strike while it is irrational for minorities to strike. This is especially true if most minorities are recent migrants, whose higher discount rates inhibit collective action.[12] Although the utility of any strategy is contingent on the structure of the situation (the relative costs and benefits), Axelrod (1984, 1986) has shown that the structure itself is subject to change over time based on the strategies of other actors. In this sense, workers' preferences may evolve over the course of an organizing drive and strike.

THE FORMAL MODEL

We are interested in the conditions that solve the "collective action problem" and cause workers to comply with union demands for inter-racial class solidarity. Following Heckathorn (1988, 1989, 1990a, 1990b), we model[13] a union organizing drive as an iterated game where the interactions of individual workers are repeated over time until either solidarity is achieved or the organizing drive collapses.[14] The model includes an *agent*, the union, that monitors and sanctions group members for defection, and a heterogeneous group of actors, dominant and minority workers. Workers are subject to both *individualized sanctions*, rewards and punishments directed at individual workers, and *collective sanctions*, which apply to all members of the worker's racial group (a "mixed sanction model," Heckathorn 1990a, pp. 366–67). Thus, an individual's action has spillover effects that affect other group members, creating incentives for all workers to regulate one another's behavior via interpersonal compliance norms (1990a, p. 367). These norms buttress the union's dictates. Represented in the model as a key to achieving solidarity is the fact that numerous small interpersonal sanctions, of little cost to the individual who implements them, may have larger effects on the recipient (such as harassment of a strikebreaker). But, as we discus below, the effect of these group norms depends upon the strength of interpersonal ties, which differ by race.

Since the union sanctions are augmented by interpersonal sanctions, we have two different levels of the free-rider problem (see Brown and Boswell 1995). The first level involves the temptation to benefit from unionization without bearing the costs of organizing and striking. Strikebreakers may ultimately receive the higher wages and benefits associated with union victory without participating in the strike. The second level involves free-riding on one's group, such as failing to rally friends and neighbors to honor the picket line (Heckathorn 1990a, p. 368; see also, Oliver 1980).

This means that workers are confronted with four different choices. *Full cooperation* involves cooperation with the union at the first level and support of intragroup compliance norms at the second. For instance, one might refuse to cross the picket line and also encourage others not to cross. This strategy minimizes the probability that the actor or the actor's group will be subjected to external sanctions, but the actor must bear the individual costs of first- and second-level cooperation. *Hypo-critical cooperation* is defection at the first level (strikebreaking), but participation in the intragroup sanctioning system (urging others to strike). Here, workers free-ride at the more costly first level, but cooperate at the second, interpersonal level. *Private cooperation* involves cooperation with the union at the first level but defection at the second (striking, but not urging others to do the same). *Full defection* is failure to cooperate with both the agent and the intragroup sanctioning system (strikebreaking and also failing to encourage others to support the union).

Finally, actors may also oppose the attempts of others to regulate their behavior. Some workers may go beyond merely withholding their support by actively undermining the strike or attacking the picket line. From their point of view, their individual costs (not only of striking, but also of being subject to normative sanctions) exceed their share of any potential collective gain. In this case, intragroup control actually creates (rather than resolves) collective action problems by generating opposition (Heckathorn 1990a, p. 377). This gives us a third level that involves oppositional control and thus adds four additional strategic choices. However, only two combinations are theoretically interesting (the other two are contradictory, both supporting and opposing compliance norms, and can be ignored). The first, *hypocritical opposition* refers to the strategy of cooperating at the first level (striking) but opposing compliance norms (active opposition to picketing, rather than just not participating). The second, *full opposition*, describes the strategy of defecting at the first level (strikebreaking) and opposing compliance norms (refusing to support the union and encouraging opposition among others).

All eight strategic choices are listed in Table 2.1. If we ignore the two illogical combinations, the remaining six strategies comprise the set of options available to each worker. Considering all these issues, a worker's strategy becomes a function of the following contextual parameters: the union's ability to monitor defections (M), the strength of individual sanctions that apply to individual defectors (Si), the strength of collective sanctions that apply to the group as a whole (Sc), the efficacy of each worker's control over others at levels two and three (E2 and E3), and the costs to each worker of cooperating at each level (K1, K2, K3). Given these parameters, we can calculate opportunities to cooperate and defect at each level and the risks and payoffs associated with each of the six strategies (see Brown and Boswell 1995). Each worker's decision to cooperate or defect at levels one, two, and three

Table 2.1

Cooperation at Levels 1–3 and Strategic Choices

Level 1 2 3	Strategy	Definition
C C C	(self-defeating)	— illogical combination
C C D	Full Cooperation	— strike and encourage others to strike
C D C	Hypocritical Opposition	— strike but encourage others to strikebreak
C D D	Private Cooperation	— strike and neither encourage nor discourage others
D C C	(self-defeating)	— illogical combination
D C D	Hypocritical Cooperation	— strikebreak but encourage others to strike
D D C	Full Opposition	— strikebreak and encourage others to strikebreak
D D D	Full Defection	— strikebreak and neither encourage nor discourage others

C = cooperate
D = defect

will impact the opportunities, risks, and payoffs subsequently facing other workers, and will thus affect their strategy selections.[15]

A worker's selection of a strategy (or "move") corresponds to a single iteration of the model, and the system variables change in accordance with each worker's choice. Thus, the context for each choice may differ at each iteration and the optimal strategy for the next worker partially depends on the cumulative effects of others' prior choices. Each worker is affected by previous workers' decisions to cooperate or defect at all three levels. After everyone selects a strategy, the first actor chooses again, this time facing a set of incentives that has been structured by others' behavior. The cycle repeats until the situation reaches equilibrium, where no actor's position can be improved through a unilateral strategy change.

RACIAL GROUPS AND HETEROGENEITY

The model becomes a bit more complex, and far more interesting, once we allow for group heterogeneity (Heckathorn 1991, 1993). In our case, heterogeneity is a function of racial subgroups. The two crucial labor market subgroups are the dominant (usually white) workers and minority workers (black or Chinese in our cases). The other important difference is between local and migrant minorities, for a total of three subgroups: dominant, local minority, and migrant minority workers. Racial differences in individual costs, benefits, and risks, as well as differences in network ties, create divergent worker strategies that reflect existing splits in the labor market. Workers may be homogeneous within subgroups (the system parameters are the same for all workers in a subgroup) but heterogeneous between subgroups (the system parameters are different across subgroups, i.e., differ between whites and blacks or locals and migrants).[16] By definition, minorities have lower incomes and thus they face higher costs for compliance (K1, K2, K3) by joining the union and going on strike. This is particularly true of recent minority migrants, who are in greater immediate need of income and who have a higher discount rate on the value of the long-term benefits of a union success.

Racial differences in workers' strategies are also affected by the normative sanctions (rewards and punishments) offered by the union and by their network of fellow workers. Collective sanctions (pickets, intimidation, blacklisting) may have a somewhat stronger effect on minorities who lack the same level of political and social resources. Most important for our model is that recent migrants will be the least affected by group norms (E2, E3) as they have far fewer interpersonal ties and allegiances that come with longstanding company or community affiliation (i.e., marriage, family, friendship, club, church, and neighborhood relationships). The more recent migrants there are in the labor market, the weaker the interpersonal norms to which they are subject or might seek to enforce. These modifications tailor the model to split labor market theory such that the main difference among workers is a high versus a low number of recent minority migrants.

Levels of solidarity are affected by characteristics of the union as well as by characteristics of the workers. We expect that a strong union will have the resources required to employ high levels of sanctions (both collective and individual) to deter defections. Because unions are membership organizations, they accrue resources only if they successfully organize workers. As such, we again modify the model to reflect a diminishing ability of the union to monitor defections and apply collective and individual sanctions over time if the overall compliance level fails to cross a specified threshold. We posit that there is an interaction between compliance levels and the ability of the union to enforce its dictates, with the union losing resources as if it fails to win a majority (that is, unions that fail to get at least 50 percent support begin to lose strength). This has a dramatic rebound effect on levels of compliance over time and reflects the fact that the initial success of union organizing may not be sufficient to ensure long-term cooperation. Because stronger sanctions increase the risks of defection, strong unions will achieve higher compliance levels. In addition, strong unions will have greater monitoring capacity, thus defectors will be more readily detected and punished.

Congruent with our discussion of split labor market theory, we posit the following propositions: (1) a strong union and a predominantly local minority labor group will produce the highest levels of compliance; (2) a strong union and predominantly migrant minority labor or (3) a weak union and predominantly local minority labor will produce intermediate levels of compliance; finally, (4) a weak union combined with predominantly migrant minority labor generates the lowest levels of compliance. Figure 2.2 presents a diagram of our model using these four separate sets of system parameters and thus graphically represents our theoretical expectations. The important comparisons are between the overall patterns of events and outcomes, not the precise compliance percentages. These patterns are consistent with the theoretical predictions. A strong union and local minorities achieve the highest and most stable level of compliance. The remaining three models predicted an initial surge in compliance, followed by a rapid breakdown as strikebreaking emerges as the most rational strategy, starting with migrant minorities. Once the efficacy of the strike declines, additional workers strikebreak and compliance rapidly falls to zero.

Reflecting collective action theory, union strength is necessary for the development of worker solidarity in a racially split labor market. This is especially important for an industrial union, which organizes low-skilled workers throughout a given industry.[17] If industrial unions pursue solidarity (and the labor market remains stable), then competitive pressure should eventually erode the racial split. In the final section below, we consider the political and ideological factors raised in the literature that mediate or condition labor relations. Historical applications of the expanded theory, including our case studies, must take union history, the political environment, and the ideological context into account. Several inductively derived factors were added in previous split labor market research or originate in alternate theories we discussed

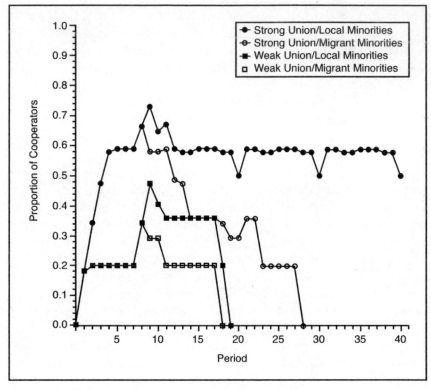

Figure 2.2 Group Compliance Levels

above. At this point, we discuss the conditions that were most important and organize them in terms of two major themes that affect actors in the market—the political conditions affecting union efficacy and the institutionalization of racial ideologies.

POLITICAL AND IDEOLOGICAL CONDITIONS

The literature frequently emphasizes the political context in which organizing occurs, notably the effects of state repression. Burawoy (1981) and others (Boswell 1986; Peled and Shafir 1987) point out that previous split labor market analyses devoted insufficient attention to the state context in which unions organize and working-class segments interact. Burawoy (1981) argued that neglecting the state is a result of analyzing racial conflict only in terms of the labor market, which limits analyses to individual or group interests. This ignores nonmarket contextual factors such as the class articulation of the state and repressive governments that increase the costs of organizing. In addition, violent repression by employers is itself affected by state tolerance or complicity. Collective behavior theory shows how the political context affects the risks and costs of workers' collective action. Patterns of strikebreaking might result more from state repression than the number of recent migrants in the labor market, while a comparatively pro-union local government might make solidarity more viable.

State policy also shapes the political context in which racially divided workers encounter each another (Goldfield 1997; Robertson 2000). This is obvious in the case of segregated labor markets, so obvious that we avoid any cases where interracial solidarity was simply prohibited. We only examine state policy in terms of state actions or legislation that indirectly affected questions of race. Related is the content of federal legislation vis-à-vis its position and impact on organized labor. Federal legislation has affected the course and strength of the labor movement, especially during the New Deal era. The National Industrial Recovery Act and the Wagner Act invigorated the labor movement and gave workers new leverage that stimulated labor organizing drives through the 1940s. Before this time, legislation was far more conservative; it inhibited strikes and did not guarantee workers' right to unionize. To the extent that the state amplifies or mitigates individual strategies and group norms, it affects the balance of power in class struggle.

IDEOLOGY AND RATIONALITY

Although not originally stated in these terms, split labor market theory explains why workers' interests may lead to divisive and self-defeating racial conflicts. The theory assumes that the behavior of actors in the market is rational, and explains why the constitution of preferences differs systematically by race (i.e., a racial split in motives and orientations, especially for sojourners and recent migrants). The dominant group invokes racist ideologies because it identifies the minority group as "cheap labor" that threatens to take jobs or cut wage levels. In so doing, a racist ideology becomes a factor in reproducing splits in the labor market. Ideology contributes to discrimination that crowds the supply of minority labor, further lowering wages. While the relationship in the theory between ideology and rationality has been addressed previously (Boswell 1986), an analysis of the institutionalization of ideologies by unions and employers is still missing.[18]

For unions, the racial tactics employed by leaders and organizers are not simply choices made under prevailing conditions. Instead, they derive from organizational strategies that have become institutionalized over time. Thus, organizational tactics may actually be at odds with current labor market or workplace conditions. Of course, some individuals may deviate from the prevailing organizational strategy, but such institutionalized patterns nonetheless potentially affect levels of solidarity. We will discuss how some CIO unions in the 1930s carried out organizing practices that effectively institutionalized policies of inclusion and promoted interracial solidarity.[19] Many other CIO and some AFL unions espoused doctrines of inclusiveness, but in practice, most of them failed to implement it (Goldfield 1993). Following McAdam (1999, pp. 43–48), we consider this kind of institutionalization tantamount to the "organizational readiness" of an insurgent group in a social movement.

Finally, employers institutionalize racial policies in their firms. As such, they may act in ways that follow policy, but are inexplicable as discrete rational choices at any particular point. Competition theory usually assumes that employer racism is an irrational taste subject to eventual elimination by the market. Marxist divide and conquer theory takes exception. Even here, employer racism is a particular strategy in response to ongoing interracial organizing. Lasting employer racism requires institutionalization in the form of racist employer paternalism.

Racist paternalism can be seen as a segregation "deal." With paternalism, employers offer personal insurance-type amenities in exchange for antiunion loyalty and low wages. Paternalism has a racial character in two situations. One occurs when paternalism has a special appeal to minorities, thus reproducing a market split by concentrating on their relatively greater dependence. The other, more common practice (at least in the South) is to offer racial exclusion of prime jobs in exchange for intense same-race loyalty and opposition to interracial unions. Racist paternalism thus explains how employer discrimination can be rational and profitable.

Each factor we have discussed—state repression, the legislated context, union institutions, and employer paternalism—could be added to the theory without contradicting the essential processes of racial competition. The ease with which factors can be added to a split labor market nucleus is due to its exclusive focus on explaining market behavior, which is inherent in any capitalist society. This parsimonious focus is also a weakness in that satisfactory descriptions of historical episodes require multiple layers of factors derived from alternate theories. Previously, these have been haphazardly added; we seek a more coherent integration.

Unifying theories can be costly. Extracting ideas and processes may leave behind theoretical context and nuances; grafting them to a singular approach pares them of any contradicting assumptions. No matter how much the approach grows, any general theory will still require revisions to explain particular histories. We contend that these costs are minor relative to the benefits of constructing systematic explanations because our game theory model offers a method for integrating alternative theoretical arguments. It translates varying contexts and institutions into specific determinants of organizational capacity and rational individual actions. Specifically, the effect of the political context on union efficacy is translated into varying levels of union monitoring and sanctioning. The costs and benefits of strikebreaking versus solidarity vary accordingly. Union institutionalization of racial inclusion has similar effects in terms of building minority solidarity. Employer paternalism, however, raises the cost of solidarity and the benefits from strikebreaking. We demonstrate the mechanics of modifying the model to consider alternate contexts in the comparative analysis. The point here is that the model allows an evolving context to affect individual and institutional behavior.

CONCLUSION

In this chapter we delineated the basic propositions of racial competition theory and provided an overview of the research carried out from the split labor market variant. In so doing, we attempted to highlight its weaknesses and limitations, and also to show which cases and periods conform with theoretical expectations. The theory has undergone revision as it has expanded to account for the reproduction of split labor markets and the role of the state. In locating competition approaches in relation to other relevant perspectives, it becomes clear that the further development of the theory will necessarily draw on the insights of other perspectives. Specifically, theories of racial and ethnic competition should take aspects of collective action, political process, and divide and conquer arguments into account. Most important is that the study of interracial solidarity is significantly underdeveloped.

Modifying a game theory model of organizational compliance to split labor market precepts provides a means to examine the dynamics of racial competition and class solidarity over time. It also facilitates the incorporation of political and ideological conditions specified in other theories, which can later be empirically assessed. We believe that this approach is useful not only because it incorporates a theoretically necessary focus on solidarity, but also because it represents a useful bridge between "analytical induction," an approach that has characterized the cumulative split labor market research, and our efforts to develop a more general and complete theory.

CHAPTER 3

Migration and Markets—
The Origins of Split Labor Markets

Migration of distinct racial or ethnic groups is the source of most split labor markets. Important in its own regard, understanding the process of migration in terms of its national and world-system context is also a worthwhile preliminary to the case studies and comparative analysis. Here we explore the roots of different forms of migration in terms of their consequences for the genesis of split labor markets, with specific emphasis on the Chinese immigration to the West Coast in the nineteenth century and on the "Great Migration" that began in 1916.

At different periods in the development of the world-system, particular combinations of imperialism, proletarianization of peripheral labor, and commodification of world markets produce different patterns of migration. The pattern of migration affects the origin and subsequent reproduction of split labor market conditions. On the basis of the historical period and degree of incorporation into the world market, three main types of migration can be identified: (1) coercive migration, where colonial populations are forced to migrate to the core; (2) sojourning migration, where temporary migrants remain in the core labor market only as long as necessary to earn a certain amount of income; and (3) wage migration, where migrants seek high wages in the core after proletarianization pushes them out of petty-commodity production in the periphery. To be sure, the conditions associated with migration will differ for each nation and each ethnic group. The form of split labor markets also depends on a number of cultural factors, such as

45

preexisting ideologies of racism, cultural distinctiveness, and ethnocentrism, which we cannot fully consider here. Since we are dealing only with the United States, we can basically assume that widespread racist ideologies and a high level of ethnocentrism already existed prior to and throughout the periods under investigation.

COERCIVE MIGRATION

In the history of capitalism and colonialism, before an external area is incorporated into the world-system, imperialists typically required coercion to acquire labor (Portes 1978, p. 11). Where populations in the initial "contact periphery" (Hall 1986, pp. 391–92) had to be forced to become colonial labor, their labor supply elasticity was equal to or greater than that of dominant workers (rather than less, as found in core split labor markets) (Berg 1961). The peripheral population was usually unwilling to enter the labor market because it was involved in noncapitalist modes of production, such as petty-commodity or communal-tribal production, and as wages increased, workers' need (or desire) for paid employment often diminished.

SOJOURNING MIGRATION

The world capital accumulation drive eventually incorporated the contact periphery and colonial areas into the world-system by commodifying economic relations (Bonacich and Cheng 1984). The process of commodification and incorporation into the world-system made the traditional petty-commodity agricultural sector dependent on the imperial enclave, which in turn was dependent on the imperial core. The double layered dependency in the peripheral society is what Portes (1978, pp. 11–12) calls a "structural imbalance," which disrupted traditional culture but did not necessarily eliminate noncapitalist modes of production. On the contrary, by reducing reproduction costs through subsistence production, the traditional noncapitalist sector lowered the cost of colonial labor to the imperial employer. Capitalist and noncapitalist modes of production coexisted, both producing for the same single capitalist commodity market (Boswell 1984; Chase-Dunn 1992).

Because economic relations have been commodified and monetized such that workers are dependent on wages, coercion is no longer necessary to create a supply of colonial labor. A steady stream of workers now voluntarily seek wages in order to acquire increasingly commodified consumption goods, but not necessarily to become permanent wage workers. Instead, workers from the traditional segment had a sojourning relationship to the labor market, seeking wage employment only during off-seasons, in order to buy land or for expedient purchases (Siu 1952; Boswell 1986). They tended to be single young males who are least enmeshed in local networks, most mobile, and garner the highest wages (Bonacich 1972; Bonacich and Cheng 1984).

Wage Migration

The third type of migration, wage migration, occurs with proletarianization, which represents the full extent of the commodification of labor. In this case, the property of noncapitalist peripheral producers is expropriated, forcing the population into the labor market on a full-time, totally dependent basis. Wage migration, where low-wage workers migrate to higher paying areas, is simply an extension of labor market forces of supply and demand across national borders (Greenwood 1975; Vickery 1977). However, during the process of proletarianization, the variation in migration is mainly determined by the social conflict at the point of origin, not the attractiveness of higher wages at the destination (Fligstein 1981). Unlike sojourners, proletarians have no agricultural plots or other subsistence production to return to and thus seek permanent employment. Labor costs are lower for recently proletarianized immigrants only because of the destitution and oversupply of labor that proletarianization entails, not because of coercion, subsistence subsidies, or temporary orientation. However, recent migrants resemble sojourners in that they tend to be mobile and have not yet formed stable networks in a community (Brown and Boswell 1995).

Colonial expropriations that created a dependent labor supply have historically taken numerous forms. The most common form has been the result of the centralization of ownership in agriculture. Most of the population in peripheral areas are peasants, sharecroppers, small farmers, or other semiautonomous agricultural producers. Class struggles revolve primarily around control over the land between the producers and landlords, and (secondarily) over access to credit between farmers and banks or other creditors (including the state). Integration into the world commodity market intensifies the struggle as landlords seek to replace subsistence production with production for the world market. The centralization of landowning by landlords expropriates the small producers, forcing them into the labor market.

The three sources of migration that fuel split labor markets are outlined in Figure 3.1. While the uneven development of world capital accumulation underlies all three migration trajectories, there is also a tiered temporal determination from the top to the bottom. In the earliest period described by the top line, colonization by core empires that leads to coercive migration also increases the integration of world commodity markets. The latter, which provides for sojourning migration between production modes (middle line), simultaneously leads to the expropriation of noncapitalist producers when coupled with imperial investment (bottom line).

It is important to point out that while proletarianization of colonial populations is a likely outcome of incorporation into the capitalist world-system, it is not an inevitable result. Coercive migration may persist for centuries (as in the case of the American slave trade) or the colonial population may be eliminated from the economy by core settlers through genocide or reservation systems (as in the case of the Native American and Aboriginal Australian populations). Nor should these three migration trajectories be seen as pure alternatives as a mixture of all three frequently occurred. The extent that migration can be described as coercive, sojourning, or wage can best be determined by examining the history of the origins of ethnic split labor markets.

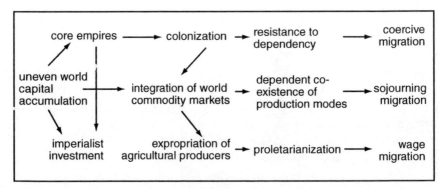

Figure 3.1 Sources of Peripheral Migration to Core Split Labor Markets

THE ORIGINS OF SPLIT LABOR MARKETS IN THE UNITED STATES

Chinese: Coercive coolie migration, a form of debt servitude, existed in Latin America but, despite popular conceptions, was not used in the United States (Coolidge 1909; Boswell 1986). Instead, Chinese migrants were sojourners drawn first by the California gold rush of 1849. They were later recruited for wage work on the transcontinental railroads and for jobs in manufacturing and agriculture. These sojourners benefited from a major difference in living costs between California and China, where they would return to resume peasant agriculture at a marked increase in status. Most Chinese migrants were from southern China where the population faced a significant "push" factor, but this was due to food and land shortages, not proletarianization. Nor was the state forcing migration. On the contrary, emigration was technically illegal in China until the 1860s (Mei 1984). Another less obvious factor was that rural Chinese culture defined social status only in terms of one's home village (Zo 1978, p. 129). A sojourner could do very poorly by California standards, but return home relatively wealthy. The expectation that hardships will be temporary often led sojourners to accept conditions other workers would not tolerate (Chen 1980, pp. 15–16; Bonacich 1973; Siu 1952). Chinese letters and documents examined by Zo (1978, pp. 152–53) indicate that most emigrants intended to return to their home villages. Chen (1980, p. 15) estimated that nearly 50 percent returned. This corresponds with U.S. immigration figures of 99,604 total Chinese immigrants and 45,322 emigrants between 1848 and 1867 (Tsai 1983, p. 22). Between 1860 and 1890, the vast majority of Chinese settled in western states, primarily California.

As discussed in the next chapter, the first Chinese migrants faced little ethnic discrimination until capitalization of production began to replace the independent producers. In this case, the source of discrimination was not capitalists seeking to force producers into the labor market, but independent white miners seeking to defend their position against industrial mining and water companies. Price standards set by the white miners for dealing with the companies were undercut by the sojourning Chinese. The dominant producers often reacted with violent discrimination during recessionary periods and through the local state, which was largely under their control. Discrimination forced the Chinese into the labor market (or alternative petty-commodity production), reducing the elasticity of Chinese labor which, ironically, provided lower cost labor to the industrial companies.

Despite white resistance and political power, the mines were capitalized. In addition to the effects of economic concentration and centralization, the economics of mining require ever more capital intensive production as the grade of ore declines and the source of ore deepens. By the late 1860s, Chinese migrants were primarily wage workers, not petty-commodity producers. The railroad companies and large agricultural employers played a major role in recruiting Chinese immigrants and encouraging the state to reduce migration restrictions, but there is little evidence that imperial capital or the state directly forced migration from China. However, employers recruited Chinese labor in part because China was politically incapable and often unwilling to protect migrants from harsh working conditions abroad. This contrasts sharply with the diplomatic pressure applied by European states on behalf of their emigrants (Zo 1978). Furthermore, the Chinese were denied the right to become naturalized U.S. citizens, which legally reinforced their status as sojourners (Chen 1980; Bonacich 1984).

While the geographic dispersion of Chinese immigrants east of the Rocky Mountains was still minuscule (3 percent) in 1880, their occasional employment in eastern factories and southern plantations attracted national media attention (Boswell 1986). Anti-Chinese discourse helped reunify white workers and farmers in the Democratic Party. A moral tone was added to appeal to the middle classes, leaving only big capital, primarily the railroads and large-scale western agriculture, in clear support of open immigration. Resistance by the latter was muted by increased immigration from other sources, primarily southeastern Europe and Mexico. The Exclusion Act was passed in 1882, which banned further immigration of Chinese workers (Saxton 1971; Boswell 1986, pp. 365–66).

Blacks: Coercive migration is obvious in the creation of an African slave labor force on plantations in the United States (Genovese 1965). Imperial capital came into contact with noncapitalist modes at two points: tribal populations in Africa and (white) petty-commodity farmers in America. Coercion was required to both commodify African labor into the world market and to sustain large-scale plantations, as opposed and in opposition to either petty-commodity or pure capitalist agriculture in America. The former was mainly accomplished by private agents of Portuguese, Dutch, and British merchants, the latter by the state acting in the interest of British colonial rule and later, American plantation owners.

As slaves, blacks did not directly compete with dominant workers in the labor market for paid positions, but the use of slavery removed positions from competition and constricted the overall size of the labor market. While slaves were mainly in agriculture, any labor intensive industry faced the option of slave labor, particularly the construction industry, an early source of union strength outside the South. Following the Civil War, sharecropping and petty-commodity farming consumed much of the black labor force. Throughout the South, the white planter elite and emerging industrial capitalists openly pursued a policy of "blacks for the land, whites for the factory" (Williamson 1986, p. 223). Planters sought to recreate a captive labor force through limiting market alternatives and to reassert the servile position of blacks through a "Jim Crow" cultural superstructure. They were joined to varying degrees after Reconstruction by other white elites whose power was threatened in the late nineteenth century by the rise of the Populists, an interracial movement. White southern workers joined the racist crusade to prevent split labor market competition once the Populists no longer offered a viable alternative (which itself often became a racist organization) (Goodwyn 1976, pp. 533–41).

A major black migration stream into the labor market did not begin until World War I and the boll weevil infestation of the 1910s. From this time on, black rural migrants constituted a low-cost alternative to dominant workers in low-skill jobs, replacing the diminished supply of southeast European peasant immigrants whose migration was legally curtailed in 1917 and restricted further in 1923 (Piore 1979; Lieberson 1980). Until the 1930s, blacks mainly left sharecropping and petty-commodity farming for wage work because the latter provided a better income. Piore (1979, pp. 159–62) suggests that throughout this period and to a lesser extent continuing to the 1960s, a large proportion of black migrants out of the South were sojourners. Like the southeast Europeans before them, southern black migrants found northern cities less repressive but more inhospitable, a place to make money, not to live. Piore's claims are only weakly substantiated, especially after the 1930s, but it is clear that the status of large numbers of blacks in the North was initially unsettled and in flux. This migration fundamentally altered race and labor relations.

THE GREAT MIGRATION

After the commencement of World War I, black agricultural workers left the South in great numbers. Marks (1983, p. 73) notes that in the two years between 1916 and 1918 more than four hundred thousand blacks, or 5 percent of the total black population, relocated to the North. Economic factors provided a major impetus. By the turn of the century, poor southern whites had begun to enter sectors of the agricultural economy traditionally dominated by blacks (Myrdal 1944; Wilson 1978). In addition, blacks were also displaced by boll weevil infestations, floods, fluctuations in the prices of crops, and mechanization. Taken together, these forces prompted many agricultural workers to seek employment in northern cities (Myrdal 1944; Wilson 1978; Marks 1989). Black workers could earn substantially more in the North than they could in the South, and thousands responded to a severe wartime labor shortage created by military recruitment combined with a sharp drop in European immigration (Florant 1942; Henri 1975; Wilson 1978).[1] Many migrants also sought better educational opportunities for their children, hoped to escape racial persecution, and believed that racial tolerance was more widespread in the North.

Once the migration was underway, lines of communication established by labor recruiters, family members, and the black press helped to reinforce the southern exodus by connecting migrants with resources and social support networks in urban communities (Myrdal 1944; Marks 1983; Dickerson 1986). Letters written by black migrants between 1916 and 1918 reveal much about their experiences after they reached the northern cities (Scott 1920). On the whole, the letters paint a relatively positive picture. They frequently mention higher wages, improved race relations, and plans to bring other family members to the North. Between 1910 and 1920, the black populations of Chicago, Detroit, and Cleveland more than doubled, and they doubled again in the next decade. Other major cities experienced comparable rates of growth. During this same twenty-year period, the percentage of America's blacks that lived in the South fell from 90 to 79 percent (U.S. Bureau of the Census 1935, p. 5).

Due to the fact that migrants often have left peripheral areas with high unemployment, a lower standard of living, and an agricultural mode of production, they enter the labor force with motives and resources that differ from those of more established, long-term workers.

Myrdal (1944), Piore (1979), Dickerson (1986), Gottlieb (1987), and others have suggested that to varying degrees the black migrant population had a temporary orientation toward residency in the North, and return migration to the South did occur in some instances (Lewis 1931; Epstein 1969; Spero and Harris 1969). According to Piore (1979, pp. 158–59), the black population was:

> fundamentally tied to the rural, agricultural South. However oppressive the cultural patterns of the communities in which they lived, they were comfortable and familiar, especially in comparison to the conditions of urban life. . . . The blacks did not, in other words, leave to escape the South. They responded to recruitment patterns of northern industry. They sought temporary economic advantages and expected to return.

To the extent that black migrants expected to return to the South, they resembled sojourners, whose primary objective is to reap a specified financial gain in the shortest amount of time and return home (Siu 1952, p. 35). Although evidence for sojourning patterns of migration among black migrants is limited, the entrance of black migrants into the industrial workforce was characterized by high rates of job turnover (see Gottlieb 1987, pp. 123–28; Grossman 1989, pp. 191–97). For instance, in 1917 Epstein (1969) interviewed 330 single black male migrants in Pittsburgh and learned that 42 percent "were going back (South) or somewhere else" (Epstein 1969, pp. 27–28). Dickerson (1986, p. 102) estimates the average length of employment of blacks in the Pittsburgh steel mills at one month. In addition, brief and long-term visits by black migrants to their points of origin were not uncommon, and migrants moved back to their southern homes in response to unemployment or economic downturns associated with the depressions of 1920–21 and the 1930s (Gottlieb 1987). Some black migrants shifted between employment in rural and urban areas, returning to family farms during months when agricultural activity was at its peak (Lewis 1931; Myrdal 1944; Spero and Harris 1969; Gottlieb 1987).

Sojourners also tend to be more willing than other workers to endure poor working conditions, lower pay, and longer hours (Bonacich 1972, pp. 551–52). Northern labor agents often convinced southern blacks to sign contracts for wages that were below the prevailing rate, and migrants frequently had to reimburse employers for the costs of transportation and housing (Marks 1983, p. 76). "Equal wages for equal work" was common in situations where blacks and whites worked side by side, performing the same tasks, but blacks and whites generally did not work side by side, and the jobs with higher pay scales were disproportionately occupied by whites (Kennedy 1930, p. 97; also see Spero and Harris 1969). Because recent migrants have less information than permanent workers about local labor disputes, employers have often used them as strikebreakers (Bonacich 1972). Black strikebreaking peaked during the early years of the Great Migration (Brown 2000), though black strikebreakers were often discharged from their jobs after the resolution of the labor dispute (Hill 1925; Reid 1930; Spero and Harris 1969). When blacks did get a foothold in a given industry, strikebreaking often provided their initial means of entry (Wilson 1978, pp. 71–74).

Despite the apparent transience of the first wave of migrants, developments in the southern economy mitigated against large-scale return migration. As a result of ongoing agricultural difficulties in the South, "at least 85 percent of rural blacks were very poor, if not starving" by 1930 (Fligstein 1981, p. 135). New Deal programs targeted the capitalization of agriculture in the South, contributing to an unprecedented concentration and centralization of agricultural production that forced many black southerners out of their traditional occupations (Fligstein 1981; Wilson 1978). Federal subsidies for farm owners and commercial producers accelerated the pace of mechanization and reduced the amount of acreage under cultivation. Both factors displaced black laborers and tenant farmers (Fligstein 1981). Despite high levels of unemployment in the North, 317,000 blacks migrated out of the South between 1930 and 1940 (Florant 1942, p. 786).[2] Mechanization of agriculture began in earnest after World War II and continued to the point that by the 1960s, migration of small farmers into urban labor markets was no longer a significant source of split labor markets in the United States.

Assessing the degree to which black migrants can be described as sojourners presents special problems because it involves the intentions of individual migrants who may or may not have actually returned to the South. What is important, however, is to recognize that black migrants from the South shared many characteristics with sojourners, regardless of whether they ever became return migrants. Despite intentions, sojourners often fail to return to their homeland for a variety of reasons, but may contribute to a split in the labor market until their temporary orientation ends. If they stay in one region, their orientation to a specific job may be short-term; even if they stay at a specific job, they have the option of returning. In short, recent migrants' orientation to a job or locale is largely economic and lacks the same degree of commitment that holds for long-term residents. We argue that all recent migrants (and especially single young males) share many of the characteristics of sojourners to the extent that they are poor, mobile, and unattached.

DISCUSSION

To what extent can the migration of blacks and Chinese to and within the United States be described as coercive, sojourning, or wage? Only blacks faced coercive migration of any major consequence. Coercive migration of Chinese was widespread in parts of Latin America, India, and southern Africa, but not North America. The exception was approximately two to three thousand Chinese prostitutes, who made up the majority of the small number of female Chinese immigrants until the late 1870s (Cheng 1984). At least in original intent, almost all other Chinese immigrants in the nineteenth century were sojourners.

During the interwar period, blacks in the South also migrated to urban labor markets, to some extent, in a sojourning fashion. Black migrants resembled the sojourners of the European immigrant populations from the semicapitalized agricultural areas that they were replacing. The uneven development between industry and agriculture that was fueling sojourning migration at the world level was also the source of migration between the South and North in the United States. After the 1930s and especially after World War II, proletarianization forced blacks into the labor market without recourse to sojourning. Blacks were increasingly wage migrants: the combination of boll weevil infestation, the Great Depression, mechanization of agriculture, and wartime and postwar industrial surge thoroughly proletarianized the bulk of the black population.

On the other hand, Chinese immigrants began as and largely remained sojourners. Like blacks, the first immigrants did not originally enter the labor market. But unlike blacks, the Chinese could remain sojourners because they were returning to China where proletarianization in agriculture was little advanced. Early mining and railroad work was also project-specific, which limited the period of employment and increased the likelihood of a return to China when the job was finished.

The prohibition on naturalization had a similar effect. Many immigrants, of course, did not return, and they usually settled in the "Chinatowns" of larger cities.

THE REPRODUCTION OF SPLIT LABOR MARKETS

Below, we outline some of the more important consequences of the world-systemic sources of migration that produce split labor markets in the United States. The effect of coerced migration and slavery set the pattern for black-white interaction once blacks entered the labor market. Coercion against blacks continued to be socially legitimate and legal in most political and social circumstances. Systematic violence and social subordination were used by planters attempting to control a low-cost labor force and by white workers attempting to continue the exclusion of blacks from direct labor market competition (Reich 1981).

The effect of continued discrimination was to perpetuate split labor market conditions even after blacks became fully proletarianized. To the extent that coercion reduced the income of blacks and confined them to low-wage, low-productivity positions, it reproduced the split in the labor market between blacks and whites. In addition to its psychological and ideological functions, segregation in the South prevented the short-term decline in white wages that would have accompanied the rise in black wages (and long-term rise in white wages) if equal competition was allowed (Reich 1981). Segregation was also supported by racist capitalists. A segregated labor market protected racist employers who hired only white labor from employers who would hire low-wage black labor.[3] Thus, the split labor market was relatively immune from the equalizing effects of competition and commodification.

The self-perpetuating split in the labor market was fractured in the North (but not completely broken) by employers after World War I when strikes and the reduction of European immigration threatened to dramatically increase white wages. The increased cost of union labor was not uniform across firms, reducing the ability of segregation to protect against competition from employers of lower cost labor. The split in labor costs was not fully eliminated in the North due not only to continued discrimination, but also to the fact that black workers were still migrating from the low-wage South (Lieberson 1980).

Sojourners were discriminated against in both cases. While this discrimination was historically important in reproducing the split in the labor market, it is not a necessary condition. Because sojourners expect a short-term duration, they willingly suffer low wages and undesirable working conditions, do not make long-term human capital investments, and have little interest in union benefits. With sojourning migration, cost differentials will be reproduced with "pure" competition (i.e., no coercion or other political interference). However, dominant workers are likely to be fiercely antagonistic and discriminate against sojourners simply because sojourners are temporary.

Finally, turning to wage migrants, barring discrimination there is no obvious reason for the split in labor costs to be perpetuated once the migration is complete and the migrants have been absorbed into the labor force. Segregation may nevertheless continue, without coercion, via abandonment of low-paying jobs by dominant workers. Although less severe than under coercive or sojourning migration, discrimination is also likely to continue. As described above for blacks, the short-term shock of wage adjustment from eliminating discrimination was a sufficient incentive for dominant labor to continue discriminating. In addition, state-enforced discrimination, such as the lack of citizenship, has a similar effect. As is the case with coercive migration, the long-term effect of wage migration is the perpetuation of split labor market conditions if discrimination continues. This occurs despite the fact that the initial cause of the split is no longer operative.

CONCLUSION

The origin of ethnic discrimination generated by split labor markets is to a great extent a function of the division of a world labor market into national segments. Except for sojourners, after initial immigration and absorption into the labor force, the perpetuation of split labor markets depends on the reciprocal effects of discrimination on the labor market.[4] With a decline in discrimination, the effects of the ethnicity of past immigrants on labor market position independent from class background or skill level, likewise decline in significance (Wilson 1978). On the other hand, with sojourning migration, a split is produced in the labor market even where no discrimination occurs. Sojourners are the quintessential economic source of split labor markets. Note that the sojourning migration we investigate occurs between different modes of production, mainly between petty-commodity and capitalist labor markets, indicating the importance of differentiating modes even within the same world-system.

In comparing Chinese immigrants and black migrants, the great irony is that the 1882 Exclusion Act indirectly benefited the Chinese who managed to remain in the United States. Lieberson (1980) points out that the intensity of racist discrimination was equally high for blacks and Chinese during the latter nineteenth century. Yet a hundred years later, Chinese Americans fare better as a group despite the Civil Rights Movement, desegregation, affirmative action, and black enfranchisement. The crucial difference is that poor blacks continued to migrate out of the rural South throughout much of the twentieth century. This continually recreated a split labor market that maintained racial antagonism, and more importantly, undercut the black wage gains of a previous generation. Unlike white ethnic slums that were passed on to new immigrant groups, black slums were replenished by new blacks. While declining migration and economic expansion produced gains in the post–World War II period, Wilson (1987) documents how the twin blows of deindustrialization and community disintegration produced a severe retrenchment in the 1970s and 1980s.

In contrast, Chinese immigration was halted in 1882 and remained minuscule until relatively recently. As a result, the remaining Chinese occupied niches and middlemen minority positions within society that allowed upward mobility for a significant number (Bonacich 1973). They also developed, often through collective action, a sizable business class. Although racism remained, the proportional decline in numbers reduced levels of active discrimination. As a result, and despite similar treatment in the late nineteenth century, the mobility patterns of recent generations of Chinese Americans and blacks have been decidedly different.

We can also look at the comparison of ethnic experiences in split labor markets from a long-term historical perspective. Proletarianization is one of the central continuing dynamics of the world capitalist system (Chase-Dunn 1987). Consequently, coercive migration of noncapitalist labor is no longer necessary and sojourning across modes of production will diminish. More salient than sojourners from noncapitalist modes will be temporary workers whose short-term orientation to the labor market is similar. If the distinction between permanent and temporary labor gets defined along ethnic lines, ethnic antagonism and discrimination are likely to follow, as evidenced by the reactions against "guest workers" in western Europe during economic recessions (Wallimann 1984). Uneven development also ensures that even in a fully proletarianized world labor market, differences in labor costs and associated split labor markets will be recreated by new waves of immigration from periphery to core. This need not result in ethnic antagonism and discrimination, but that is likely as long as dominant workers identify their interests in market and national—rather than class and global—terms.

CHAPTER 4

Sojourner Labor—The Pattern of Discrimination against Chinese Immigrants, 1850–1882

> [T]ime and experience have shown that we can gain nothing from these people. . . . Although an industrious class of beings, they will not partake of our habits; even their breadstuffs and habiliments they bring with them from the "flowery kingdom."
>
> —*Mining and Scientific Press*, 1860

In nineteenth-century America, Chinese immigrants were largely sojourners. They moved between the labor market and self-employment under conditions of constant racial prejudice, and periodically, they faced discrimination on a mass scale.[1] While historical studies of Chinese immigrants treat ethnocentric prejudice as a constant factor in race relations, scholars generally focus on three periods of market contraction in which discriminatory actions were particularly violent and organized.[2] These include: 1852–54, when independent miners rioted against the first major Chinese immigration; 1867–69, when white mineworkers combined anti-company strikes with anti-Chinese discrimination; and 1876–82, when white workers and white small business owners formed a political alliance in the Democratic Party in order to secure national anti-Chinese state action.

In Table 4.1, we outline the central events and actors during each of these periods. The case study follows this outline: in the first section, we explain the initial racial difference in labor costs and the origins of the racist ideology; in the following sections, we describe the formation of the split labor market and explain its reproduction; in the final section, we examine the sources of the interclass racial alliance against the Chinese.[3] Because the split labor market originated in mining, where the Chinese were initially concentrated, we focus on labor relations in that industry and make comparisons to labor relations in the railroads, skilled trades, and manufacturing. This chapter addresses the following theoretical issues: (1) how are split labor markets and the resulting racial antagonisms formed?; (2) how do changes in the relations of production shape (and even reverse) patterns of discrimination?; (3) how does a split labor market and the corresponding racist discourse become self-perpetuating?; and (4) how can split labor markets engender interclass

Table 4.1

Central Actors and Events for Major Periods of Competition and Discrimination

	1852–1854	*1867–1869*	*1876–1882*
competing actors:	white vs. Chinese independent producers	white unions and craft workers vs. Chinese workers	white alliance in Democratic Party vs. Chinese (as a race)
principal industries:	independent mining; water companies	industrial mining; skilled trades; local manufacturing; railroads	industrial mining; local and national manufacturing; railroads
market conditions:	initial Chinese immigration; recession	release of Chinese railroad workers; Civil War ends	recession; release of Chinese railroad workers
effects of discrimination:	push Chinese into wage labor; invoke racist ideology	segregate market; push Chinese into self-employment	push Chinese labor into Chinese shops; Exclusion Act

political alliances? To answer these questions, the narrative will show how the forms and effects of discrimination differed according to changes in technology and class relations in mining and other industries.

THE INDEPENDENT PRODUCERS: 1852–54

Prior to 1852, the small numbers of immigrant Chinese were mainly merchants. They were tolerated and sometimes officially welcomed by state authorities in the sparsely populated West (Shen 1942; Nee and Nee 1973). The California gold rush, however, lured thousands of Chinese to America. Chinese immigration to the West Coast jumped tenfold from 2,716 in 1851 to 20,026 in 1852 (see Coolidge 1909, p. 498). White gold miners reacted to the initial influx of Chinese immigrants with racial violence. When a recession and drop in gold prices in 1853–54 intensified competition for profitable mining claims, they forcibly drove Chinese (and Mexican) miners out and confiscated those claims that were highly profitable (Saxton 1971; Lingenfelter 1974; Chiu 1967; Coolidge 1909).

Racist behavior of the white miners was directed against the Chinese as competing commodity producers and property owners. During the initial gold rush of 1849, most mines were placer mines consisting of small surface digs that yielded the highest grade of ore. Placer mining requires little skill or capital. Picks, shovels, pans, and especially water were the primary means of production. The placer miners typically owned their own diggings, individually or in partnerships. Others might work a claim for a percentage or for a fixed daily income, expecting the work to be a temporary condition. However, even those who worked for a fixed income were independent producers. They controlled their own work and owned the means of production, including having to pay for the water used in mining (Paul 1947; Lingenfelter 1974; Boswell and Brueggemann 2000).

Miners were not wage workers in the usual sense, even when they did not own the mining claim and received a nominal "wage" (Paul 1947, p. 119). Instead, this was a variant of petty-commodity production in which ownership of the property rights (the mining claim) did not include ownership of the means of production. Commercial relations (prices) instead of wage relations governed the labor process. As independent petty-commodity producers, the white miners shared something close to the Jacksonian ideal of an egalitarian "producer ethic."

This egalitarianism did not extend to outsiders, however, particularly the Chinese (Saxton 1971).

Whites accused the Chinese of accepting a lower standard of living, which with continued large-scale immigration, diluted the income of the white miners. There is no doubt that Chinese immigrants were generally poor. Most emigrants were peasants from southeastern China where arable land was limited, the population was increasing, and the price of rice was rising, factors that created a substantial migration "push" even before gold was discovered in California (Zo 1978; Tsai 1983). Compared with white migrants from the East, the Chinese were burdened with passage loans requiring repayments as high as $100 for the $40–$50 ticket, which depressed their ability to demand or search for higher incomes (Zo 1978, pp. 95–96). It is these initial differences in national incomes that led to the identification of job competition with racial competition, and to the generation of racial antagonisms. However, Chinese and white placer miners were competing producers, not competing wage workers. Chinese miners who worked their own mines were under no constraints to take less gold from the land than white miners. Unlike a labor market where employers set wages, petty-commodity property owners keep what they produce.

White miners discriminated against the Chinese in defense of their status as independent producers in the face of declining placer mines and competition from capitalist production. The threat from capitalist production initially came from water companies that built irrigation systems to bring water to the placer mines, once those near natural water bodies were exhausted. By controlling the water, the companies could control the mining process and charge high prices for water use. Water companies became the targets of "strikes" by the white placer miners, which usually concerned the price of water (*Mining and Scientific Press* 1860). As such, they were actually a type of boycott peculiar to petty-commodity production (Paul 1947). The participants were reacting as independent producers to the increasing control of the water companies. Included in these strikes or boycotts were riots and other actions against Chinese miners, whom white miners saw as diluting their position in relation to the water companies. The white miners resented the loss of income and the loss of independence the water companies could inflict upon them. They treated the Chinese as scapegoats for "accepting" a low living standard that did not challenge the water companies' high prices (Chiu 1967; Saxton 1971).

ANTI-CHINESE IDEOLOGY

The white miners identified Chinese labor competition with the negative influence that both capitalism and slavery were having on independent petty-commodity production (Coolidge 1909; Zo 1978). According to the ideology of the white miners, competition with the Chinese was unfair because the Chinese were neither independent producers nor wage workers. Instead, low-cost Chinese labor was considered a type of slavery. Whites accused Chinese immigrants of being slaves to gang bosses, to capitalists, and even to the Emperor of China (Wyman 1979; Seward 1881; Nee and Nee 1973). A paradoxical mixture of abolitionist rhetoric and racist ideas arose in the discourse of the white miners. They considered Chinese immigration "a more abominable slave traffic than that of the African slave trade in its most odious features" (*Mining and Scientific Press* 1860, p. 4). The same source refers to Chinese as "filth, depravity, and epidemic" (1860, p. 4). The abolitionist and prejudicial beliefs of the white miners were the economic and cultural components of the same racist ideology, and the Chinese suffered a stereotyping similar to that practiced against blacks during the same period (Locklear 1978; Seward 1881; Saxton 1971). For instance, anti-Chinese legislation in California was modeled on anti-black laws found in the Midwest in the 1850s (Saxton 1971).

Although the white miners borrowed from the racist discourse of black slavery, they referred to the importation and exploitation of Chinese labor as a system of "coolie" slave labor. Technically, Chinese "coolie" labor was not a slave system, but a system of indentured labor exchanged for passage loans and minimal wages. It was mainly used to undercut the wages of the former black slaves in Latin America and several British colonies. Chinese immigrants to the United States, on the other hand, were not slaves or indentured workers. Chinese migrants forced into prostitution were an important (and illegal) exception (Cheng 1984). Contracts for passage loans to North America required a monetary repayment instead of a servile one (Seward 1881; Zo 1978; Coolidge 1909; Campbell 1969; Mei 1984).[4]

The ideology that Chinese immigrants to the United States were "coolies" came into being as a result of the property competition in the placer mines. "Coolie" only replaced "Celestial" as a common moniker for the Chinese in the California newspapers after 1852 (Coolidge 1909, pp. 48–49). Prejudice and ignorance about the differences between the monetary and servile contracts explain part of the confusion over the term *coolie* (Coolidge 1909; Zo 1978; Seward, 1881). Coolidge reports that "the newspapers were full of references to the cruelties of this (Latin American) contract coolie trade and . . . the casual reader might readily infer that the Chinese laborers who came to California were of the same class" (1909, pp. 45–46). Below, we examine how working conditions facing the Chinese in North America were analogous to an indentured labor system in two situations, which probably contributed to the spread of the "coolie" myth.

RACIAL DIFFERENCES IN WORKING CONDITIONS

Chinese migrants usually needed passage loans. Chinese clan associations established in California, known as the "six companies," and later, capitalist employers, were a ready source. This included the railroad companies, who recruited labor in China. The immigrant Chinese were likely to seek employment through the six companies or other creditors who were a reliable contact in a strange country (Coolidge 1909; Zo 1978; Hilton 1979). It was also the manifest purpose of the clan associations to aid and protect their constituents (Tsai 1983). The state government allowed the six companies to enforce contracts for passage loans and to prevent the emigration of Chinese debtors. The state even supplied police to the Chinese merchants who controlled the associations (Saxton 1971; Chen 1980). As a conduit for low-paid labor and a coercive collector of debts, the six companies functioned as middlemen in the interests of the capitalist class. By enforcing contracts and otherwise policing Chinese behavior, the six companies acted as an unofficial arm of the state that the white miners could not control through the electoral process. On the surface, a "coolie"-type exchange with private enforcement seemed to be taking place.

A second factor whites considered unfair and slavish was the hiring of Chinese labor in gangs. Large employers, such as company mines, railroads, water companies, and manufacturers, contracted Chinese labor from gang bosses who could speak English. Pay for each gang went only to the boss who kept the difference between the wages he paid to the gang workers and payments made by the company for their work (Seward 1881; Coolidge 1909; Gibson 1877). The gang boss was essentially a middleman subcontractor who had an economic interest in exploiting his subordinates. White wage workers, on the other hand, were individually hired. They considered the gang labor and the enforcement of contracts by Chinese associations to be in contradiction to the principles of a free labor market (Wyman 1979). Because of these racial differences in working conditions, the belief that the Chinese were slaves spread with the development of wage labor. The "coolie myth" legitimized discrimination against the Chinese without upsetting the equally widespread belief in free markets and individual competition.

EFFECTS OF DISCRIMINATION

While the Chinese were never entirely excluded from the gold fields, discrimination created a barrier in the property market that crowded them into non-mining jobs. Discriminatory laws made mining less profitable and less attractive to them. In 1852, the state of California levied on all foreign miners a tax of $3 a month. The tax applied primarily to Chinese miners, because the state had prohibited Chinese immigrants from becoming citizens in 1854. However, the tax was an important source of state revenue (from 25 percent to 50 percent in some counties). Financial dependence on the tax placed a limitation on further legal anti-Chinese activities conducted by the state. Recognizing the importance of this constraint on legislated discrimination, Chinese merchants asked that the tax be increased to $4 in 1853. The tax was declared unconstitutional in 1870, shortly after the placer miners were thoroughly exhausted and the resulting tax revenues had evaporated (Coolidge 1909; Chen 1980; Seward 1881; Shen 1942).

White independent miners tolerated the Chinese where they had pushed them into non-mining wage labor (Shen 1942). White migrants from the East had made the trek to the West Coast to seek their fortune, not to work as laborers or servants (Coolidge 1909; Carranco 1978). Chinese were particularly welcomed in positions that the white miners (who were almost all males) considered female work, such as cooking, housekeeping, or laundry, even though only a handful of the Chinese immigrants were women. Chinese women traditionally did not leave their home village and only about 3 percent of Chinese immigrants were women. The six companies, which kept records on their clan members, estimated that 80 to 90 percent of the approximately six thousand Chinese women in California in 1876 were prostitutes, many of whom were forcibly imported (Tsai 1983, pp. 17, 34; see Coolidge 1909, p. 502; Tsai 1983, p. 22 for immigration statistics on

Chinese women). What was a gender-based division of labor in the East was reproduced as a racial division on the West Coast where women were rare. This division remained even after the white miners left the placer mines to become wage workers, but once wage labor proliferated, a new round of racial antagonism arose.

THE TRANSITION TO WAGE LABOR

In the early 1850s, the average income from wage labor tended to be lower than the average income from self-employment in placer mining, but wages and yields varied together. When a mining field was played out, miners flooded the labor market, depressing wages. When someone discovered a rich field, all types of workers left their wage work, creating a scarcity of labor. Thus, wages rose at precisely the same time the placer mines were most profitable (Chiu 1967). During the mid-1850s, companies began to replace individuals as the owners and operators of placer mines in the West. Once the initial surface digs of a rich field were played out, only more extensive operations were profitable. A drop in bank interest rates in 1858 accelerated the accumulation of claims from miners by companies. Mining companies had easy access to or were owned by banks (Chiu 1967). At the same time, the spread of costly and dangerous explosives in mining further shrank the prospects of individual miners. The use of explosives also reduced water use in the mines, driving many water companies out of business, except those owned by the mining companies themselves. Where miners could not independently contract for water, their dependence on the mining companies made it possible for the company to set piece rates rather than pay prices for the gold or silver ore. The independent miner was quickly becoming a wage worker (Paul 1947; Chiu 1967; Saxton 1971).

By the late 1850s, the market situation had changed (see Perrow 2002). Wages tended to be higher than incomes from independent mining as the high-grade placer mines diminished and the mining companies bought up claims. In 1851, the ratio of income from placer mining to wages for skilled labor ranged from 1.00 to 1.60, and was twice the wage for unskilled labor. By 1853, the incomes from placer mining and wage work were about the same, and five years later, the ratio of income from placer mining to skilled wages ranged from .60 to .67 and was even worse for unskilled labor (Boswell 1986). As a result, there was an exodus of white miners out of the placer mines and into wage work.

By the 1860s, lode mining had supplanted placer mining. Lode mining was a capital-intensive process that traced a vein of ore into hard rock far below the surface. Employees of the lode mining companies needed to be skilled in drilling, using explosives, timbering, tunneling, and working in dangerous underground conditions. As early as 1859, with the discovery of the Comstock Lode in Nevada, the capital requirements of lode mining began to make mining an industrial occupation rather than the independent petty-commodity production associated with placer mining. An industrial revolution was taking place in a matter of decades (Paul 1947). The longer a miner waited to switch from independent placer mining to wage labor in the lode mines, the worse the pay and job in the lode mine were likely to be (Shen 1942). There was a heavy demand for wage workers when the lode mines first opened. Experienced Mexican miners were the first to work in the lode mines. They were later supplanted by skilled Cornish and Irish immigrants (Todd 1967; Wyman 1979; Lingenfelter 1974). By the late 1860s, whites from the East increasingly worked in the mines, prompted by high wages rather than by the possibility of a bonanza find. As the industry was capitalized, wages had become the predominant economic incentive.

By the 1860s, the relationship between the white miners and the Chinese had been transformed. The Chinese placer miners had not become lode miners, due both to a lack of skill and to discrimination. Instead, the Chinese bought the placer mines that white miners were abandoning. White placer miners who wished to unload their claims now welcomed the Chinese buyers, and white wage workers ignored the Chinese placer miners, with whom they did not compete (Saxton 1971; Chiu 1967; Zo 1978; Wyman 1979). Because they had been forced into low-paid wage labor by discrimination throughout the 1850s, the Chinese found the ratio of income from independent mining to income from wage labor much more favorable than did the whites. Chinese wages were usually about half white wages in the West, but ranged to as low as one-third (Coolidge 1909; Shen 1942; Lingenfelter 1974; Paul 1947). Despite the greater returns it provided, independent placer mining was also attractive to the Chinese because it allowed them to avoid competition with whites and the sometimes violent discrimination that competition engendered (Seward 1881). This is the opposite of the situation in the early 1850s, when placer mining was more profitable and independent white miners forced the Chinese into low-paying wage labor.

CLASS CONFLICT AND SEGREGATED LABOR MARKETS: 1867–69

As a result of the limited competition between the white wage-earning mineworkers and the Chinese independent petty-commodity miners, the early 1860s were largely free of anti-Chinese riots (Zo 1978; Chiu 1967; Wyman 1979). During this period, the state moved to protect the Chinese from violent attacks, recognizing the benefits of Chinese miners working the abandoned claims. Also important in dampening discrimination against the Chinese was the absorption of surplus labor during the mid-1860s by the building of the transcontinental railroad (Nee and Nee 1973). The next period of extensive discriminatory action did not take place until the late 1860s, when the reworked placer mines had become unprofitable, even at the reduced incomes of the Chinese. By this time, white workers conducted discriminatory actions in response to the potential of wage competition with Chinese labor. We examine four industries—railroads, mining, skilled trades, and manufacturing—where racial antagonism eventually resulted in segregated labor markets.

THE RAILROADS

In early 1865, the Central Pacific Railroad had specifically advertised for several thousand white laborers, but only eight hundred applied (Seward 1881; Shen 1942). The railroad company turned to recruiting Chinese immigrants. As with split labor market conditions for blacks in the steel industry and elsewhere (Bonacich 1976), the Chinese were first hired as strikebreakers (Zo 1978), yet more important over the long term was the inability of the railroad company to retain white labor. Except for an initial group of Irish workers brought from the East, most of the white railroad workers hired in the West were failed prospectors who had a sojourning-type relationship to wage work and would quit the railroad as soon as they had enough money for a new grubstake (Seward 1881; Saxton 1971; Nee and Nee 1973). The labor market for railroad labor became passively segregated as white workers responded to class conflict over wages by abandoning their jobs for more lucrative possibilities. By the time the rail line was completed in 1869, 83 percent of the 12,500 Central Pacific employees were Chinese (Seward 1881, pp. 23–24). Except in higher-paid skilled or authority positions, Chinese workers filled the abandoned jobs because they lacked better alternatives. In a rare attempt, two thousand Chinese in 1867 went on strike for wages and hours comparable to those paid white labor. Lack of support from white workers and the company's ability to import new labor from China defeated the strike. Afterward, the Chinese were known for a marked disinclination toward labor organizing and strikes (Nee and Nee 1973).

THE LODE MINES: COMSTOCK AND BEYOND

The scarcity of wage workers and the alternatives of independent placer mining or railroad work kept wages high in the 1850s and early 1860s. Unions were essentially nonexistent. After the Civil War, however, former soldiers returned (or ventured) to the western mining fields just as the placer miners were disappearing. These factors increased wage competition to the extent that by 1870 mining wages had declined about 25 percent for skilled mineworkers and 36 percent for unskilled mineworkers (Chiu 1967, pp. 20–21; Lingenfelter 1974, pp. 66–107). As a result, the white miners revived dormant "protective" associations and turned them into labor unions.

Strikes were widespread in the mining fields between 1867 and 1869. The principal strike demands were: $4 a day, union recognition, ban on the use of dynamite (which threatened to deskill black powder users), ban on single jacking (drilling that required only a single mine worker instead of the customary two), often the firing of a foreman, sometimes payments for a hospital fund, and always the exclusion of the Chinese from the mines. White mineworkers were generally successful in segregating the labor market by banning Chinese from underground work and sometimes from mining altogether. They often achieved most of their other demands, at least in the short run, except banning dynamite. The strikes were most successful in the more settled communities, except where Cornish-Irish conflict divided the mineworkers (Lingenfelter 1974; Jensen 1950; Wyman 1979; Zo 1978).

The major precipitating factor in the anti-Chinese character of the 1867–69 mining strikes was the dramatic increase in wage competition resulting from the release in 1869 of Chinese workers from the completed Central Pacific Railroad (Coolidge 1909). Many recently released Chinese railroad workers had acquired skills in drilling and using explosives, making them real competitors for skilled lode mining positions (Seward 1881; Saxton 1971). Most, however, were simply low-paid laborers whom the skilled Cornish mineworkers could easily keep out of underground work. Above ground, mining and water companies hired Chinese construction workers and ditchdiggers. They also hired Chinese to work the mine tailings or do other unskilled labor (Chiu 1967; Todd 1967).

The events of 1869 constituted a classic example of racial conflict in the face of a split labor market. Moreover, these events provided an example to other miners, as indicated by their widespread emulation. As the transcontinental railroad was nearing completion, the miners and other workers held a statewide convention in July concerned mainly with the possible threat of Chinese employment in the mines and mills. In January, a vigilante group from the newly formed "Workingman's Protective Union" had run about sixty Chinese mill workers out of Unionville (Lingenfelter 1974). In what became a trend, the union first marched through town (led by a band) on the way to the Chinese houses.

During this time, William Sharon, superintendent of the Bank of California, which owned or controlled the local railroad, mills, and much of the mining stock, began a railroad from his mills in Carson to the mines. He hired Chinese railroad construction workers, probably released from the transcontinental. On September 29, about four hundred miners assembled to prevent the soon to be released Chinese from staying in the area. The local deputy sheriff read them the riot act, which they greeted with cheers as he had no intention of enforcing it (the elected sheriff belonged to the union). They marched to the Chinese camp, tore down the shanties, and chased some sixty Chinese out of the district (Lingenfelter 1974). William Sharon returned on October 6, but instead of protesting the racist crime, as the newspapers had done, he proclaimed to the striking miners that he opposed hiring Chinese in the mines. He followed the speech with a signed oath. William Sharon may have had a "taste" for discrimination against Chinese, as most whites did at the time, but he also knew that a long strike would inflict significant costs (Lingenfelter 1974).

White workers repeated such incidents throughout the mining districts of the West. Note that the mineworkers were able to exclude Chinese labor from the mines, while a few years earlier, Chinese workers had replaced striking railroad workers and had gone on to fill almost all railroad jobs. Unlike the skilled white workers in the underground mines, where danger and confinement generated a strong sense of interdependent solidarity, the low-skilled white railroad workers were unable to form labor organizations capable of segregating the labor market. Whites leaving the labor market passively segregated railroad work, while organized white mineworkers actively segregated the mining labor market.

APPRENTICESHIP AND ASSIMILATION IN THE SKILLED TRADES

A second source of active segregation occurred in the craft shops and building sites, where white artisans and craft workers considered it impossible to compete fairly with the Chinese. Skilled labor was apprenticed; along with developing the necessary technical proficiency of the craft, apprenticeship included a studious imitation of the habits of the master. Chinese immigrants had maintained their cultural identity over years of subjugation. It was thus not unreasonable for the white craft workers to believe, at minimum, that they could not easily apprentice Chinese. Skilled craft workers claimed that employers were obtaining "slaves to manufactures at a nominal price, thereby depriving regularly apprenticed mechanics, who have spent years to acquire their trade, and white laborers, of their own legitimate field of labor at a fair price" (*Mining and Scientific Press* 1860, p. 4). In addition, they deemed the Chinese workers impossible to assimilate due to deep cultural differences and strong ethnic enclaves (Zo 1978).

Craft unions in the late 1860s and 1870s attempted to protect the income of their members by limiting the number of apprentices to the number of employed craft workers (Coolidge 1909, p. 397), or by imposing long apprenticeship terms (Chiu 1967, p. 122). Chinese workers were accused of undermining the traditional apprenticeship system by only serving the short period necessary to acquire the skill and capital needed to open their own shop (Chiu 1967, pp. 94–95). Newspaper reports claimed that Chinese apprentices would feign illness to avoid their apprenticeship obligations, then recommend another Chinese worker to replace them who would then repeat the process (cited in Chiu 1967, pp. 94–95). The veracity of such claims is nearly impossible to verify, but the widespread belief in these accusations marred relations between white craft workers and potential Chinese apprentices. The white craft workers' beliefs became a self-fulfilling prophecy. Control over the labor process and over apprenticeship enabled them to actively segregate the labor market in skilled trades (Saxton 1971; Wyman 1979).

THE DEVELOPMENT OF MANUFACTURING

In concert with the development of the labor market, small-scale manufacturing expanded in the West during the 1860s. Chinese immigrants had long substituted for women in domestic service. With the development of manufacturing, companies employed Chinese in those manufacturing positions that women and children filled in the East (Coolidge 1909; Seward 1881; Senate Committee 1876). For example, the owner of a jute factory that manufactured grain bags reported that the labor force was "almost entirely Chinese, except the foreman. We tried to get Scotch help, white girls. We imported them for that very purpose, but could not keep them a fortnight. They ran away" (quoted in Seward 1881, p. 84).

It is important to note that the labor and consumer markets in the West were regionally bounded before completion of the transcontinental railroad in 1869. Chinese wages were about half the wage of white males in the West. Compared to eastern wages, however, the Chinese were paid within the same range or only slightly less. A rough comparison of wages in the three areas of manufacture with the largest percentage of Chinese workers in 1867 is presented in Table 4.2. The upper range of Chinese wages in all three industries on the table is about the same as the lower range of white wages in the East (see tabular notes describing data sources for eastern and western wages). Chinese wages were lower than wages paid to women in boot and shoe manufacture but about the same in cigar manufacturing. In the woolen mills, Chinese wages were about 7 percent to 30 percent higher than those paid to children in the East (Boswell 1986).

With the end of the Civil War and completion of the transcontinental railroad, western manufacturers would increasingly have to compete with industrial manufacturers in the East. Competition generated pressure to cut wages. The railroad also rapidly increased the

Table 4.2
Daily Wages for Industries with Chinese Labor Competition

Type of Work	Year	Chinese Wage	White Wage (West)	White Wage (East)	Source
Boot and Shoe Manufacture	1870		$4.00–$5.00	$1.50–$2.50	Coolidge (1909, pp. 360–61)
	1870		$2.00–$2.50 (women)		Coolidge (1909, pp. 360–61)
	1870s		$2.88		Chiu (1967, p. 111)
	1876	$.50–$1.00	$2.00–$2.50	$1.00	Shay (1876, pp. 50–51)
	1880	$.75–$1.25	$2.00–$4.00		Chiu (1967, p. 114–15)
	1880			$1.50–$2.50	Coolidge (1909, 360–61)
	1882	$.83–$1.25	$1.50–$2.17		Saxton (1971, p. 170)
Cigar Manufacture	1876	$1.00	$1.83		Seward (1881, pp. 108, 343)
	1878	$1.00–$1.08		$4.00/1000 cigars	Coolidge (1909, p. 367)
	1880	$.65–$1.75	$1.25–$2.00		Chiu (1967, p. 124)
	1880		$.50–$1.25 (children)		Chiu (1967, p. 124)
	1885	$1.00–$1.50	$2.00	$1.50–$2.25	Coolidge (1909, p. 367)
	1885			$1.00–$1.50	Coolidge (1909, p. 367)
Woolen Mills	1873	$1.08	$3.00	$1.75	Coolidge (1909, p. 374)
	1873			$.83 (boys)	Coolidge (1909, p. 374)
	1870s	$.95–$1.50	$2.50		Chiu (1967, p. 124)
	1870s		$1.25–$1.50 (women)		Chiu (1967, p. 124)
	1870s	$1.00–$1.25	$1.17–$4.00	$.83–$2.90	Coolidge (1909, p. 373)
	1870s		$1.00 (boys)	$.69–$1.16 (children)	Coolidge (1909, p. 373)
	1876	$1.12			Coolidge (1909, p. 372)

Note: All wages are for adult males per day unless otherwise noted. Data on Chinese and white wages in the West are from San Francisco where most mills and shops were located. Eastern wages are from the East Coast, primarily New York and Massachusetts. Weekly wages have been converted to a daily figure by assuming a six-day week. Percent Chinese in 1867 is for San Francisco only (Coolidge 1909, p. 359); for 1880, it refers to the state of California (Chiu 1967, p. 65).

labor supply by releasing Chinese workers and transporting new workers to the West, further depressing wages. For the Chinese, active segregation in the mines and skilled trades crowded them into the labor market for manufacturing jobs. Accustomed to high wages, white workers in manufacturing formed "anti-coolie" clubs that blamed wage cuts on competition with the Chinese rather than on competition with eastern manufacturers (Seward 1881; Coolidge 1909; Shen 1942).

As was the case of the railroads, employers first hired Chinese workers in boot and shoe manufacturing as strikebreakers in 1869 (Nee and Nee 1973). While the white manufacturing workers actively discriminated against the Chinese, they lacked the skill levels and interdependent solidarity found in the skilled trades and mines. They were unable to form labor organizations strong enough to prevent competition from low-wage Chinese labor. Also, manufacturing faced national markets while craft workers (and possibly some unskilled labor) in fields such as the building, maritime, and metal trades faced regionally limited markets that were relatively free from national competition. As a result, unskilled manufacturing jobs in the West, like railroad work, became an increasingly Chinese occupation (Saxton 1971).

While different in content from the racial competition in the property market in the early 1850s, the intense labor market discrimination in the late 1860s had similar long-term effects on the ideological orientation of the white workers. They considered competition with Chinese labor unfair because pay for Chinese labor fell below the prevailing market wage. Active segregation in mining and the skilled trades reproduced split labor market conditions by crowding Chinese labor into other industries, where passive segregation occurred as whites abandoned low-paying jobs. The belief that the Chinese were "coolie" slaves had the real effect of reducing Chinese wages. Thus, the racism of the white workers became self-perpetuating in that it encouraged exactly the labor cost differences upon which it was based.

ELECTIONS AND STATE ACTION

In 1868, the United States signed the Burlingame Treaty, which was primarily intended to open China to American trade by codifying reciprocal relations of equality. The treaty included a clause on the reciprocal right of voluntary emigration. Emigration was not the central focus of the treaty, which was negotiated before the intensification of racial antagonism during the recession of 1868–69, but the emigration clause served as a legal barrier to exclusion until renegotiation of the treaty in 1880 (Coolidge 1909). According to Tsai (1983, p. 11), the Chinese government paid little attention to the treatment of émigrés. Emigration was considered disgraceful; before 1868, Chinese emigration was even a rarely enforced crime. Their home government's refusal to protest the maltreatment of the overseas Chinese prior to the Burlingame Treaty surely contributed to their plight.

At the local level, actions by the state generally lagged behind the conflicts in the mines and manufacturing shops. There was a general dearth of discriminatory state activity after the mid-1850s, but in 1870 several states and municipalities passed ordinances that discriminated against the Chinese. These included the following: minimum lodging space laws, bans or taxes on the use of poles to carry laundry or vegetables, bans on the wearing of queues (braids), prohibitions from owning land, and prohibitions on hiring Chinese for municipal works (Chen 1980, pp. 137–39). While supported by the mineworkers, few of the state regulations were specifically directed to the conflict in the mines or mills, since by 1870 the labor market was already highly segregated along racial lines. State activity intensified with the onset of elections and with changes in tax revenues, neither of which were directly related to racial competition in the labor market.

Discriminatory state actions were particularly extensive in 1870 because elections that year included large numbers of naturalized European immigrants who had come west to work in the mines in 1868 and 1869. In California, anti-Chinese agitation became the racial rallying point under which ethnically diverse white workers could unite in the Democratic Party yet, as workers, still oppose slavery (the "coolie" slave system) (Saxton 1971). Also, by 1870 the foreign miners tax no longer contributed to state revenues. Nevertheless, the discriminatory laws were declared unconstitutional under the Civil Rights Act of 1870 (Chen 1980; Tsai 1983).

CHINESE CAPITALISTS AND THE ANTI-CHINESE ALLIANCE 1876–82

Labor market segregation and a general economic expansion reduced the arenas of direct racial competition and dampened antagonism in the early 1870s (Saxton 1971). Segregated from the underground mines and skilled trades, and crowded into low-wage agricultural or sweatshop work, Chinese immigrants often tried to escape the wage system entirely. Stories in the press noted their penchant for self-employment (Chiu 1967, p. 94). Chinese acquisition of placer mines that white miners had given up must be seen in this light. Another alternative to wage labor was still the option of providing low-cost, gender-stereotyped services, such as laundering or cooking. In combination with stereotypes that the Chinese had a "feminine way of handling tools" that made them inefficient in manufacturing (Chiu 1967, p.11), this mix of racial and gender discrimination in the labor market pushed Chinese into forms of petty-commodity production that otherwise might not have existed. Self-employed Chinese were a common sight in mining camps where Chinese mineworkers were banned (Saxton 1971).

Where segregation produced sizable Chinese community enclaves, Chinese merchants were at an advantage over outsiders due to location, racial loyalty, and access to traditional Chinese products. The Chinese merchants subsidized traditional Chinese cultural and clan activities in part to maintain their trade monopoly. In the enclaves (especially in San Francisco), Chinese apprentices could set up their own shops. Chinese merchants could invest in small-scale manufacturing, often with backing from the clan associations (Zo 1978; Saxton 1971; Senate Committee 1876; Hilton 1979).

During the 1870s, mechanized factory production began to replace handicraft labor in manufacturing with the growth of large-scale monopoly capitalism. The availability of low-paid Chinese workers hastened factory openings. For example, introduction of the self-acting spinner into woolen mills between 1873 and 1875 allowed the owners to replace skilled white craft workers earning $3.00 a day with unskilled Chinese labor at $1.08 per day (Coolidge 1909, p. 374, see also p. 360 on boot and shoe manufacturing; Seward 1881; Coolidge 1909; Shen 1942; Saxton 1971). In the midst of this technological change, a recession in the mid-1870s heightened racial wage and job competition. White workers used the old anti-coolie club structure to form trade unions that forced the mass discharge of Chinese workers from white-owned manufacturing shops in 1876 (Saxton 1971; Chiu 1967). The mass discharges increased the availability and lowered the wages of Chinese workers employed by Chinese-owned firms. For instance, the number of Chinese-owned shops in California in 1877 increased 36.4 percent in the cigar industry, 142.9 percent in the clothing industry, and 41.9 percent in the shoe industry (Chiu 1967, p. 135). Low-cost Chinese labor made it possible for Chinese manufacturers to compete in markets where they otherwise would not have had sufficient capital or adequate technology.

Nationally, white labor, small manufacturers, and merchants were coalescing into a populist alliance to oppose the rapid growth of monopoly capital during this period. In the West, anti-Chinese and antimonopoly politics combined against "big capital," which the coalition saw as the only beneficiary of Chinese immigration (Saxton 1971; Nee and Nee 1973, Coolidge 1909; Bonacich 1984). Chinese-owned manufacturing shops and the employment of Chinese labor became a major focus of antagonism by white manufacturers in the 1870s (Saxton 1971; Hilton 1979; Miller 1969). The growth of Chinese capitalists created an economic basis for the formation of an interclass anti-Chinese alliance between white workers and white manufacturers who employed white labor (because of union provisions or geographic isolation from Chinese labor). White merchants also joined in the anti-Chinese alliance in the Democratic Party. They foresaw no major drop in sales from banning Chinese immigration because of the cultural trade monopoly held by Chinese middleman merchants (Saxton 1971). The political potency of the anti-Chinese alliance was evidenced in a new wave of local discriminatory ordinances enacted from 1879 to 1882 that reintroduced legal distinctions between whites and Chinese of the type declared unconstitutional in 1870 (Chen 1980; Tsai 1983).

White workers formed an alliance with white small capitalists rather than demand equal pay for white and Chinese labor, in part because white workers nostalgically identified with the interests of self-employed producers instead of proletarians (Hilton 1979; Bonacich 1984). This was more true of the skilled trades where movement in and out of self-employment was common, than of the mine or railroad workers. Manufacturing workers fell somewhere between. More important than misplaced class identity, however, was that all white workers opposed racial competition that would lower their wages. During a strike in 1876 against reduced wages, at least one group of white mineworkers did demand that employers pay Chinese labor the white wage rate. However, the intent of the demand was to exclude the Chinese from employment, not build class solidarity (Lingenfelter 1974). Given the loose market, the white mineworkers expected employers to hire only whites, once the market incentive to replace white with Chinese labor had been eliminated. Instead, the employers offered to exclude the Chinese and hire white children, but still pay the white miners the reduced wages.

Had the employers agreed to equal pay, an unintended consequence would likely have been a decrease in racism among white workers and integration of the labor market once demand increased. But, whether intentional or not, integration increases the supply of labor. It therefore would have been increasingly difficult for an integrated union to maintain the same wage level as that paid in white-only workplaces. This is especially true where low-wage Chinese immigrants continued to arrive. Long-term success of a "radical strategy" requires political action to secure equal wages in all sectors of the labor market, but no major political party (including the Socialists) took up this strategy. The Chinese could not vote, and the white workers voted according to their market interests and racist beliefs (Saxton 1971).

NATIONALIZATION OF ANTI-CHINESE MOVEMENT

Originally concentrated in California, employment on the railroads and declining employment in the mines dispersed the Chinese to other western states. The concentration of Chinese immigrants in California dropped from 100 percent in 1860 to 72 percent in 1880. Yet, only 3 percent of the Chinese lived east of the Rockies in 1880 (U.S. Census 1892, p. 474). Racial antagonism generated by split labor market conditions explains why discrimination periodically intensified in the western states, especially California, where the racial competition took place. However, in 1882, Congress passed the ten-year Exclusion Act that banned immigration of Chinese labor. The Exclusion Act required national legislation and took place several years after the recession of 1876 had sparked violent discrimination. How and when did the question of Chinese immigration become a national issue?

Although the amount of labor market competition was minuscule, the importance of the accelerated dispersion of the Chinese population after 1869 should not be overlooked. Even a small presence of the culturally distinct Chinese was politically important for making the issue salient to nonwestern audiences. In Massachusetts, seventy-five Chinese strikebreakers brought to a shoe factory in 1869 catalyzed a decades-long debate in the local newspapers and labor journals (Miller 1969). Loewen (1971) describes the long debate during the 1870s in Mississippi newspapers over the importation of about fifty Chinese to work on plantations and the widely reported 1873 revolt over working conditions by Chinese plantation workers in Louisiana, where a few hundred were employed (see also Tsai 1983). To protect women workers, the Knights of Labor launched one of its first boycotts in New Jersey against Chinese laundry workers in 1886 (Voss 1993). Chinese were the only group excluded by the Knights, who otherwise managed to recruit and hold together a membership that was 10 percent black and 10 percent female (Voss 1993). Less surprising is that the founding meeting of the AFL in Pittsburgh in 1881 included a petition for Chinese exclusion (Zo 1978).

The lack of widespread competition between whites and Chinese outside the West, along with the attention paid to minor conflicts, suggests that nationalization of the anti-Chinese movement was the result of political and ideological forces that spread beyond their economic origins. Saxton (1971) documents the organization of the anti-Chinese alliance in the Democratic Party along with its political efforts to secure the Exclusion Act. His description is extensive and need not be repeated at length, but his central contention is that prejudice against the Chinese was an important ideological element in reunifying southern white Democrats with the populist alliance of white workers and small capitalists in the West. Slavery, which whites in the West and North strongly opposed, tainted organized racism in the South. The peculiar combination of prejudice and abolitionist rhetoric in the anti-Chinese ideology, described above, condemned slavery (in the form of coolies) without condemning racism. This combination created an ideological bridge between antislavery populists and "Jim Crow" southerners.

Post-Reconstruction was also a period of renewed unifying nationalism in the United States during which one would expect ethnocentric antagonism against unassimilated sojourners to intensify (Stryker 1959). During this period, the discourse of the anti-Chinese ideology was altered to include a greater stress on opposition to the Chinese as a threat to American culture, with less emphasis on labor market competition. "Cheap labor" was reinterpreted as a moral problem instead of an economic one (McKenzie 1928; Feldman 1931; Saxton 1971). As was common of the times, moral arguments were often framed in gender terms. The Chinese were increasingly accused of driving white women into prostitution by taking traditionally female jobs. By emphasizing the threat to the morality of white women, union leaders garnered middle-class support for banning Chinese immigration (Frish

1984; Miller 1969). Politicians could not frame exclusion in strictly economic terms without simultaneously exposing class differences, and instead, the articulation of economic interests centered on middle- and working-class opposition to monopoly capital (Coolidge 1909).

Nee and Nee (1973, p. 47) suggest that white capitalists supported exclusion in the face of the widespread violence in 1876, "as the only way of regaining domestic order," rather than out of economic interests. However, they fail to distinguish between the motives of the white manufacturers and other small capitalists, and the interests of large-scale employers. Nor does their argument explain the continued support for exclusion by small capitalists and merchants, and the docile opposition by large-scale capitalists long after the violence abated. Saxton (1971, p. 178) points out that rapidly increasing immigration from southern and eastern Europe in the 1880s meant that large-scale capital had little to lose from Chinese exclusion. Although some western capitalists suffered, completion of the railroads mitigated their opposition by providing easier migration of low-wage labor from the East. Also, the Exclusion Act specifically required renewal every ten years for the purpose of reopening Chinese immigration if European immigration proved insufficient for the large employers.[5]

Regarding the timing of enactment, the following factors contributed to preventing federal action before the 1880s: the concentration of Chinese in the West; the lack of white small capitalist support until the 1870s; the opposition of large capitalists before increased European immigration; and the unifying effects of the anti-Chinese ideology on the Democratic Party after Reconstruction. The national and international changes in political relations that occurred independently of the split labor market conditions in the West were also important. The end of Reconstruction broadened the institutional limits on racist politics and state actions. Abolitionist Republicans declined in political influence and southern Democrats increased, leading Republican politicians to abandon their antiracist politics. President Hayes cited international obligations to China under the Burlingame Treaty in his veto of an exclusion bill in 1880, but the treaty was renegotiated in time to pass the Exclusion Act before the 1882 elections (Coolidge 1909). We can point to two precipitating factors in 1882: immigration from China peaked at 39,579 (Tsai 1983, p. 19), and the completed Northern Pacific and Canadian Pacific Railroads released Chinese laborers (Feldman 1931).

Finally, we should not see enactment of the Exclusion Act as a clear-cut "victory" for white labor, despite union support for the act. On the contrary, one reason the state acted to restrict Chinese labor was to stem unionization. Chinese exclusion had been one of the most popular and unifying demands of the radical Western Federation of Miners and other unions (Wynne 1978; see also, Locklear 1978; Zo 1978; Frish 1984; Miller 1969). With the Exclusion Act, the unions lost a principal organizing tool.

CONCLUSION

The case of the early Chinese immigrants provides a model of split labor markets that is sensitive to developments in the mode of production and that predicts the sources of racial discrimination. In the first phase, independent petty-commodity production dominated nascent capitalist production. An initial racial difference in the cost of labor led to racial competition and discrimination in the property market among the independent producers, whose independence was threatened by encroaching capitalism. They invoked a racist ideology adapted from preexisting ideologies of slavery. The egalitarian politics of petty-commodity producers were modified to exclude minorities identified by the racist ideology with the threat of both capitalism and slavery. Local state action followed at lagged intervals according to the timing of elections, and thus was largely autonomous from discriminatory actions generated by market forces.

A second phase emerged as capitalist wage labor relations became predominant. Previous discrimination in the property market and by the state disproportionately forced minorities into the labor market, depressing their wages. Along with continued immigration, the depressed minority wages reproduced the initial racial difference in the cost of labor. This secondary racial difference was centered in the labor market instead of the property market, and was thus the origin of a split labor market. As employers attempted to replace dominant workers with cheaper minority labor, racial competition resulted in renewed racial antagonism and segregation of the labor market by unions. This is Bonacich's (1972, 1976) thesis, to which we add labor market segregation resulting from the effects of the racist discourse on apprenticeship and from white abandonment of low-paying positions. Labor market segregation pushed minorities into self-employment, where conflict was lower, and along with the state, crowded them into new industries. The crowding effect expanded the racial wage differential, reproducing split labor market conditions in new industries.

A third and final phase emerged when self-employed minorities began to become small capitalists by employing other minorities. Racial competition and discrimination existed in both the labor market and the product market, where dominant workers and small capitalists were under economic pressure from nascent factory production and the nationalization of markets. Here, the racial politics of workers and small capitalists dominated class politics to the extent that the racist discourse was articulated in nonclass terms, the political demands were consonant with other movements against monopoly capital, the minority group was disenfranchised, and an increase in the immigrant labor supply muted resistance from industrial employers. However, as previously described, the international context and electoral cycle mediated the timing of state action. The effects of a racist discourse were important in this case for explaining the perpetuation of racial wage differences and the spread of racial antagonism.[6]

CHAPTER 5

Racial Competition in the Great Steel Strike of 1919

> They would drag—these pickets—would drag black workers from the
> streetcars and beat them up. And I saw that. The only explanation my
> brothers could give me was, "Look they are scabs and they are trying to
> break our union." The union was broken up, of course, and there were
> some very bloody fights.
>
> — Stanley Nowak, UAW organizer

The Chinese Exclusion Act of 1882 provided a legislative precedent
for racial segregation in the coming decades (Gyory 1998). In 1896,
the Supreme Court ruled that requiring separate accommodations for
blacks and whites was not unconstitutional, which provided the legal
foundation for the establishment of Jim Crow institutions throughout
the South. In much of the North, less formal but no less pernicious
forms of segregation limited blacks' options in education, residence,
and employment. Supported implicitly (and often explicitly) by the
craft unions of the AFL, the color line permeated the American
workplace as the country's economy shifted from small-scale craft
production to the massive industrial manufacturing oligopolies of the
early twentieth century. In this context, an infusion of cheap, minority
labor was all that would be required to racially split America's urban
industrial labor markets.

85

The months immediately following World War I witnessed un-precedented levels of labor conflict in the United States. Labor militancy peaked in 1919, when more than four million workers went on strike. This was more than double the number of strikers in any year between 1880 and 1937 (Peterson 1937, pp. 20–21; Griffin 1939, pp. 43–44).[1] As labor insurgency swelled, racial conflict divided many unions and com-promised important strikes. Dramatic examples include the AFL's efforts to organize America's steelworkers and stockyards employees in 1919. In both cases, the unions were vulnerable to black strikebreaking, discrimi-nation, and racial violence. The failure of these strikes foreshadowed more than a decade of decline in the labor movement and represented a lost opportunity to solidify wartime union gains (Perlman 1968).

The national steel strike involved more than 350,000 workers (Whitney 1920, pp. 1506–07).[2] The size of the strike, its coincidence with a period of massive southern black migration, and its implications for the labor movement all make the 1919 steel strike a particularly important instance of working-class racial conflict. Although the cam-paign collapsed for many reasons, most historical accounts underscore the significance of black strikebreakers and the failure of AFL organiz-ers to aggressively encourage black membership (Foster 1920; Inter-church World Movement 1920; Brody 1987). According to several authors, southern blacks who migrated to northern cities during this period resembled sojourning workers; they sought short-term employ-ment and intended to return to the South.[3] As discussed previously, we hold that all recent minority migrants share important characteristics with sojourning workers to the extent that they are poor but mobile. This is true even if the migrants never return to their home commu-nities and helps to explain the emergence and racial dynamics of split labor markets.

The prevalence of split labor markets in the North provides an opportunity to examine the effect of racial antagonism on union insurgency. In particular, the 1919 steel strike underscores the division that existed between black and white workers during the early years of the migration and is a critical case for our theory. Bonacich (1976), Wilson (1978), and others point to the unions' failure to incorporate blacks as a fundamental weakness of the labor movement during this era (also see Foster 1920; Brody 1987, 1998; Spero and Harris 1969). This chapter explores the factors that inhibited interracial solidarity in this important case.

THE HISTORICAL CONTEXT: LABOR ORGANIZING, 1858–1918

Iron production in Pittsburgh dates back to 1804, and by the mid-1820s, Pittsburgh had become a major producer of finished iron goods (Ingham 1991). Pittsburgh's skilled workers, often immigrants from the iron-producing areas of England, Scotland, and Wales, made the first efforts to organize iron and steel production during the 1850s (Robinson 1920). In 1858, they formed the Iron City Forge of the Sons of Vulcan, which grew and eventually became a national organization (the Grand Forge of the United States, United Sons of Vulcan) in 1862. The Sons of Vulcan soon established locals in New York, New Jersey, Maryland, Pennsylvania, Ohio, West Virginia, Kentucky, Illinois, and other states. By 1873, there were 3,331 members in eighty-three locals in twelve states, making the Sons of Vulcan one of the nation's strongest unions (Robinson 1920; Gulick 1924; Brooks 1940; Brody 1998).

Two other major unions emerged in the Chicago region. The first of these was the Associated Brotherhood of Iron and Steel Rail Heaters, established in 1861. By 1873, the union had twenty-two locals with 480 members in Illinois, Missouri, Kentucky, Ohio, Pennsylvania, and New Jersey. The union subsequently became the Associated Brotherhood of Iron and Steel Heaters, Rollers, and Roughers of the United States and established a lodge in Pittsburgh in 1875. Like the Sons of Vulcan, the Associated Brotherhood only admitted skilled workers. A third organization, the Iron and Steel Roll Hands of the United States, was founded in Chicago in 1870 and attained national status in 1873. Although it failed to develop the membership of either the Sons of Vulcan or the Associated Brotherhood, the Roll Hands did not limit membership to the craft trades. In 1876, the three unions merged to form the Amalgamated Association of Iron and Steel Workers (AA). The Sons of Vulcan dominated the newly formed Amalgamated Association and limited membership to those employed in the skilled aspects of iron and steel making (Robinson 1920; Gulick 1924; Brooks 1940; Brody 1998).

As the AA grew, the arrival of millions of immigrant workers from eastern and southern Europe increased the ranks of unskilled labor and fueled the expansion of mass production technology. Because this story has been told many times, we refrain from repeating it here except to note its obvious importance for our subject.[4] Pittsburgh's burgeoning iron and steel industries attracted many immigrants, so that by 1890, nearly 70 percent of Pittsburgh's population was first or second generation immigrants. Scottish and Irish immigrants arrived first and together comprised the largest group, followed by Germans, Croats, Serbs, Slovenes, Slovaks, Lithuanians, Bohemians, Poles, Ukrainians, Russians, and finally, Italians and southern blacks. By 1907, 76 percent of the workers in the Carnegie Steel plants identified themselves as foreign born (Ingham 1991, pp. 52–53). Union locals sometimes established separate branches for members of various immigrant or ethnic groups, although the national opposed this practice (Robinson 1920, pp. 39–40). In general, the unionized, skilled craft workers tended to be longer term residents while nonunion, unskilled workers were more often recently arrived immigrants. As a consequence, prejudice against recent immigrants marked the early years of American craft unionism (Barrett and Roediger 1997).[5]

Black workers' entrance into the Pittsburgh mills dates to the era of the AA's formation. In January 1875, the Pittsburgh Bolt Company imported black steelworkers from Richmond, Virginia, to break a strike.[6] The strikebreakers were escorted into the mills by soldiers and enabled the company to win the strike. This victory initiated a long and frequently violent history of iron and steel employers using black labor to break strikes by predominantly white unions. Even when blacks did not serve as strikebreakers, rumors often fueled racial hostility and reinforced the perception that black labor threatened the union cause (Montgomery 1987; Spero and Harris 1969; Dickerson 1986). Although black workers represented an increasing proportion of the industrial labor force beginning in the 1870s, they were most often limited to unskilled work. This was particularly true in the South. In the 1890s, blacks comprised 90 percent of the furnace laborers in southern mills (Montgomery 1987, p. 24). In addition, the practice of hiring close relatives as helpers preserved white control of the apprenticeship system through which workers learned their craft.

Black workers became eligible for AA membership in 1881, although it is unclear how many blacks joined or the degree to which the union actively cultivated their loyalty. Where possible, the union organized black members into separate lodges (Robinson 1920). Dickerson (1986, pp. 12–15) suggests that although the union extended membership to "colored lodges," whites frequently treated black members of the AA with contempt. Moreover, the shifting stance of the AA toward black steelworkers "engendered cynicism among blacks and encouraged them to eschew union membership" (Dickerson 1986, p. 15; also see Montgomery 1987). As a result, few blacks actually belonged to the AA and employers often relied on black strikebreakers in the Pittsburgh area. Employers imported black labor during strikes in 1875, 1888–89, and 1892 (Dickerson 1986, pp. 15–17; also see Spero and Harris 1969). Racial antagonism and segregation was even worse in many of the southern mills, where any degree of integration was anathema (Robinson 1920; McKiven 1995).

During the 1880s, AA membership fluctuated. When employers met union demands following strikes in 1883, membership increased to 11,800. Over the next two years, the union lost several strikes, which nearly cut membership in half, but AA membership rebounded to 15,000 by 1888 (Robinson 1920, p. 19). Various estimates suggest that between 15 and 25 percent of the eligible workers were members of the union during the 1880s. As the revolution in steel production prompted expansion in the industry, "there was a growing consensus that the mill owner had the right to direct the operation of his plant without outside interference, whether by the union or even the individual craftsman himself" (Ingham 1991, p. 130). Most notorious was Andrew Carnegie who, with the aid of Henry Frick (operating chief of the Carnegie Mills), succeeded in eliminating the AA from his massive Edgar Thomson works in 1885 and vigorously fought the AA in his other plants.[7]

The Knights of Labor also challenged the AA's jurisdiction in the 1880s. The Knights was the largest labor organization of the nineteenth century and was the most successful in establishing a broad-based working-class movement before the New Deal (Conell and Voss 1990; Dubofsky 1988; Voss 1993). At its height in 1886, the Knights of Labor had more than 750,000 members, including 60,000 blacks and 65,000 women (Conell and Voss 1990, p. 258). The Knights originated in Philadelphia in 1869 and differed markedly from the AA in at least two key respects. First, a chief objective was to organize all workers despite "nationality, sex, creed, or color." Second, the Knights were not oriented around a particular job, craft, or industry, and did not exclude unskilled workers. The Knights' inclusive stance attracted black labor in the southern states (Robinson 1920). There was frequent conflict between AA locals and the Knights of Labor in mills where both were present. As a result, the AA prohibited its members from joining the

Knights of Labor in 1888. The threat posed by the Knights encouraged Secretary Martin of the AA to implore the local unions in 1888 to "[b]e liberal and admit to membership the men whom the Knights of Labor are playing to reduce wages. . . . We mean the unskilled workmen. . . . Yes, even the daily laborer. We have nothing to lose and all to gain by the admittance of these men. All they ask is recognition. Failing to get that, they naturally seek and get in the Knights of Labor" (Robinson 1920, p. 50, also see pp. 48–49). However, the 1886 Haymarket Square riot in Chicago contributed to the Knights' demise; after that, the union did not represent a significant challenge to the AA (Dubofsky 1988).

Relations between the AA and steel industrialists began to unravel in 1889. For skilled workers, wages were a function of output and were based on a tonnage rate. As mechanization and technological innovation rationalized production, employers needed to ensure that the benefits of increased efficiency did not unilaterally accrue to the workers (Brody 1987). At Carnegie Steel, Henry Frick attempted to undercut the union's hold on the Homestead mills and break the link between employees' output and their compensation by imposing wage reductions and individual contracts (as opposed to union contracts) on the Homestead steelworkers. The demands prompted a strike in July 1889. Carnegie Steel imported strikebreakers, but ultimately, William Abbott (president of the Homestead plant) relented. His three-year agreement with the union recognized the AA as the exclusive bargaining agent in the plant in exchange for significantly reduced wages (Ingham 1991, p. 132).

The 1889 strike underscores the fact that technological changes had undermined craft unionism as the heavily mechanized steel industry eclipsed skill-intensive iron production (Brody 1987, 1998; Conell and Voss 1990; Brueggemann and Brown 2000). Skilled workers became expendable because they were increasingly replaceable. Throughout the 1880s, the union accepted wage reductions where technological improvements or the introduction of machinery simplified workers' tasks or decreased their labor (Brody 1998, pp. 50–53). Publicly, Carnegie Steel maintained that it fairly divided the advantages of improved machinery between the company and the workers, but every technological change brought renewed conflict over wages (Brody 1998).

By 1891, the AA had twenty-four thousand members, and the struggle between capital and labor was particularly salient at Carnegie's Homestead plant, which had become the center of the organized labor movement in the steel industry (Robinson 1920; Brody 1987; Ingham 1991). In an effort to undercut the AA's hold on the Homestead steel works, Carnegie used the expiration of Abbott's 1889 settlement to force a confrontation. Carnegie proposed a new wage scale that reduced pay by 18 percent and ordered Frick to fortify the Homestead mills in preparation for a strike. After negotiations failed to yield an agreement, Frick locked out the Homestead workers in late June, initiating a struggle that lasted nearly five months. The strike's decisive moment came early, however. On July 7, striking workers' attempt to prevent the entry of nonunion labor prompted a bloody clash with Pinkerton guards that resulted in sixteen deaths and hundreds of injuries. Troops arrived to restore order and protect the operation of the mills, which tipped the balance of power decisively in Carnegie's favor. When the strike finally ended on November 20, unionism in the steel industry was effectively crippled for decades (Foster 1920; Robinson 1920; Brecher 1972; Brody 1998; Ingham 1991).

Following the Homestead strike, economic depression further inhibited the possibility of union gains, and other steel producers aggressively challenged the AA. Employers purged union activists from their plants, implemented wage cuts, and gradually dislodged the AA by laying off union employees and forcing new workers to sign "ironclad" contracts, which stipulated penalties for joining a union. After 1892, steelworkers occasionally engaged in strike activity and achieved some modest gains, but on the whole, the AA was in decline. Membership dropped sharply over the next thirty years and the union never regained the position it had held before the Homestead strike (Robinson 1920; Ingham 1991; Brody 1987, 1998).

UNIONIZATION AND THE U.S. STEEL CORPORATION

The trends that had been set in motion during the 1890s did not bode well for steelworkers in the new century. The sale of Carnegie's vast steel enterprises helped to create the United States Steel Corporation, which represented a new threat to the AA. The merger brought together two leading figures in the industry at the turn of the century: Charles Schwab, president of the Carnegie Company, and Elbert Gary, president of the Federal Steel Company (Fisher 1951). In promoting the merger to J. Pierpont Morgan (who financed the consolidation), Schwab argued that:

[i]nstead of having one mill produce ten, twenty, or fifty different products . . . the greatest economies could be realized by having one mill limit itself to a single "line" such as rails or beams or plates and make that one product continuously. To accomplish [this] . . . no existing concern was large enough. Only a corporation larger than any then existing . . . encompassing ore fields, transportation facilities, all kinds of mills and finishing plants, could achieve the degree of integration which would place the steel industry on a really scientific basis. (Fisher 1951, p. 21)

Schwab convinced Morgan to purchase the Carnegie Company, and U.S. Steel was incorporated on February 25, 1901.[8] Schwab was the first president of U.S. Steel, and following his resignation in 1903, Gary chaired the Board of Directors from 1903 until his death in 1927 (Fisher 1951).

Instantly, U.S. Steel became one of the most powerful corporate entities in the world. The corporation controlled "60 percent of the basic steel industry, including the Carnegie, Morgan, and Moore properties, and nearly the entire capacity of the finishing lines" (Brody 1987, p. 19). In addition, U.S. Steel's interests in mining and shipping companies meant that the corporation had extensive involvement in the nation's metals, fuel, and transportation industries (Foner 1964). However, consolidation raised the possibility of industry-wide labor organizing and massive strikes (Garraty 1960). The economic boom of 1898–1903 created a strong demand for labor that gave new impetus to the union movement (Montgomery 1979), and U.S. Steel adopted a strong antiunion policy to combat potential labor disruptions. Publicly, the corporation granted individual companies autonomy regarding labor disputes and contract negotiations. However, U.S. Steel officially opposed the extension of unionization into its unorganized plants (Gulick 1924, pp. 96–99; Brody 1987).

Almost immediately, the company refused to honor existing union contracts, thus forcing the AA into a strike on July 1, 1901. The 1901 strike began with the workers at the American Steel Hoop Company, the American Tin Plate Company, and the American Sheet Steel Company, but ultimately, the AA called on all steelworkers in U.S. Steel plants to strike. After several months of strike activity involving more than sixty-two thousand workers, the union capitulated. The AA lost its hold in fourteen mills of the American Tin Plate Company and agreed not to attempt to extend its influence into other mills controlled by U.S. Steel. In addition, the strike settlement gave employers the right to discharge workers for union activities and permitted union and nonunion employees to work together (Foster 1920; Gulick 1924; Brooks 1940; Brody 1998).

After the 1901 failure, the AA concentrated its efforts on retaining its very tenuous position in the industry. Often, it had no choice but to concede to the demands of U.S. Steel (Brody 1998; Foner 1964). The union did not penetrate unorganized mills and the AA conservatively sought to secure slight advantages for skilled workers at the expense of the unskilled (Foner 1964). At the same time, U.S. Steel directed less work toward unionized mills, creating higher unemployment where the unions were located (Gulick 1924).[9] "After prolonged unemployment, mill officials would suggest that if the workmen circulated a 'voluntary petition' to leave the union, they would get work. That was the source, the Association claimed, of the loss of many of its lodges" (Brody 1998, p. 69).

Despite the setbacks experienced by steelworkers, union membership in the United States was on the rise. Between 1900 and 1904, membership in American trade unions more than doubled, AFL membership tripled, and twice as many strikes occurred in 1903 relative to 1900 (Foner 1964, p. 27). During this period, business and labor leaders formed the National Civic Federation, which sought to facilitate capitalist production by minimizing disruptive labor conflicts (Montgomery 1987; Weinstein 1968). The basic strategy of the NCF was to recognize and make some concessions to craft unions in exchange for labor's tacit assurance that it would not organize the masses of industrial workers. Samuel Gompers, president of the AFL, and John Mitchell, president of the United Mine Workers and vice-president of the AFL, were both members of the NCF; their involvement provided a relatively conservative bridge between capitalists and the labor movement (Foner 1964; Boswell 1981).

The NCF's relations with Gompers and the AFL were part of an effort to cultivate a "conservative unionism" within the mainstream labor movement that would counterbalance more radical organizations such as the Industrial Workers of the World (IWW) (Weinstein 1968). With its principle of "bottom-up" organizing, the IWW represented a significantly more radical model of labor organizing than the AFL

(Boyer and Morais 1975; Montgomery 1979; Boswell 1981).[10] Gompers instructed AFL unions not to support IWW strikes and to guard against infiltration (Dubofsky 1988, p. 94). Ironically, this conservative stance indirectly contributed to the IWW's rise. Dubofsky (1988, p. 12) writes:

> More and more after 1900 . . . [the AFL] . . . sought to sell itself to employers and to government officials as *the* alternative to working class radicalism. It could do so because its members were by and large those workers most satisfied with the status quo, those least alienated. . . . So long as wages rose, and they did, hours fell, and they did, security increased, and it appeared to, the AFL could grow fat while neglecting millions of laborers doomed to lives of misery and want . . . [the IWW] offered to do that which the AFL declined to attempt: organize the Negroes, the new immigrants, and the workers in mass production industries where craft lines dissolved under the pressures of technology.

In steel, members of the AA were generally forbidden to participate in the IWW on the grounds that the latter constituted a "dual union."[11] Given the persistent internal working-class cleavages of race, ethnicity, and skill level in the steel industry, it is not surprising that the IWW's success in organizing iron and steel workers was so limited.[12]

By 1908, only twelve operating U.S. Steel mills remained under the control of the AA, and in June 1909, U.S. Steel announced that it would operate all its plants under the principles of the open shop (Brody 1987; Gulick 1924). For U.S. Steel, the open shop was a "defense of personal liberty" and, as a U.S. Steel spokesperson proclaimed, of "the principles on which the government of this country was founded" (Brody 1987, p. 27). In 1909, U.S. Steel supported a move by the American Sheet and Tin Plate Company to operate its mills without unions. The company proposed a wage cut, and in response, the union called a strike on June 30. Despite AFL support and sympathy strikes by other workers, the union was vulnerable to strikebreaking and repression by authorities. After more than a year, the steel companies announced a wage increase above the union wage scale, effectively crushing the AA (Gulick 1924; Brody 1998). To consolidate its gains, U.S. Steel pushed its antiunion agenda into its other industries, including its ore and coal mines, limestone quarries and coke plants, and railroad and shipping lines (Brooks 1940).

The demise of the AA resulted in large measure from the union's inability to respond to the changing circumstances of production. Although mechanization and technological change continuously eroded skilled labor's role in the production process, the AA resisted building a more inclusive union. Brody (1987) argues that the continued need for skilled labor in some declining areas of steel production (such as wrought iron, sheet, and tin plate manufacture) obscured the more general threat of deskilling, thus inhibiting the development of industrial steel unionism prior to World War I. Increasingly significant, however, was the AA's racially segregated and generally exclusive membership structure.

THE RACIAL CASTE SYSTEM

Between 1910 and 1920, the percentage of blacks performing industrial labor increased from 18 to 31 percent; in 1920, nearly 10 percent of blacks in industrial jobs worked in steel plants (Greene and Woodson 1930, pp. 342, 344; Reid 1930, p. 14). At the end of the World War I, black workers represented 11.4 percent of the steel workforce in Illinois, 14.2 percent in Indiana, and 10.9 percent in Pennsylvania (Brody 1987, p. 46). By 1920, black workers in iron and steel numbered more than 125,000 (Spero and Harris 1969, pp. 84–85). As black workers entered the steel industry, their presence as cheap labor increased racial job competition and threatened to undermine existing wage levels. As a response, white workers and their labor organizations informally established caste systems that reserved the more desirable jobs for union members, members of particular ethnic groups, or workers with seniority or experience. Although the trends that promoted industrial deskilling made workers increasingly interchangeable, caste systems helped to protect the interests of more expensive and generally white workers by preventing direct competition with black recruits.

One clear manifestation of the racial caste system in steel involved the division of labor. In his study of black steelworkers in Western Pennsylvania, Dickerson (1986, p. 50) reports that 54.4 percent of the black workers in the mills held unskilled positions in 1920 (compared to 13.6 percent for whites and 31.7 percent for foreign-born). Spero and Harris (1969, p. 154) support these findings: data from the Illinois

Steel Company show that blacks "constituted 2.57 percent of the skilled workers, 10.6 percent of the semiskilled, and 21 percent of the unskilled." By the onset of the Depression, blacks in western Pennsylvania had achieved few gains compared with whites and continued to be relegated to the lowest paying positions (Epstein 1969; Dickerson 1986). Buttressed by racial antagonism, the racial caste system ensured that black migrants entered the steel industry through the worst jobs and then circumscribed their prospects for moving up internal job ladders.

Blacks were less costly to employ because few belonged to labor unions. Widespread discrimination inhibited black participation in the labor movement, and unions viewed blacks as strikebreakers rather than as potential allies. Several of the unions involved in the 1919 AFL campaign to organize steelworkers excluded blacks by constitutional provision and many more had few black members (Reid 1930, pp. 101–102). When strikes occurred, many blacks took advantage of opportunities to enter new and better positions by crossing the picket lines (Gordon, Edwards, and Reich 1988; Spero and Harris 1969). In part, black strikebreaking was a function of union discrimination, but it also resulted from the precarious economic situation of many of the black migrants. In addition to the migrants' often acute need for resources, their mobility further inhibited interracial unionism because it undermined the formation of community networks and norms that might have otherwise promoted labor solidarity. Indicative of blacks' higher rates of geographic mobility is the fact that they were much more likely to have been born out of state than whites in key northern steel producing cities. Table 5.1 shows that in 1920, 70 percent or more of the black residents of Akron, Chicago, Cleveland, Gary, Pittsburgh, Toledo, and Youngstown had been born out of state. In most cases, these figures tripled or even quadrupled the comparable rate for whites.

Heightened racial antagonism marked the entrance of southern blacks into the urban labor markets of the North as competition for jobs became acute (Nelson 2001). Labor conflicts helped to precipitate the race riots that occurred in East St. Louis and Chicago in 1917 and 1919 (see Rudwick 1964; Tuttle 1969, 1985; Foner and Lewis 1981). Racial divisions within the industrial working class contributed to the failure of labor organizing drives during World War I and through the twenties. The inability of labor to cohere around class interests enabled employers to exploit racial differentials in labor costs and to use minorities as strikebreakers during periods of intense class conflict. At no time were these dynamics more evident than in 1919.

Table 5.1
Population Born Out of State for Selected Northern Steel
Producing Cities, 1920

	Blacks		*Whites*	
Akron, Ohio	4,736	85.4%	6,915	46.6%
Chicago, Ill.	91,095	84.0	401,630	22.5
Cleveland, Ohio	27,907	81.9	112,804	21.6
Columbus, Ohio	13,484	60.9	32,542	16.4
Dayton, Ohio	5,998	66.7	26,657	20.4
Gary, Ind.	4,924	93.5	18,375	54.7
Pittsburgh, Pa.	26,106	69.7	47,764	11.1
Toledo, Ohio	4,106	73.4	50,237	25.2
Youngstown, Ohio	5,488	82.8	29,564	32.2

Source: U.S. Bureau of the Census (1922, pp. 661–65).

LABOR AND WORLD WAR I

Woodrow Wilson addressed the AFL convention in 1917, the first president to do so, calling for labor peace in a time of war. Gompers took
full advantage of the war to make the AFL a junior partner in the
government's effort to administer the economy. He also enlisted the
AFL in the war at home against socialists, the IWW, and other leftists
who might oppose the war (Brody 1980). Since Wilson's election in
1912, mainstream politics had co-opted many socialist objectives, which
Perlman (1968, p. 132) claims had already resulted in "a decimation of
the socialist ranks." While this may be an overstatement, wartime repression and subsequent Red Scare hysteria in 1919 seriously wounded the
socialist movement and dealt a mortal blow to the IWW (see Murray
1951, 1955).

The AFL offered a conservative alternative to more radical organizations; its membership soared during the war, especially after Wilson
made protection of labor rights a wartime policy in March 1918 (Brody
1987). Increased unionization in building, shipbuilding, the railroads,
munitions, and textiles tended to dilute more radical ideologies, and
union leadership realized that as new (and less committed) workers
joined the ranks of organized labor, the movement's sense of purpose

became diffuse (Perlman 1968). Employers could grant pay raises, im-prove working conditions, and give promotions more readily during the war-driven prosperity, and the labor shortage generated by the military's manpower needs and the cessation of immigration meant that these gains did not require costly union mobilization. Perlman (1968, p. 133) states, "[I]t was a case where reform was accomplished by the action of the market rather than by pressure group activity." The market in this case was driven by the state, which also provided protection for union orga-nizing (albeit only for the AFL). AFL success in the Chicago meat pack-ing houses in December 1917, for instance, derived from a settlement negotiated by the President's Mediation Council (Brody 1980).

Until the war, U.S. Steel had maintained firm control over its labor force. There were many localized strikes in the prewar period, but the fragmented alliance of workers and the relative strength of the U.S. Steel Corporation virtually ensured defeat for labor. Significant strikes during this decade occurred at South Bethlehem, East Youngstown, and Pittsburgh. Strike losses forced the AA out of basic steel production and the union survived only in a few small companies (Brooks 1940). Thus, the commencement of World War I brought new prosperity to the steel industry and consequently gave steel workers new leverage. The forces that increased the relative strength of the steel workers would culminate in the 1919 strike effort, which sought to achieve the development of a national union for workers in the industry. The outbreak of war also provided the impetus for the massive black migration from the South, which resulted in the first large-scale interactions between black and white workers in the industrial sphere. This would ultimately weaken organized labor by exacerbating existing fissures that union leadership had never adequately addressed.

During and immediately following the war, strikes in the steel industry began to increase and involved larger numbers of workers (Whitney 1920). As insurgency spread, steel officials used increasingly repressive measures to prevent the development of a national union. This was particularly apparent in the Pittsburgh area, where the steel interests freely used the machinery of local government to thwart organizing.[13] Owners of the steel mills (and the U.S. government) could not risk interruption of wartime production due to labor disputes (Brody 1987). As a response to labor disturbances in Youngstown, employers increased wages by 10 percent in 1916. This was the first of seven voluntary wage increases over the next year and a half. Employers also extended company welfare benefits to unskilled workers (Brody 1987; Rees 1997). In spite of the concessions offered by U.S. Steel, AFL leaders recognized the advantages associated with organizing the steel industry in 1918, and as the AFL mobilized, the federal government began to take a more active role in mediating labor conflict (Brody 1987).

THE 1919 STRIKE

In August 1918, the AFL formed the National Committee for Organizing Iron and Steel Workers, which sought to unify more than twenty-five major unions with jurisdiction in the steel industry. This represented the first significant effort to transcend craft and skill level differences in a labor organization of steelworkers. Although the AA was the largest of the National Committee's constituent unions, the AFL unions of shipbuilders, miners, bridge workers, electrical workers, and machinists were prominently represented. As the organizing campaign began in earnest in the fall of 1918, production cutbacks resulted in worker firings and layoffs. Frequently, union members were singled out for discharge, although U.S. Steel denied such practices. Company officials stated, "We don't discharge a man for belonging to the union . . . but of course we discharge men for agitating in the mills" (quoted in Brody 1987, p. 89).

Although labor organizing carried significant risks, the National Committee could barely contain workers' enthusiasm for a confrontation with U.S. Steel. Workers joined the union in large numbers, ultimately organizing more than 150,000 employees (Foster 1920). Brody (1987, p. 99) points out that the momentum of the organizing drive had created its own dilemma: either the National Committee could engage in a premature strike with a low probability for success, or it could risk losing control of the movement to the unorganized but militant workers. In addition to these pressures, a flurry of localized labor disturbances threatened to fragment the national organization. These events forced the National Committee to hold a union vote on a proposed work stoppage in August 1919: 98 percent of the workers favored a strike in the event that employers did not meet their demands (*New York Times* 8/21/19; Foster 1920, p. 78). The chief objectives of the National Committee included the right to unionize, a reduction in the length of the work day and work week, and wage increases (*New York Times* 8/21/19; Gadsby 1919; Interchurch World Movement 1920; Brody 1987).

The U.S. Steel Corporation refused to acknowledge the legiti-macy of the National Committee, much less grant concessions. As a result, the National Committee called a strike for September 22, 1919. President Wilson made several efforts to resolve the dispute, but when solutions were not forthcoming the union implemented its strike plan. William Foster (1920), secretary-treasurer of the National Committee, reports that by the end of the first week of the strike more than 365,000 (about half) workers had left their jobs, halting production in many plants. Labor organizers had hoped that sympathetic strikes would follow the commencement of the steel strike, but such movements failed to take hold on a large scale. Despite its initial success, the movement began to crumble and workers gradually returned to the mills. In December, 109,300 workers were still on strike and the pro-duction of steel had risen to between 50 and 60 percent of normal (Brody 1987). Although the strike remained strong in a few areas (such as Cleveland, Wheeling, Buffalo, and Joliet), it was apparent by the end of December that the strike could not continue. On January 8, 1920, The National Committee formally called the strike to an end, Foster resigned his post, and the National Committee disbanded.

Several factors contributed to the failure of the strike and the larger effort to unionize the employees of U.S. Steel. The coalition of more than twenty-five unions quickly became fragmented and skilled workers were particularly reluctant to strike (Foster 1920; Interchurch World Movement 1920; Asher 1978). The financial strength of the steel companies was substantial due to the inflated levels of production that had existed during the war, and the demand for steel declined prior to the onset of the strike. From this standpoint, the timing of the strike gave U.S. Steel a strategic advantage (Asher 1978). Also, the political influence of steel officials in particular communities resulted in the mobilization of local and state authorities on behalf of the industry in many steel towns (Murray 1951). Rumors of a Bolshevist conspiracy proliferated, diverting attention from the grievances of the steel workers and turning public opinion against a strike that the press increasingly linked to foreign radicalism (see Foner 1988; Murray 1951, 1955; Scheuerman 1986; Mohl and Betten 1986). U.S. Steel undermined the efforts of the National Committee by manipulating the mass media and by disseminating misinformation (largely through the Pittsburgh press). Employers also used violent intimidation and widely employed strike-breakers (Foster 1920; Interchurch World Movement 1920; Murray 1951).

As important as the foregoing factors were, labor historians frequently cite the effectiveness of strikebreakers in this particular case (see Foster 1920, p. 207; Yellen 1974; Foner 1974; Dickerson 1986; Nelson 2001). Many strikebreakers were southern blacks, who responded to the recruitment efforts of the industry.[14] Foster (1920, p. 207) reports that the steel companies successfully recruited thirty thousand to forty thousand black strikebreakers, most of whom came from the South (also see Brody 1987, p. 162). The black migration, which had been under way for several years, created conditions favorable to the differential participation of blacks in the movement to organize steel production. Other factors, such as white discrimination, inhibited the incorporation of blacks into the developing steel union. But working-class racial cleavages, cultivated long before the commencement of the strike, enhanced the effectiveness of black strikebreakers. Although the National Committee (and William Foster in particular) made some efforts to encourage black participation during the organizing drive, the union realized only the most limited success in this regard (Foster 1920; Spero and Harris 1969; Brody 1987, p. 162). Some influential black leaders believed that the union would use black workers to win the strike and then exclude them from the union (Spero and Harris 1969) and many of the labor organizations involved in the drive segregated or excluded blacks (Brody 1987).

As discussed in chapter 2, split labor market theory posits that sojourning or recently migrated workers have less to gain from labor organizations and are a key source of working-class divisions. This insight helps to explain the general pattern of racial divisions that emerged during the 1919 steel strike. Although the steel strike was a national effort, the path to failure resulted from events that unfolded in particular communities. For these reasons, it is also important to explore the circumstances that favored or inhibited the development of interracial working-class alliances in the key locations.

DISCUSSION

The history of the Great Steel Strike suggests that many factors limited the ability of workers to form an interracial labor coalition. Presumably, the differential incentives for black and white participation discussed in chapter 2 explain the absence of solidarity. Of particular importance for this case is the premise that sojourning workers have a short-term orientation toward employment and working conditions, and are less affected by their fellow workers. Consequently, they are less likely than members of the permanent workforce to participate in labor organizing campaigns and strikes.

Comparisons of sixteen major steel cities shows that those communities with higher proportions of recent black migrants were more likely to experience black strikebreaking (Brown and Boswell 1995). The cities that experienced sojourning migration before the strike did not achieve interracial solidarity, and the racial differences in commitment to the developing labor movement were a significant source of working-class weakness. Many authors have noted the transitory nature of black employment during this period, especially among the population of recent migrants.[15] However, minority migration is only one of several factors important for explaining instances of black strikebreaking and white racial antagonism.

Government repression also affected the viability of an interracial labor movement. In locations such as Bethlehem, Buffalo, Gary, and the Pittsburgh area, local authorities served the interests of the steel companies by inhibiting the ability of labor to organize. In some cases, city politicians or officials were also owners of the local steel mills. The convergent interests of the local government and the steel employers enhanced the ability of U.S. Steel (and other companies, such as Bethlehem Steel) to suppress the union. Interracial labor coalitions are unlikely to develop under such adverse conditions for two reasons. First, local authorities' attacks on labor organizers greatly diminish the ability of a union to cultivate support from rank and file workers. Given the tenuous grasp of the labor movement on black workers before the 1919 strike, such local repression is likely to have a disparate impact on black recruitment. Second, the political weakness of blacks in the steel industry's split labor market made them more vulnerable to the use of force and more likely to acquiesce when the use of force was imminent. At the same time, political weakness exacerbates racial groups' divergent interests. Because blacks were politically weak and vulnerable to discrimination, they sometimes worked during strikes to enter occupations from which they would otherwise be excluded. As a result, the importation of black strikebreakers is likely to augment existing racial strife and promote a further breakdown of working-class alliances where racial solidarity is already problematic.

The effectiveness of black strikebreaking is clear in cases where interracial solidarity was already low. Conversely, the use of black strike-breakers was not an effective strategy where workers' interests cut across racial lines. Perhaps the two most notable contrasting examples are Gary and Cleveland. (We take up the case of Cleveland below.) In Gary, employers paraded black strikebreakers through the streets, which exacerbated racial animosity and further fragmented workers (Interchurch World Movement 1920). The riots that developed in Gary between black strikebreakers and white strikers are symptomatic of the racial split that existed before the onset of the strike (see *New York Times* 10/2/19–10/6/19; Brown 1998). The nonparticipation of blacks in the walkout meant that employers could exploit racial divisions. Similar conflicts occurred in western Pennsylvania and at other locations where black/white alliances were tenuous or nonexistent (Spero and Harris 1969, pp. 262–63).

Interracial solidarity was also less likely in those cities with a history of failed steel strikes (Brown and Boswell 1995). It is possible that an underlying sense of futility in these areas resulted in a lower degree of enthusiasm and a higher estimation of the risks associated with participating in the strike. A history of failed steel strikes in a given region may reflect the relative strength of the steel employers vis-à-vis their workforce over time. Where unions are weak, community members have difficulty mobilizing against antiunion local governments, and where unions are strong, labor's interests should be more clearly represented in local politics. Of the communities that participated in the strike, cities with repressive political environments often had a history of failed strikes, making organizing doubly difficult. If a history of failed strikes suggests that steel companies are relatively strong, then it is possible that employers cultivated racial divisions to forestall class-based collective action. It is clear that in a split labor market situation, employers benefit from the divisive effects of cheaper minority workers. However, employers also benefit from labor cost differentials in the sense that they erode white wage scales. Thus, racial competition not only inhibits the crystallization of labor militancy, but it also keeps wages lower than they might otherwise be.

The race riot that occurred in Chicago was the most serious of the numerous racial clashes that occurred in 1919. In a kindred fashion to the steel, Chicago's racial strife was fueled (in part) by the packinghouse employers' use of black strikebreakers. In this context, whites employed violence to resist classic split labor market conditions, as described in the quote from Nowack that opened this chapter. Tuttle's (1985) analysis of the Chicago riot found that the massive black migration during the war had more than tripled the number of blacks working in the Chicago meat-packing plants. Few blacks had been incorporated into the unions of the Chicago meat-packing industry, and in the days preceding the riot, white workers walked off their jobs and refused to work with nonunion blacks (Tuttle 1985). Strikes threatened in other Chicago-based industries as well, and willingness of blacks to cross hostile white picket lines contributed to the animosities that subsequently fueled the violence.

Competitive conditions in the labor market clearly played a role in the development of racial violence in Chicago. Further, split labor market dynamics racially divided workers due to their differential support for organized labor. The Chicago case demonstrates the association between racial violence and an absence of interracial labor solidarity. This occurs regardless of whether the violence is a cause of working-class racial divisions or merely a symptom of underlying conflict rooted in labor market competition. It may also be that the effects of the Chicago race riot (and other race riots) spread to other cities; a city may not have to have actually experienced a race riot for the threat of racial violence to compromise union organizing. In the racially charged context of the "Red Summer" of 1919, violent racial clashes undoubtedly had widely dispersed effects.

Comparing the histories of the communities that participated in the 1919 strike reveals several key determinants of the ability of workers to generate and sustain an interracial labor movement. An examination of the historical evidence (at both the national level and at the community level) supports the importance of recent minority migration, union strength, repression, and racial violence for explaining patterns of interracial cooperation and conflict during the 1919 steel strike. Clearly, racial divisions become salient not only because of sojourning migration and race riots, but also where the working class was politically weak and was confronted by a strong capitalist class.

THE EXCEPTIONS

Sojourning migration, an antiunion local government, a history of failed strikes, and instances of racial violence—any one of these was sufficient to inhibit interracial solidarity during the 1919 steel strike. In contrast, interracial labor solidarity did develop in Wheeling and Cleveland (Foster 1920, p. 206; Brody 1987, p. 162; Spero and Harris 1969, p. 260; Yellen 1974, p. 283; Kusmer 1976, p. 197). Although the preconditions necessary to achieve interracial solidarity rarely converged in the racially split labor markets of 1919, a brief look at the similarities between Cleveland and Wheeling will help to delineate the salient factors. We should note, however, that the success experienced in Cleveland and Wheeling was fleeting: the defeat of steel workers in other important cities eventually brought down the National Committee drives in Cleveland and Wheeling as well.

In contrast to cities such as Gary, Cleveland had developed a high degree of racial solidarity before the strike (Spero and Harris 1969, p. 260). Consequently, no local blacks crossed the picket lines as strikebreakers. It is possible that employers in Cleveland realized that the importation of black strikebreakers would prove to be ineffective. Recruits might refuse to break a strike representing the interests of fellow black workers. The effectiveness and duration of the strike in both Cleveland and Wheeling and the absence of racial violence during the conflict are linked to the solidarity of workers across racial lines. At the very least, the absence of factors that intensify racial divisions countered the tendencies of the split labor market to erode class solidarity. Several authors suggest that the general race situation in Cleveland tended to be better than in other areas (see Kusmer 1976; Boryczka and Cary 1982). Specifically, Kusmer (1976, p. 186) suggests that the diversification of Cleveland industries did not provide a focal point for racial hostility, in contrast to the stockyards of Chicago and the steel mills of Gary. Further, the fact that Cleveland's black steelworkers joined the union during the National Committee campaign served to undercut another potential source of racial friction. Kusmer (1976) argues that another factor was the pattern of residential segregation. Due to the distribution of black neighborhoods in relation to Cleveland's industries, black workers could travel to and from work without having to pass through predominantly white areas. Again, this was not so in Chicago. During periods of racial friction, the location of Cleveland's blacks may have minimized contacts that could have potentially become violent and escalated into large-scale conflicts. Additionally, Kusmer (1976, p. 187) suggests that integration of schools and neighborhoods was more widespread in Cleveland, possibly promoting a degree of racial tolerance not evident elsewhere.

Cleveland also had a history of political radicalism. The Socialist Party created an organization in Cleveland soon after its founding in Indianapolis in 1901 (Millett 1972). Charles Ruthenberg, a Cleveland native, joined the party in 1909 and became a prominent member. He ran unsuccessfully as a Socialist candidate for public office every year between 1910 and 1919 (Millett 1972, pp. 195–97). For May Day 1919, Ruthenberg organized a demonstration of five thousand marchers in Cleveland with the support of the Socialist Party, the IWW, and several unions of the AFL, and Ruthenberg became Executive Secretary of the Communist Party of America when it formed on September 1, 1919 (Millett 1972). This radical political backdrop may have contributed to the interracial labor solidarity that developed in Cleveland during the steel strike. However, accounts of the steel strike do not emphasize any connections between the National Committee and Cleveland's Socialist or Communist Parties. In fact, Millett's (1972, p. 205) account of Ruthenberg's life suggests the opposite: these radical organizations were small in terms of membership, were vigorously repressed by the government in the later part of 1919, were internally divided, and had little influence with labor unions. As such, Communist Party activity does not appear to have been a decisive factor in interracial labor organizing efforts during the 1919 strike.[16]

In Wheeling, the strength of the labor movement in this region appears to have facilitated the development of interracial labor solidarity during the 1919 steel strike. The historical strength of the Wheeling working-class, as suggested by the absence of failed strikes and the autonomy of the local government from the steel industry, resulted in a higher level of working-class consciousness that transcended racial lines. It is also critical that an absence of sojourning migration appears to underlie the sources of interracial solidarity in Wheeling (Brown and Boswell 1995).

The duration of the strike effort in both Cleveland and Wheeling is indicative of the benefits that accrue to members of inclusive labor unions. Although the failure of the strike in other areas meant the eventual defeat of the Cleveland and Wheeling workers, the absence of a racially divided working class contributed to the relative local success of the steelworkers in these two areas. Undoubtedly, unions would still have to overcome the effects of discrimination. But, in an atmosphere where workers' interests are aligned, the goal of class solidarity is more likely to be achieved. It would be another generation, however, before that goal was realized.

CONCLUSION

The Great Steel Strike of 1919 was a disastrous defeat for the labor movement in America. It was one of the largest and most important in a string of strike losses that prefaced a rapid decline in unionization and a costly split in the labor movement. When the war ended, so did the government protection of the AFL. U.S. Steel was one of many companies that responded by cutting wages and restoring open shops, inciting the massive strike wave of 1919–20, one of the nation's most intense periods of class conflict (with similar events happening across Europe). Labor suffered a devastating defeat. Changes in the nature of production and the organization of work away from skilled labor had long weakened the position of AFL trade unions. With the socialist aspects of the labor movement stripped away by the repression of the IWW and onset of the Red Scare of 1919–20, the AFL was no longer the moderate alternative. Employers imported strikebreakers, including large numbers of southern blacks, while at the same time cutting production and firing union workers. Repression went unchecked. Organized labor not only failed to sustain its wartime gains once the war ended, but it retreated into a conservative business unionism that was increasingly disconnected from conditions facing industrial workers.

The consequences for race relations were perhaps even worse. Because the AFL's organizing efforts coincided with the black migration, the labor movement's response to a new (and rapidly growing) segment of the industrial workforce institutionalized rather than obviated longstanding divisions in organized labor. Race riots followed broken strikes and a lasting enmity toward white unions settled into the black community. Overcoming these divisions would fall to one of the oldest and most racially inclusive unions, the United Mine Workers. But even the UMW would fall to racial antagonism and strikebreaking before it discovered the formula, quite literally in this case, for institutionalizing its commitment to racial inclusion.

CHAPTER 6

The Formula—Interracial Solidarity in the Coal, Steel, and Auto Unions, 1927–1941

[T]he words didn't amount to anything, not worth the paper they were printed on, for in deeds discrimination was rank everywhere.

— William Boyce, NMU vice president

I always said that whatever the leadership of any organization does it reflects on the membership. And it most certainly happened at Ford during the organizing drive in the UAW. Those in charge of . . . organizing the UAW in the Ford plant exhibited and carried out in their own way and handed it on down to the membership; and nowhere in the UAW have I witnessed any examples of brotherhood more than I have seen in the Local 600.

— Dave Moore, UAW activist

On the heels of severe defeats in 1919, followed by recession, red scare, and Republican presidents, the labor movement collapsed in the 1920s. Union membership dropped from 18.9 percent of the nonagricultural labor force in 1920 to 10.7 percent in 1930 (Troy 1965). As noted in the last chapter, labor unions lost most of the institutional gains from supporting the war and skilled workers continued to lose from deskilling. It is not surprising then that workers became disenchanted with the craft orientation of the AFL leadership. The AFL had catered to the interests of the most skilled tiers of workers, who constituted increasingly small proportions of the workforce. Organized labor's position continued to deteriorate throughout the twenties, even in industries such as mining that had the strongest union traditions.

The worst blows came during the depths of the Great Depression, which contributed further to the emaciation of unions (Bernstein 1970, 1985). But, this fall would be followed by an unprecedented rise. The Depression ultimately transformed the role of labor in American politics. An initial effect was that the economic crisis discredited business leadership; decision-making freedom normally afforded employers became assailable. More important is that the declining efficacy and diminished credibility of capital marked a deepening class schism and corresponding decay of the unquestioned business orientation of the state (Milton 1982, p. 73). In conjunction with general economic insecurity, this schism provided the basis for a new militancy among American workers. Yet despite these changes, the response of the AFL leadership remained tepid.

It was in this context that a wave of labor unrest broke out in 1933 and 1934. Some union leaders considered this period to be a unique window of opportunity for organizing on an industrial basis, rather than the traditional skill or craft union (Bernstein 1966, pp. 89–90). Thus, in the early thirties the debate between the old guard craft unionists and proponents for industrial unionism was alight. The three unions who initially took up the mantle for industrial unionism, according to Bernstein, were fortunate to have "vigorous and imaginative leadership, superior to that of virtually all other unions and to that of the Federation itself" (1970, p. 90). Of these leaders, John L. Lewis, the self-assured, cantankerous president of the United Mine Workers, emerged preeminent. With Sidney Hillman of the Amalgamated Clothing Workers and David Dubinsky of the International Ladies Garments Workers Union, Lewis led the attack on the AFL's craft orientation. This resulted in the formation in 1935 of the "committee for industrial organization," within the AFL, and then ultimately the Congress of Industrial Organizations, which split off from the AFL in 1936 (see Bernstein 1970).

This new industrial unionism marked an important turning point in interracial labor dynamics (see Cohen 1992; Brueggemann and Brown 1998). Black workers in most industries were among the least skilled, least empowered, and lowest paid. A series of organizing drives in various industries took place during the Depression, in which the CIO figured prominently. The motives and significance of the CIO's efforts to include blacks remain a subject of debate (see Hill 1988; Goldfield 1993; Nelson 1996; Lynd 1996). Anticommunist, anti-egalitarian, and racist views were common among prominent CIO leaders. Nevertheless, the industrial organizing drives of the thirties and early forties stand in stark contrast to the efforts of the AFL craft unions in terms of successful recruitment of African American workers and new precedents of interracial labor solidarity (Goldfield 1993; Zieger 1995). The CIO's inclusive racial orientation was surely central to this efficacy.

From a different viewpoint, the various drives are linked in a single sequence as part of the emergence and rise of the CIO. The same CIO leaders were influential in several different industries throughout the decade. For example, John L. Lewis, Philip Murray, Van Bittner, John Brophy, and David McDonald were all UMW organizers who were involved with the early CIO and then later the Steel Workers Organizing Committee (Nelson 2001). As leader of the CIO, Lewis was, of course, involved in almost all drives to some extent.

The CIO was certainly not a monolithic entity that acted with single-mindedness. It was rather a conglomeration of organizations with varying policies and ideologies, and different constituencies and personnel.[1] However, key lessons of past victories and defeats were embodied in the leadership of the CIO and passed on to its member unions. This would prove crucial in the development of industrial unionism and the implementation of new strategies related to class struggle in general, and interracial solidarity in particular. We examine seven incidents of interracial labor organizing linked to the origins of the CIO, which include the drives of 1927–29, 1931, and 1933 in the coal mining industry, 1934 and 1937 in the steel industry, and 1937–38 and 1940–41 in the auto industry.[2] These successful cases of interracial organizing reflect historically rare circumstances, which are of particular theoretical interest.[3]

THE UNITED MINE WORKERS DRIVE OF 1927–29

This narrative begins in 1927 with the United Mine Workers organizing drive in the coal industry that culminated in 1928 and wound down, finally ending in 1929. Despite a long and rich history, the UMW suffered many defeats throughout the early and mid-twenties, growing increasingly impotent and acquiescing to management's policies

(Green 1980). Wage rates dropped and membership declined. During the mid-twenties, waves of black migrants fled the failing agrarian economy of the South. Many of them successfully found work in West Virginia, Ohio, and Pennsylvania (Lewis 1987). Most black miners remained in the South, but a substantial number poured into the northern coalfields, altering the racial composition in a region unused to extensive interracial interaction. The most important coalfields in the North were in the central competitive district (i.e., eastern Ohio, northern West Virginia, and western Pennsylvania).

In 1928, the Pittsburgh Terminal Company employed almost one thousand black workers, more than 40 percent of the work force (Spero and Harris 1969, p. 228). By 1930, out of 267,654 miners in Pennsylvania, 7,574 were black (Lewis 1987, p. 192). Conditions varied from one mine to another, but thousands of blacks gained access to mining jobs as strikebreakers. There was little other work and hardly any avenue into the coal mining industry for blacks other than strikebreaking. Such "scabbing" enraged the resident white mineworkers.

Coal mining did not have large skill differentials compared to other industries. But, black mineworkers were clustered in the most arduous, lowest-paying stages of the mining process (e.g., coal loading) and as displayed in Table 6.1, their wages were typically much lower than those of whites (Northrup 1944; Foner 1974; Nyden 1977). The most significant skill division among the mineworkers was between miners and loaders—who comprised about 60 percent of the work force—and all others. The others included employees who worked underground, but were not miners or loaders, and all employees who worked outside the mine (see *Monthly Labor Review* 1940). Miners and loaders were paid on a tonnage or piecework basis, whereas others were paid in terms of hours worked. A further division existed between miners and loaders, some of whom operated machines, some of whom were hand loaders, and some of whom were miners' and loaders' assistants. As Nyden (1977) explains, most black workers were hand loaders, which was among the most backbreaking and dangerous work in the mine. Although it varied from place to place, about 60 to 75 percent of black workers were employed as hand loaders (Northrup 1944, p. 160; Nyden 1974, p. 10; Trotter 1990, ch. 4). Lewis explains that black workers worked inside the mine at much higher proportions than native and immigrant whites (1987, p. 145). Miners, and especially loaders, were paid lower wages than employees in other work. In this

Table 6.1

Earnings of Employees in Bituminous-Coal Mining, 1929–36

	Miners and Loaders		Others		Ratio
All States	*Wage Earners*	*$/Week*	*Wage Earners*	*$/Week*	
1929	99,405	—	52,806	—	—
1931	90,063	15.54	47,725	19.25	.81
1933	78,896	10.69	41,438	13.90	.77
1936	51,791	24.19	33,735	25.99	.93
Pennsylvania					
1929	29,665	—	12,935	—	—
1931	28,519	16.40	11,819	22.00	.74
1933	25,814	9.52	9,480	13.21	.72
1936	17,207	24.29	8,945	26.97	.90
W. Virginia					
1929	20,421	—	14,675	—	—
1931	17,578	15.79	11,295	17.72	.89
1933	17,002	11.04	10,503	12.91	.85
1936	12,956	25.27	9,143	25.84	.97
Ohio					
1929	7,625	—	2,783	—	—
1931	6,840	12.75	2,392	17.35	.73
1933	6,656	10.58	2,243	15.01	.70
1936	3,989	23.11	2,093	28.05	.82

Source: *Monthly Labor Review* (1940, vol. 5)

way, black mineworkers earned disproportionately lower wages than most white mineworkers.

Since many entered the industry as strikebreakers, the mines where blacks were clustered were typically nonunion, company towns. Although there was a good deal of variation between regions, companies, and mines, black workers generally were more materially desperate. They had no organization or leadership to speak of and were willing, at this point, to work under unpleasant conditions for below-average wages (Bernstein 1966; Long 1989; Seltzer 1985).

African American attitudes toward the UMW in the twenties were mixed. Various leaders, such as W. E. B. DuBois, praised the union for having "organized the black miners without discrimination . . . throughout the country" (quoted in Foner 1974, p. 169). The UMW stood out among the AFL unions as the most inclusive. Even before the turn of the century, the early UMW leadership included blacks (Gutman 1976; Spero and Harris 1969; Letwin 1998). Foner concludes that "the UMW, though hardly committed to thoroughgoing racial integration, was still far superior to most white trade unions in the period between 1890 and World War I so far as the black worker was concerned. It was one of the very few unions affiliated with the AF of L that admitted blacks (although in segregated locals in some areas), did not prevent them from working at the trade (although keeping them out of better-paid jobs), and imposed a fine on any local that discriminated on the basis of color" (1974, p. 100).

Despite its distinctive legacy of racial inclusion, blacks' dissatisfaction with their treatment by the UMW grew following World War I (Foner 1974, p. 194). While black UMW members were treated better than blacks in other unions, they still fared worse than white UMW members (Goldfield 1993; Letwin 1998). This disparity may have worsened in the twenties, and with the influx of black migrants, racial hostility escalated. William Boyce, quoted at the beginning of this chapter, was a respected black miner who attacked the UMW's covert racism in the 1920s. He pointed out that black miners " 'usually receive the worst place in the mine, dangerous and unfit to work in.' If they complained their grievances got 'a merry-run-around' and were buried. The truth, he noted, was that 'the UMW did not really want Negro members' " (quoted in Foner 1974, p. 194). Hill (1988; see *Labor History* 2000) amplifies the criticism, claiming that the portrayal of the UMW as inclusive by Gutman and others was far too optimistic.

During the twenties, the rights of African Americans, which were already quite limited in the South, were deteriorating in the North (as described in the previous chapter). Segregation in the South had been institutionalized by Jim Crow laws in the prewar period and a postwar conservative reaction further polarized race relations. Throughout the decade, many coal companies only hired blacks as strikebreakers. Although discrimination, job segregation, and other racist policies were not a legal obligation on the owners, neither were they legally prohibited (see Lewis 1987; Nyden 1977). The policy in most cases for black employment was "The last to be hired, the first to be fired" (Foner 1974, p. 188). Thus, based on seniority alone, black miners were severely disadvantaged. "In the early months of 1929, with the economy supposedly flourishing as never before, 300,000 Negro industrial workers, about one-fifth of all blacks employed in industry, had already been thrown out of work" (Foner 1974, p. 188). Whereas the general Depression began after 1929, many black workers began to feel it in 1926. Employment in the mining industry began to drop steadily in 1926, during which it was 1,185,000. In 1927, the industry employed 1,114,000 workers. After a decline in 1928, to 1,050,000, and a slight increase in 1929 to 1,087,000, there was a sharp drop in employment, which reached a low of 731,000 in 1932 (Bureau of Labor Statistics, Bulletin No. 1312–6). These trends affected black miners disproportionately, who were generally less senior and more vulnerable. Clearly, there were major differences in resources between black and white workers. For blacks, wages were lower, expectations were more modest, the capacity for political organization was much more limited, and the options for alternate work were significantly more narrow.

The basis for these differences was partially linked to the recent relocation of many black workers. Migrants having arrived recently from the depressed South were poor. Although most blacks did not move to the North with the intention of being strikebreakers, many crossed a picket line as a temporary expedient (Lewis 1987). On the other hand, as Nyden (1977) suggests, most black workers did not plan to organize alongside other white workers. White miners, including previous and recent immigrants as well as Appalachian mountaineers, did little to instill trust among black migrants (Seltzer 1985). They were racist in the first place, and hostile to strikebreakers, thereby reinforcing the expectations of newly arrived black migrants (Wilson 1978; Lewis 1987).

In the North, the largest concentration of black miners was in Pennsylvania. The big coal companies in the region tried to eradicate the union throughout the mid-twenties. One of the largest conglomerations of coal companies in the world was located there: the Pittsburgh Coal Company (PCC), run by Andrew and Richard Mellon (Gottlieb 1987). As Lewis explains, soon after it signed a contract with the UMW in 1924, the PCC began ignoring various provisions of the agreement (1987, p. 234). The company closed down numerous mines operating under union contracts, claiming poor business conditions. Then gradually it began reopening mines on a nonunion basis, with wage rates set back to the level of a 1917 contract. When the union struck in response, the PCC hired strikebreakers from western Pennsylvania and other, more distant places (see Gottlieb 1987, p. 234). Strikebreakers, who included many whites as well as blacks, generally

did not cross the picket line out of any particular loyalty to the operators, but out of material need (Nyden 1977; Lewis 1987).

In 1927, the UMW began a general organizing drive. The conflict
with coal companies in northern West Virginia and western Pennsylvania soon turned so violent that it became known as the "Panhandle
War." The political conditions of the era explicitly favored employers.
There were few legal barriers and little enforcement related to the
violent repression practiced by many coal operators. The alignment of
local police with coal operators, coupled with the inactivity of other
state actors, demonstrates as much. One miner in southwestern Pennsylvania recalled, "They were always fighting. Between them and the
'yellow dogs' they brought in, the company coal and iron police, they
would ride around town on them horses, and they had them clubs; they
would chase everybody off the street and everything else" (quoted in
Bodnar 1982, p. 95). Another industrial worker in Pennsylvania com-
mented on the widespread influence of the companies. "The companies
controlled the towns. They controlled the courthouse. They controlled
the police. They controlled the state police, the coal mine police"
(quoted in Bodnar 1982, p. 69).[4]

During this strife, according to Nyden, the UMW constantly
emphasized the damage caused by black strikebreakers, downplayed the
significant role of white strikebreakers, and neglected to report on black
miners who supported the union (1977, pp. 77–84). The UMW newspaper sometimes printed racist jokes (Trotter 1990; Goldfield 1993).
The following remarks of a white UMW organizer exemplify such a
portrayal:

> We have a strike on at this time with Pittsburgh Coal
> Company and three-fourths of the men working as strike-
> breakers are Negroes—and bad ones too. They were the first
> to enter the mines. . . . They [PCC] are bringing colored
> men here to take the place of men who are resisting the
> thing the company is trying to do. We have some white
> scum also, but the Negro is in the majority. (quoted in
> Nyden 1977, pp. 76–77)

From the outset, many blacks considered the choice between a
lower wage from the employer versus a racist union and possible loss
of work an easy decision, and sided with the employer. Employers used

many tactics to overpower labor, including violent repression. Such strategy contributed in no small part to the operators' victory in the Panhandle War. However, regarding racial discrimination, employers were not as culpable as the union. They were essentially willing to hire the cheapest workers. White workers did not try to exclude black labor altogether, but there were clearly conceptions about tiers of work, "white man's work," and the arduous and dangerous work of black mineworkers (Northrup 1944, p. 160; Nyden 1977, p. 74; Lewis 1987, p. 170). Maintaining a caste system was clearly a goal of white workers.

The drive culminated in a series of strikes that were eventually defeated through the combination of violent repression and the use of strikebreakers. The union was crushed. Strikes became lockouts and the mines that remained open did so with nonunion labor. Operators took steps to prohibit access to the strikebreakers, and deter those workers who might consider leaving the mine. Fences were erected with the notorious iron and coal police posted at every corner (Nyden 1977, p. 81; Gottlieb 1987, p. 235; Bodnar 1982; pp. 94–95). Machine guns were mounted in many mines because, as Richard Mellon explained, "you could not run without them" (quoted in Lewis 1987, p. 113).

In this case, there was an increasing difference in social conditions between blacks and whites. The lower rates of employment for blacks in the mines and their relegation to lower paying jobs contributed to their already inferior material position. During the 1920s the UMW was rarely militant and was sometimes racist in its policies (Nyden 1977, p. 69). Many blacks who had recently migrated, and who were met by a hostile white union, perceived little choice but to cross the picket line. Racial antagonism thus developed most poignantly in the form of black workers who were alienated from the union and felt few disincentives to strikebreaking.

THE NATIONAL MINERS UNION DRIVE OF 1931

The UMW's defeat in the Panhandle War remained bitterly salient for mineworkers in the early thirties. With the crash in 1929, companies cut back or closed and the remaining strikers "slunk back to the pits" (Lewis 1987, p. 112). Operators rolled back wages and working conditions to pre-1900 standards. Union membership shrunk from approximately 600,000 in the mid-1920s to between 60,000 and 150,000 by the end of the decade (Nyden 1977, p. 87). One report counted a drop in membership in Pennsylvania from more than 100,000 members in the 1920s to fewer than 1,500 in 1932 (Dubofsky and Van Tine 1977, p. 156).

Criticism of John L. Lewis's leadership surfaced from communists within the UMW. The "Save the Union" movement of the mid-twenties, led by John Brophy, was the first major expression of such unrest. This faction had organized a national convention in 1928 to address the shortcomings and backsliding of the UMW. It was during this convention that the National Miners Union (NMU) was formed (see Draper 1972; Howard 2001). The NMU sought to "organize the unorganized," explicitly including black workers. The goals of the new union included industrial organization of the entire coal industry, nationalization of the industry, and the formation of a Labor Party (Spero and Harris 1969). Of these, "no task in the 1930's was more formidable than interracial organizing" (Gerstle 1993, p. 3).

William M. Boyce, the prominent black miner quoted above, was named NMU vice president (Draper 1972). The practice of employing a black unionist as vice president of a local became known as the "miners' formula." According to the strategy, a union local has a white president, secretary, and treasurer and a black vice president and minor officers (Foner 1974, p. 218). This approach was first used in Alabama at the turn of the century by the UMW on a limited basis (Kelley 1990; Letwin 1998). It included hiring rank and file black workers as organizers and sometimes included outreach to the black community. The formula was a concrete demonstration of union commitment to racial inclusiveness designed to appeal to black workers alienated from the union by racially inclusive but empty rhetoric. Its application would be expanded later by the UMW and then, through the CIO, by the Steel Workers' Organizing Committee and the United Auto Workers. The miners' formula was later associated with the UMW and became known as the "UMW formula" (Nyden 1977). This organizing strategy, which we discuss below, would prove a crucial tactical innovation.

The desperate needs of workers and their families precipitated by the failed 1927–29 strike and the other factors noted above provided miners the impetus to join the NMU. At first, few blacks joined, remembering previous discriminatory union experience (Nyden 1977, p. 90). Then the NMU got support from the Communist Party and the Trade Union Unity League (TUUL). Both groups sent black leaders to the NMU, which still had to fight internal racism. While John L. Lewis headed up the UMW and struggled to maintain union control, he was challenged by John Brophy, the emerging leader of the NMU (Howard 2001).

In the summer of 1931 the NMU held one of the largest strikes of the era (Nyden 1977). More than forty-two thousand (including six thousand blacks) workers struck in Pittsburgh and West Virginia, notably in "bloody Harlan" county (Dubofsky and Van Tine 1977, pp. 171–72). Numerous mass marches (led by the NMU and the Communist Party) took place and more than twenty-five thousand joined the union. The NMU treated strikebreakers differently, appealing to their interests, trying to meet their needs. By addressing racism among white miners, and specifically recruiting black members, the NMU was much more successful than the UMW had been at winning over potential black strikebreakers (Nyden 1977; Spero and Harris 1969). Many black miners who had been strikebreakers during the twenties became active union members, and helped lead strikes.

In a characteristic response, operators undertook a brutal campaign of terrorism. They harassed and beat a number of union leaders, members, and sympathizers. In one company ambush on six hundred NMU pickets at Butler Consolidations Wildwood Mine, a striking miner was killed. Forty-two NMU members were charged with the murder (Nyden 1977, p. 95). Often, the law stood behind the operators, blaming union members for the deaths of other union members. By August, the NMU's District Strike Committee claimed that "terror, arrests, evictions, threats of evictions and starvation" had broken the strike and told each local to decide whether to return to work (reported in Nyden 1977, p. 97).

The NMU deteriorated after losing the strike. Its leaders concluded that the operators and federal government would only deal with the UMW, and what was left of the organization merged with the UMW between 1933 and 1935. Nevertheless, the NMU greatly influenced the whole future of organized coal miners. "W. E. B. DuBois remarked that the struggle of the blacks in the NMU should be enough to compel 'colored thinkers and writers' to leap to the defense of trade unionism, especially when black workers were involved" (Foner 1974, p. 195). The 1931 strike, though defeated, was the largest expression of labor unrest since the Depression had begun. The NMU set a precedent for black participation and nondiscrimination. Another significant development was that the Communist Party played an important role in building the union and in fostering interracial solidarity. The NMU influenced the reconstructed UMW in general and John L. Lewis in particular.

Because Lewis and the UMW were so prominently involved in the emergence of the CIO, the NMU had an important impact, albeit indirect, on the policies of the CIO. Nyden explains that although the NMU ultimately crumbled, its militant approach and commitment to racial inclusiveness remained influential in subsequent labor organization, through the UMW in particular and more broadly via the CIO (1977, p. 101). In 1936, the CIO started the largest organizing drive in American history. As noted above, the CIO was not a monolithic entity, despite Lewis's authoritarian leadership. This "union of unions" had multiple leaders and constituencies with differing ideological perspectives. As part of the principle of organizing unorganized industrial workers, however, an important general goal was to organize black workers (Goldfield 1993). Emulating the miners' example, the CIO leadership attempted to be inclusive and egalitarian. It forbade segregated locals or other Jim Crow status policies, and it hired black organizers to prove its commitment (Foner 1974, p. 216).

THE UNITED MINE WORKERS DRIVE OF 1933

"As the Depression deepened, the black and white miners were on the point of starvation" (Foner 1974, p. 196). The depths of the economic crisis were felt throughout 1933 and early 1934, during which unemployment reached unprecedented levels. Employment in the coal mining industry was approximately 750,000 (compared with 1,100,000 during the mid-twenties). Wages for all workers had fallen. According to Johnson, mining wages ranged from $3 to $6 per day among the remaining unionized companies in the North, to less than $2.50 for more than one-third of the industry, with some as low as $1–1.50 (1979, p. 125). Systematic wage inequalities were still common in early 1933. The most dramatic contrast was North/South (i.e., wages were often 50 percent lower in the South). Because there were proportionally more blacks in the South, the racial differential was pronounced. There was also a racial wage differential within the northern fields. As described above, operators clustered black workers in loading jobs that paid by tonnage, and most earned far less than those paid hourly wages (see Table 6.1).

In 1933, the options black miners had for employment were diminished further. Operators tended to hire white workers before black workers, except when the need for strikebreakers arose. As they were systematically "last hired, first fired," accruing seniority was difficult for blacks. There was, of course, no legal barrier to deter this kind of discrimination. In January 1931, a report from the Census Bureau (based on a sample of thirteen U.S. cities) indicated that approximately one-third of the white industrial workers were unemployed compared to more than one-half of black industrial workers. And as economic conditions deteriorated, the racial differential in unemployment increased (Foner 1974, p. 190).

Although the economy in the rural South was devastated, there were no jobs in urban areas drawing migrant workers, which made for relatively little migration in the early thirties (McAdam 1999, pp. 78–80). The black miners who were in the central competitive district in the early thirties had, for the most part, been there since before the beginning of the Depression. Unstable jobs made for some turnover. According to an article in *Opportunity*, black workers around Philadelphia held steady jobs an average period of 3.8 years (compared to the average white workers' stability of six years). Nevertheless, many of these black workers were in the area, exposed to working conditions for a longer period than the black mine workers of the twenties had been (see Foner and Lewis 1981).

Black mineworkers became more economically desperate as wages fell and unemployment continued to increase. They were not, however, as trusting of employers as the recent migrants of the late twenties and they were far less mobile. Exit was not an option. Black-sponsored publications, such as the NAACP's *Crisis* and the Urban League's *Opportunity*, bear witness to this increasingly militant worker consciousness of the early thirties (see Foner and Lewis 1981).

As the story of the National Miners Union demonstrates, the expectations of black miners were more militant and more pronounced in 1933. Their experience of the Depression and their treatment by operators of nonunion mines had fostered this militancy (Nyden 1977). Black miners were still largely unorganized as a group in 1933, but as with white miners, there was little esteem or trust for the coal operators. At the same time there were other developments reflecting the declining credibility of capitalists.

Roosevelt's New Deal established the National Industrial Recovery Act in June 1933, which was essentially an effort to steer the country out of depression. Its proponents emphasized the effort to empower labor, and Roosevelt surely wanted to engender labor's support. Immediately after its passage, however, the concrete effects of the Act were mixed. The National Recovery Administration often had inadequate mechanisms for enforcing its measures. It did, nevertheless, serve a critically important symbolic function—to mobilize labor. John L. Lewis, leader of the UMW, seized the implicit message of the Act, capitalizing on it in the slogan, "The President wants you to join the union!" (Brecher 1972, p. 150). A miner in southwestern Pennsylvania echoed this perception, saying, "The New Deal was a blessing. You can say what you want, but you better be a Democrat if you are a laborer working for a living. You better vote Democrat. You better work for the Democratic Party and the people because when Roosevelt got in office his first program was that NRA" (quoted in Bodnar 1982, p. 99).

Just as industrial labor would become central to Roosevelt's coalition, the New Deal was crucial to the miners' efforts. Already ardent due to material destitution and motivated by the sense of possibility and impending social change, passage of the NIRA and the implicit federal support it symbolized roused miners further (Dubofsky and Van Tine 1977, p. 185; Edelman 1956, p. 168).

McAdam asserts that an organization must have "structures of solidary incentives," which refer to the "myriad interpersonal rewards that provide the motive force for participation in these groups. It is the salience of these rewards that helps explain why recruitment through established organizations is so efficient" (1999, p. 45). The degree to which the federal government was supportive of labor's interests fundamentally shaped such structures. If workers perceive low costs and high rewards for joining a union, especially compared to other options, they are more likely to participate (Hechter 1990). Labor legislation was the most important form of federal action during the period in question, an issue we return to below.

The UMW waged a massive organizing drive in 1933, successfully recruiting members in many areas where they had previously been unsuccessful, both in the North and South. Mine workers joined the union in droves, including many blacks. A huge wave of strikes erupted throughout 1933 in the central coal fields (i.e., eastern Ohio, northern West Virginia, and western Pennsylvania) (Johnson 1979). As Green explains, union organizing became like a "religious revival" among the rank and file "once the miners realized that the state might no longer be their implacable enemy, and that the government might even protect the miner's right to organize" (1980, p. 140). Amidst the spreading fervor, one miner observed the following:

> As far as I am concerned, I have to give those boys a lot of credit. They were fighting for better working conditions, for more pay, because they were down in the dirt for so long working for nothing and starvation wages. My God, they had to do something, and you have to give those people credit. So what appeared after they give them the right to organize, they come out for the United Mine Workers. Everybody joined the UMW. (quoted in Bodnar 1982, p. 100)

As the UMW mobilized, threatening to disrupt coal mining through a national strike, Roosevelt established the Bituminous Coal Code (as part of the NIRA) in October 1933 (see Fritz and Veenstra 1935; Schlesinger 1960). Among various changes, such as an eight-hour day, and a five-day week, the Code established a minimum daily wage of $4.20. This substantially diminished the differential between northern and southern miners, and more importantly between black and white miners (see Kelley 1990). *Opportunity* reported that among a sample of mines around Pittsburgh there was no differential in pay on the basis of race (see Foner and Lewis 1981, p. 126). All these mines were operating under the NIRA codes, eliminating some of the advantages of operating nonunion. During the fall of 1933 operators throughout the region recognized the UMW (Dubofsky and Van Tine 1977, pp. 196–97).

In what must have seemed an overnight change, the political context had become particularly favorable for the UMW. Roosevelt's New Deal in the early thirties had both material and symbolic implications for the miners. The Code enhanced the benefits of joining the union and reduced the incentive to strikebreak. This provision and the New Deal in general reflected labor's political success, demonstrating the effectiveness of the union. A perception of government support reduced the risk of union organizing and invigorated the drive.

To be sure, there were pockets of violent repression on the part of northern operators in response to the strikes of 1933 (see Bernstein 1970, pp. 50–56; Coleman 1943, p. 149). Overall, however, the operators were divided and uncharacteristically passive. Furthermore, there was virtually no state support of employer repression. According to Coleman, "Organizers shouted their summonses under the noses of the horses of the coal and iron police. The sullen riders did not dare attack men who seemingly had behind them the support of the federal government. Nonunion operators were loathe to order the terrorization of such numbers of their workers who were obviously eager to join the once-outlawed organization" (1943, p. 149).

Many northern operators were aware of the potential effects of a strong national union. The Depression took its toll on employers as well as workers. Declining profits left many operators weak and vulnerable to the union's efforts. More importantly perhaps was the fact that southern operators had, for the most part, maintained nonunion mines and consequently had undercut northern operators who were forced to pay higher wages in unionized mines (and generally higher wages for all labor). Thus, the prospect of a strong national union was not completely unappealing in the eyes of northern operators (Johnson 1979). Few of the conventional strategies, such as strikebreakers, propaganda, racial divide and conquer tactics, or violent repression, were used in these labor disputes (Coleman 1943).

In contrast, the union was aggressive. Its leadership, who was aware of the progressive origins of the UMW, the failures of the late twenties and the positive example of the NMU, took dramatic steps to include black miners. With John L. Lewis as president, the UMW leadership invested in the principle of interracial solidarity. The union utilized the miners' formula on a widespread basis, developing mixed leadership in numerous locals. After its first success on such a large scale, the strategy then became known as the "UMW formula" (Foner 1974, p. 214; Lichtenstein 2002, p. 84).

Communist influence contributed to the UMW's development of the miners' formula and to general support for interracial solidarity (see Kelley 1990; Letwin 1998). However, the UMW leadership, especially Lewis, was quite hostile to the Communist Party. That communist organizers were generally utilized reflects an instrumental and calculated strategy by UMW leaders as opposed to ideological sympathy (Levenstein 1981, pp. 48–49).

The white rank and file followed its leadership in this drive. An article in *Crisis* published in 1935 described the UMW as racially inclusive and egalitarian (see Foner and Lewis 1981, p. 339). In addition, the role of black leadership was crucial in facilitating the recruitment of the black rank and file. After being convinced of the union leadership's sincerity, black leaders solicited support from black miners who participated in the union drive and later strikes in large numbers. There had always been a few black unionists, but at this time a strong cadre developed that was effective in recruiting the black rank and file (Nyden 1977).

Wages and working conditions (including hourly and weekly limits on working periods, and minimum wage laws) became fairly even for black and white workers after the NIRA Bituminous Coal Code was established. Although there were legal barriers to racial equality, the expectations of black miners became much more similar to those of their white counterparts in terms of relations with operators. These attitudes were characterized by a lower perceived risk of organizing, higher expectations of victory, and a shared distrust of employers. The one factor in the 1933 UMW case that portended an increasing racial gap in economic resources was the decreasing options black miners had for alternative employment. White mineworkers at the time also had decreasing options, but the trend was more pronounced for blacks. Overall, however, the economic trend in this case was toward an equalization of resources and motives.

Differences in political organization also became somewhat muted. Following the defeats of the twenties, the union was not particularly strong at the beginning of the decade. In terms of black political organization, national institutions such as the NAACP and the Urban League were outspoken about black miners' interests, even though they were not directly involved in labor matters. As noted, however, an important black leadership among miners evolved, one that was effective in mobilizing the support of the rank and file behind the union.

In terms of political mobilization, there was a substantial convergence between black and white miners. Besides the increasing militancy of black miners described above, the stability of the black workforce, in contrast to the recently relocated migrant labor of the late twenties, contributed to a growing concern about economic and political conditions. At this point, dominant white labor, represented by the UMW, adopted a new tactic in appealing to the needs and interests of black workers, offering incentives not to strikebreak. Institutionalized into the UMW formula, this new strategy reflected a historic turning point of union commitment to racial inclusiveness. This example of success and the UMW's organizational trajectory made the miners' efforts a template for subsequent campaigns in other industries. However, additional factors shaped whether unions were willing and able to successfully utilize the formula.

THE AMALGAMATED ASSOCIATION OF IRON, STEEL, AND TIN WORKERS DRIVE OF 1934

Most steel production in the early thirties took place in western Pennsylvania. The industry was relatively stratified as to skill and wages. There were basically three tiers of workers: highly skilled (i.e., smelters, puddlers, shearmen, rollers, roughers, and heaters); mechanical tradesmen (bricklayers, machinists, boilermakers, riggers, electrical workers, and blacksmiths); and semiskilled operatives and unskilled laborers (Cayton and Mitchell 1939, p. 48). A wide gap in wages divided unskilled workers on one hand and semiskilled and skilled workers on the other (see Table 6.2). Northrup reports that "heaters and rollers in bar mills in the North earned an average of $1.07 and $1.71 per hour, respectively, and unskilled workers in the same branch of industry but $.63 per hour" (1944, p. 177). While changes during the early decades of twentieth century in steel production made these skill differences increasingly less significant, management maintained the stratified categories and wage differences to facilitate control (see Nyden 1984; Braverman 1974; Stone 1975; Brown 1998).

Table 6.2
Hourly Wages in the Iron and Steel Industry by Skill, 1928–36

Year	Unskilled	Skilled and Semiskilled	Ratio
1928	$0.495	$0.695	.70
1929	$0.511	$0.681	.75
1930	$0.469	$0.679	.69
1931	$0.422	$0.622	.68
1932	$0.347	$0.499	.69
1933	$0.367	$0.515	.71
1934	$0.468	$0.656	.71
1935	$0.477	$0.686	.69
1936*	$0.479	$0.689	.70

Source: Beney (1937, pp. 114–15)

*Wage rates for 1936 are based on first six months.

Whites were disproportionately represented in skilled jobs and blacks among the unskilled (Cayton and Mitchell 1939; Northrup 1944). In 1930 blacks constituted 16.5 percent of unskilled laborers, 6.9 percent of semiskilled operatives, and 8.5 percent of skilled, blast furnace workers and rollers (Cayton and Mitchell 1939, pp. 44–45). In short, there were substantial differences in the economic resources commanded by white versus black workers.

Organized labor in the steel industry during that period was still very much associated with the American Federation of Labor, and was thereby based on a craft orientation. The Amalgamated Association of Iron, Steel, and Tin Workers (AA) had never recovered from defeat in the 1919 strike and was largely impotent in advancing the interests of workers, particularly the unskilled, throughout the twenties. Since labor in the steel industry was organized on a craft basis in the early thirties, the racial skill differential had critical implications for the racial gap in political resources. Because black workers were mostly unskilled, had no organization of their own, and no voice in the craft union, this gap was also pronounced.

As with the Coal Code, Roosevelt established the Steel Code in August 1933 as part of the NIRA. Wages for workers above the position of "common labor" were increased by 15 percent. Minimum rates were also established for common labor, but this varied a good deal in different districts (Cayton and Mitchell 1939; Harbison 1937). However, even after minimum wage standards were established by this code, racially based wage differentials remained. The minimum wage varied from 25 cents to 40 cents, the lower rates being prominent in districts with a preponderance of black workers. In addition, the Code did nothing to address the disproportionate number of blacks in low-skilled, low-paying jobs. Therefore, despite the regulation of wages in the steel industry, black workers still had far lower wages than their white counterparts, and white workers in general. Cayton and Mitchell (1939) suggest that the wage differential between blacks and whites was directly related to the differences in bargaining power.

The major steel mill owners, all of whom employed significant numbers of black workers, included Bethlehem Steel, Republic Steel, Jones and Laughlin, and the behemoth United States Steel Corporation. In addition, there were many other smaller companies spread out over western Pennsylvania (Dickerson 1986). The Iron and Steel Institute was an organized conglomeration of these and most other companies, representing more than 95 percent of the country's steel producers (Progress Publishers 1977, p. 374).

The main mechanism of social control utilized by employers at the time was an institutionalized system of paternalism—the company union. The company union or employee representation plan system had worked effectively in the late twenties, preventing or coopting any independent labor organizing. Company unions had become unnecessary during the depths of the Depression, but were reinstated in the early thirties (Cayton and Mitchell 1939). The system was based on a personal, "accommodating" relationship between employer and employee. Organized labor was recognized, workers' needs were addressed, and legitimate collective bargaining was practiced. However, the organization was monitored by the steel mill owner, the services (i.e., housing, stores, etc.) were all company owned, and the bargaining took place within very limited parameters. Employers effectively portrayed the system as in the interests of both workers and owners (Nelson 2001).

Black steelworkers, who were largely excluded from the AA, were welcomed in company unions. Although the company union was essentially a controlling mechanism for employers, to some real degree it represented a positive and egalitarian institution for black steelworkers. Cayton and Mitchell portrayed black affiliation with the company unions as follows: "In summary, it may be said that Negroes accepted company unions because they were first accepted by the company unions, and because the paternalism which these unions offered on the one hand, and the mock equality which they embodied on the other, combined the best elements of both the North and the South. At the same time, the hostility of the white workers made the relative favors of the employers all the more welcome" (1939, p. 63).

In 1934 there were not many recent black migrants to Pennsylvania (see McAdam 1999, pp. 78–80), but black steelworkers had a different image of the operators and the union, as compared with white workers. The union had never made a concerted effort to include black workers in the industry, whereas the operators, although controlling, provided black workers with some basis for loyalty (Brown and Brueggemann 1997; Nelson 2001). Part of this difference was based on the much more severe economic insecurity for blacks. The rule of "last hired, first fired" for black labor was still very much in effect, which was reflected in black unemployment rates. There was an abundance of labor, both black and white, which made this norm particularly salient.

Although black steelworkers typically constituted between 5 and 10 percent of the work force, in parts of western Pennsylvania they represented as much as 30 percent of unemployed steelworkers (Dickerson 1986, p. 129; see also Foner 1974).

Cayton and Mitchell provide substantial anecdotal evidence illustrating the fears of black steelworkers of being fired (1939, pp. 132–35). Being associated with the Amalgamated was grounds for dismissal. With higher unemployment rates (and no outreach from the union), black workers faced a much higher disincentive to unionizing. By 1934, operators were employing armed guards to monitor and inhibit union activity. Dickerson suggests that black steelworkers were quite conscious of the unfair treatment they received, in terms of hiring discrimination, wage differentials, seniority, etc. (1986, pp. 125–29). However, the few incentives provided by the company, the threat of repression, the exclusiveness of the union, and the lack of alternative employment made for a relatively greater commitment to employers.

National unemployment rates began to drop in 1933 and then even more so in 1934 (Darby 1976). In June 1933, the AA reported a membership of fewer than five thousand. It initiated an organizing campaign in August 1933. Within several months, there were more than 125 new local unions. By April 1934, membership was estimated between fifty thousand and two hundred thousand (Cayton and Mitchell 1939, p. 126; Lynd 1973, p. 191). The "guaranteed right to organize," established by the National Recovery Administration (part of the NIRA) inspired the rank and file in steel as it had in coal, although not with the same unanimity. The NIRA did not guarantee the right of independent unionism, so many employers in steel (and elsewhere) established company unions (Fleming 1957; Wilcock 1957; Brody 1987). As steelworkers joined the company unions as well as the AA, the overall position of organized steel was still precarious. And while adoption of the Steel Code electrified the rank and file, the AA's leaders remained rather tepid. The official leadership was conservative, often compromising with or even siding with employers against its own locals.

At the AFL's annual national convention in April 1934, held in Pittsburgh, a militant left-wing opposition confronted the conservative, craft union–dominated leadership (Cayton and Mitchell 1939, p. 128). The younger, more radical voices became known as the Rank and File Committee. They supported the many demands being made by local unions, including a resolution against the North/South wage differential, support for racial inclusion, and at least the threat of a national strike (Cayton and Mitchell 1939). A rank and file leader explained, that "the mass of steel workers wanted industrial unionism, and so did we. But it wasn't clear to us until we set out to get it that we would have to fight not only the companies but our own international officers and even the Government. The process of learning was slow and painful, and a lot of us dropped by the way" (quoted in Lynd 1973, p. 194). One of the intellectual leaders of organized steel, Harold Ruttenberg, more succinctly declared that "social revolution was at hand" (Lynd 1973, p. 199).

The Rank and File Committee was making demands and advocating strikes, and most rank and filers were somewhere in between—uninformed and confused but nevertheless energized. Roosevelt himself had a good deal of clout among steelworkers and William Green of the AFL was considered closely associated with him, so rank and file workers were pulled in different directions. Another important difference between the dominant leadership and a large portion of the rank and file, perhaps unique to this case, pertained directly to interracial solidarity. Many white workers, according to Cayton and Mitchell, were sincerely interested in racial inclusion, despite the indifference or even racist stances of the top leaders (1939, p. 189). Unlike 1919, most blacks in the mills were now long-time residents. Also different was that the legacy of 1919 (and related events) convinced officers and members of the white lodges of the necessity of organizing black workers.[5]

As labor unrest developed in the spring of 1934, negotiations followed involving the national office of the AA, the employees' committee, the Steel and Metal Worker's Industrial Union (a small communist-led union), and the American Iron and Steel Institute. The latter organization, the conglomeration of steel mill owners, was often a decisive actor in national labor disputes in the steel industry throughout the 1930s. Negotiations continued, with many disagreements, and the threat of a national strike always looming. Eventually, William Green proposed a compromise, a new board to mediate labor disputes. The workers' faith in Roosevelt, even including the Rank and File Committee, facilitated the acceptance of Green's proposal. "On June 28 President Roosevelt appointed the National Steel Labor Relations Board and with this act the strike threat in the steel industry was terminated" (Cayton and Mitchell 1939, p. 144). It was no compromise. Before the NIRA was declared unconstitutional employers had not recognized outside unions. The board rarely came to conclusive decisions and, when it did, had no means to enforce them (Cayton and Mitchell 1939, p. 153). In short, the leadership had sold out the rank and file.

Several other factors were important in this drive. In addition to company unions, the racial divide and conquer tactics of employers were quite effective. They spread propaganda in white communities about black troublemakers, and among black workers about destructive unions and the threat of unemployment (Cayton and Mitchell 1939). On the one hand, for example, the Duquesne Steel Works circulated a leaflet with the following message in May 1934: "To the Decent people of Duquesne: Strikes are threatening to shut down the Duquesne Steel Works. A Bunch of Hoodlums, Hunkies and a few Negroes banded together for their own greed are trying to dictate to the management of the steel workers" (quoted in Cayton and Mitchell 1939, p. 135). According to one source, the Iron and Steel Institute had more than 375 newspapers at its disposal (Progress Publishers 1977, p. 374). On the other hand, company officials warned black workers against the union. As one black steelworker explained in Pittsburgh (July 1934), "The bosses in the plant claim that if the union gets in it will cause colored to lose out. The superintendent said to me about the union not to pay any attention to them" (quoted in Cayton and Mitchell 1939, p. 136).

Company repression, often with the support of state officials, was also common. One steelworker remarked, "When we were first organizing the union in Aliquippa, the police department was against us, the fire department, every governmental group was against us" (quoted in Bodnar 1982, pp. 124–27). Another steel worker recalled, "And there was never a meeting held, it seemed, that there wasn't a stooge of the company there. It seemed the meeting wasn't half over sometimes and someone would walk out, probably call a raid by company police. The company could deputize the police then. The deputies were like the old coal and iron police and they had [the] authority of state policemen. And the company used that to the fullest" (quoted in Bodnar 1982, p. 133).

On top of such potent employer tactics, the union had its own internal problems. Although the white workers had militant tendencies, its leadership was conservative. No concerted effort was made in the interests of, or for the recruitment of, black workers. The skill and wage differentials and their caste-like hierarchies were tolerated and perpetuated. The AA leadership retained a craft orientation that did not represent the interests of the vast majority of the rank and file, black or white. Many unskilled workers, including a preponderance of blacks, were alienated from the AA, perhaps more so than from the company unions. After the establishment of the Steel Labor Relations Board, the rank and file movement collapsed. The outcome of this drive, which produced no gains on the part of labor, and no interracial solidarity, must be attributed to the union leadership as well as to the steel mill owners and their company unions (Cayton and Mitchell 1939; Northrup 1944).

Although the NIRA lacked necessary enforcement mechanisms and the Steel Code did not go far enough in correcting wage inequalities in the labor market, the political context nevertheless remained quite favorable. "In 1933, the New Deal and the NRA had an 'electric effect' up and down the valleys where steel towns were located," according to Harvey O'Connor, a labor journalist (quoted in Green 1980, p. 141). Moreover, the NIRA was the precursor to more important and concrete legislation. Roosevelt's intentions were not altogether clear, but the union leaders had his attention and the Steel Code constituted an important step toward better conditions for workers.

In this case, the conditions were met for a split labor market. The skill wage differentials between white and black workers were substantial, and the economic insecurity precipitated by the Depression exacerbated these differences. Unemployment for black steelworkers was substantially higher than for whites. Thus, the possibility of finding alternative employment for blacks was much smaller. In the context of starkly differentiated tiers of skill, and a craft-oriented union, the concentration of black workers in lower occupational levels made for a significant difference in political resources.[6] In addition, because of historical experiences in the South, economic insecurity, and the union's stance on racial inclusiveness, black workers were more inclined to the paternalistic company union system.

While not averse to employing black labor, employers propagated racially charged information and threatened black employees with dismissal and violence. In fact, blacks were hired in front of white unionists as long as they did not join the union. Therefore, for blacks, there was both a "push" away from the union and a "pull" toward the employer.

The most variation between whites and blacks in this case stemmed from the differing resources: wages, skill levels (and thereby political organization), and opportunities for alternative employment. Employers capitalized on all these differences to ensure the loyalty of black steelworkers. Despite some interest in racially inclusive organization among white rank and filers, the white unionists maintained the hierarchical system, which contributed further to the black workers' loyalty to employers.

In this case, black workers did not cross a picket line per se, as a strike never materialized; it was sold out before it ever began. The organizing effort ended with white and black workers still estranged. In its entire existence, as Cayton and Mitchell note, the AA "had not made a single serious attempt to include Negroes in its ranks in a position of full equality with white union members" (1939, p. 81).

THE STEEL WORKERS' ORGANIZING COMMITTEE DRIVE OF 1937

In 1935, Roosevelt signed the National Labor Relations Act (NLRA), or "Wagner Act" (see Brueggemann 2002). It remains the most important U.S. labor legislation in the twentieth century. At the time of its passage, however, its initial impact was symbolic, like that of its precursor, the National Industrial Recovery Act. Unlike the NIRA, though, it would later have important concrete effects. The Wagner Act guaranteed workers the right to organize, provided election machinery to determine union representation, and mandated collective bargaining between employers and elected union representation (Fleming 1957). For workers in the steel industry, the most significant change was that the Act prohibited company unions (Edelman 1957).

Also in 1935, John L. Lewis formed the Committee for Industrial Organization, a group of nine industrial labor unions, as part of the AFL. It would leave the AFL in 1936 and become the Congress of Industrial Organizations. The Steel Workers' Organizing Committee (SWOC) was established in 1936 as part of the CIO (Rees 1997). Although the SWOC had a top-down political structure, it was organized on an industrial basis from its inception and was explicitly inclusive of unskilled and black labor—workers whom craft unions had often excluded (Nelson 2001).

In the mid-thirties, the nation's economic recovery crawled forward and by 1935 unemployment had dropped significantly. But in 1937 another, shorter recession took place—the "Roosevelt recession." In 1938, unemployment went up again, remaining high until 1940 (Darby 1976).

In the steel industry there remained substantial wage differentials between skilled and unskilled workers. Northrup explains that blacks were laid off in disproportionate rates during the mid-thirties (1970). By early 1935 (as Table 6.3 indicates), however, black steelworkers who were still employed were increasingly accessing semiskilled and skilled positions in larger proportions than white workers. That is, steelworkers in all racial groups were gaining access to the skilled and semiskilled occupations. But for blacks, the proportions that gained access were larger. Nyden argues that, in the mid-thirties, steelworkers began to recognize the decreasing importance of genuine skill differentials (1984, pp. 18–20), an important realization for their nascent militancy. In Pittsburgh during 1935, black steelworkers occupied the skilled and semi-skilled categories in even higher proportions (compared to blacks in the steel industry in general). In that year, of the black workers in the Pittsburgh district, 18.6 percent were in skilled jobs, 22.5 percent were

Table 6.3
The Skill Distribution of Racial Groups in the Steel Industry, 1910–36*

		Total	Whites	Foreign-born Whites**	Blacks
1910	Skilled	12.9%	18.1%	15.2%	8.2%
	Semiskilled	11.4	13.5	22.5	10.7
	Unskilled	48.0	25.0	67.1	73.6
1930	Skilled	13.1	15.2	11.4	6.2
	Semiskilled	21.6	22.5	22.0	16.4
	Unskilled	38.0	25.6	49.2	73.5
1933	Skilled	23.9	30.4	19.4	8.4
	Semiskilled	30.0	33.5	28.3	21.3
	Unskilled	46.5	36.1	52.3	70.3
1935	Skilled	35.7	38.1	—	15.0
	Semiskilled	29.2	29.8	—	23.9
	Unskilled	35.1	32.1	—	61.1
1938	Skilled	33.8	36.1	—	12.5
	Semiskilled	40.4	40.6	—	38.3
	Unskilled	25.8	23.3	—	49.2

Sources: For 1920, 1930, 1935 see Cayton and Mitchell (1939, pp. 25–45). For 1933, see Daugherty et al. (1937). See Cayton and Mitchell (1939, p. 22) on differences in skill classifications in 1933. For 1938, see Northrup (1970, p. 263).

*These categories exclude several nonproduction occupations.
**Native and Foreign-born Whites are aggregated for 1935 and 1938.

in semiskilled jobs, and 58.9 percent were unskilled laborers (*Monthly Labor Review* 1937; Northrup 1970). As displayed in Table 6.3, less than one half of all black steelworkers in 1938 held unskilled positions.

In the mid-thirties, real wages in steel increased substantially (Nyden 1984). And there is some evidence that wage rates narrowed across skill grades. "Increases of a higher relative percentage were given lower-paid workmen in November, 1936" as most all wages increased ten cents an hour (Harbison 1937, p. 16; see also Beney 1937). Although still substantial, the racial wage differentials in the steel industry declined somewhat in the mid-thirties.

A more important factor was a growing alignment in the organizing expectations of black and white steelworkers. Decreasing economic insecurity among black steelworkers altered their trust and expectations of employers. They saw that better conditions were possible, and what is more important, wanted to do what was necessary to realize those conditions (Kelley 1990). Part of this class consciousness was based on certain disillusionment with the company union system (Dickerson 1986). During the mid-thirties, company unions did not adequately address the needs of workers. As was often the case, those members who expressed interest in outside organizations were harassed, beaten, or simply dismissed. Eventually, the company union system lost what little credibility it had, even before it was banned (Cayton and Mitchell 1939).

In conjunction with increasing black militancy, a cohesive black leadership evolved. At various Carnegie, and Jones and Laughlin mills, among others, black rank and file workers and particularly their leaders recognized the importance of independent union organization (Cayton and Mitchell 1939; Dickerson 1986). When the Wagner Act prohibited company unions, black and white steelworkers alike were even more drawn to independent unionism.

During the mid-thirties, according to one estimate, steel mill owners employed some 5,235 black workers in western Pennsylvania. Most of them (81 percent) worked at Carnegie, and Jones and Laughlin steel plants in Pittsburgh and Aliquippa and the Monongahela mill towns of Homestead, Braddock, Duquesne, and Clairton (Dickerson 1986, p. 146). Virtually all of these mills were politically charged in the late 1930s, which was fostered by a strong black rank and file leadership (see Dickerson 1986, pp. 144–47). Almost all the black workers in the area had been there for some time and exhibited a lasting commitment to organizing against the owners (Cayton and Mitchell 1939; Dickerson 1986).

The drive to organize the steel industry was initiated with formation of the Steel Workers Organizing Committee in June 1936 (Sofchalk 1996). As a new union, the SWOC did not have the benefit of its own history of success. Racism continued to permeate relations among rank and filers. Said one SWOC Women's Auxiliary leader:

> There's something about colored men that makes you *afraid*.
> I don't know what it is, but you have a certain *fear*. . . . I know
> that Negroes *are* workers, and I suppose that, really, they *are*
> human, but there's just something about them—that black
> skin—I guess the trouble with us is really that we're not
> liberal enough. You know, the thing is that you would like to
> be nice to them yourself personally, but other people don't
> feel that way. Perhaps if you were just with a colored person
> away from the eyes of everyone, you would act quite different;
> but with the eyes of everyone on you, you don't feel that
> way." (quoted in Drake and Cayton 1945, pp. 332–33)

Despite this context of cruel racism, SWOC's reputation was instantly established because it was linked to the CIO and, importantly, the UMW. Thus, in contrast to the astonishingly ineffectual AA, the achievements of those organizations contributed to the prestige and promise of the new steel union. In addition, the SWOC enjoyed the substantial resources of the CIO and its supporters.

In the fall of 1936, there were approximately eighty-two thousand SWOC members. This figure would jump to 125,000 by the end of the year (Progress Publishers 1977, p. 377). The campaign was massive, and the CIO threw great resources behind the effort. Energized organizers, white and black, recruited all over western Pennsylvania, eastern Ohio, and in scattered other cities, such as Chicago (Goldfield 1993). By May 1937, membership was up to three hundred thousand and by the end of the year, 550,000 (Progress Publishers 1977, p. 377; Foner 1974, p. 224).

The SWOC capitalized on the experience and leadership of many UMW unionists (Nelson 2001). SWOC officials, who were even more authoritarian than UMW leaders, used some sixty to two hundred communist organizers. Again, though, union leaders strategically controlled the efforts of communists. Leaders were not active in or even sympathetic to communist agendas, except insofar as such work served their own purposes, which in this case included the recruitment of black steelworkers (Cochran 1977, p. 101).

Many locals implemented the UMW formula (Northrup 1944, p. 180; Drake and Cayton 1945, p. 327; Brown and Brueggemann 1997). This arrangement proved successful in demonstrating the commitment to racial inclusion, but the number of black unionists is uncertain. Foner suggests that by the end of 1937 there were eighty-five thousand black members (1974, p. 224) and there is evidence that blacks joined in at least as great proportions as whites (Cayton and Mitchell 1939; Dickerson 1986; Bernstein 1970).

One of the most significant moments of the drive came in 1937. The union confronted a powerful employer organization called "Little Steel," which represented several companies, including Republic, Bethlehem, Youngstown Steel and Tub, Weirton Steel, and Inland Steel (Sweeny 1956, p. 32). The union had seventy-eight thousand members working at these various mills. With the support of the CIO, the SWOC demanded recognition in collective bargaining and living wages in a series of strikes over the next eighteen months. The Little Steel companies responded with intensely violent repression and various racially divisive tactics. In Youngstown, Ohio, for example, the steel company hired black workers as special police so as to identify blacks in opposition to the union (Cayton and Mitchell 1939, p. 214).

Cayton and Mitchell (1939) explain that aggressive black unionists who maintained the pickets offset the effect of such tactics in many strike settings. For example, in some cases black strikebreakers were called in to attack a picket line and were met by black strikers. This pattern negated the stereotype of the black scab. Many white workers did not overcome this stereotype of blacks, but recognized the necessity of solidarity (Cayton and Mitchell 1939). One white steel worker said in November 1937, "I tell you the truth too, at first I wouldn't like a Negro boss even if he was smarter than anybody in the plant. Maybe later on, I would get used to him—then I wouldn't care. I think the CIO will get us away from thinking so much about color" (quoted in Cayton and Mitchell 1939, p. 224).

The most extreme case of violence came on Memorial Day of 1937. The strike on Little Steel, which involved more than seventy-eight thousand workers and spanned seven states, was only hours old (Sweeney 1956, p. 32). A thousand strikers gathered at the Republic Steel's South

Chicago mill. After being ordered to disperse, some started to leave. The Chicago police, who had lined up next to the mill, then opened fire, killing seven and injuring ninety. The company had also hired black police to be a part of this force (see Cayton and Mitchell 1939, p. 214; Sweeny 1956, pp. 32–33). Bernstein provides the following account:

> According to Ralph Beck's testimony, which appears to be reliable, a marcher about twenty feet behind the line of confrontation threw a branch of a tree toward the police. Before it reached the peak of the arc, a policeman fired his revolver into the air and this was followed immediately by two more shots. Several marchers threw clubs and rocks. The police in the front ranks then fired their guns point blank (Beck estimated hearing 200 shots) and tossed tear-gas bombs directly into the crowd. Those marchers who were not dead or seriously wounded broke into full flight across the field. The police advanced, continuing to fire their guns and beating the fallen, now lying in tangled masses, with billies and hatchet handles. (1970, p. 488)

The SWOC, however, was not defeated. John L. Lewis had been negotiating secretly with U.S. Steel (Sofchalk 1996). The company wanted a stabilized price-wage structure and looked to Lewis's "practice of disciplined unionism" (Brody 1987, p. 22; see also Cayton and Mitchell 1939; Bernstein 1970). He secured major concessions, including minimum wage standards and a forty-hour week. The momentum of the SWOC drive had facilitated a bargaining position for such negotiation, and this agreement added to the momentum.

Coming off such victory by way of the threat of a strike however, the SWOC was not prepared for the devastating force of Little Steel. No major concessions were won from the companies of Little Steel during this drive. But, the outcome must be considered in a broader context. Loss of this battle did not portend defeat in the longer struggle. The union was not smashed, which was momentous in itself. Both black and white workers increasingly considered the violence of the steel companies to be unreasonable (Cayton and Mitchell 1939). In addition, there were other victories encompassed within the SWOC drive. The contract with U.S. Steel was particularly important, especially given the declining demand for steel due to the recession of 1937–38.

The Wagner Act was constitutionally validated in April 1937 and a number of gains for the union followed. Validation hinged directly on a dispute with the Jones and Laughlin Steel company. The NLRB ordered the company to reinstate previously dismissed steelworkers with back pay. Republic Steel lost a similar case. At this time, as a result of the Wagner Act and the U.S. Steel contract, the company union system basically collapsed (see Bernstein 1970; Brody 1987; Wilcock 1957). This was of course important for all steelworkers, but especially blacks, whom the independent unions had neglected but whom the company unions had included. Clearly, the political context favored labor's interests. Federal legislation contributed to a new conceptualization of the role and rights of labor in American society.

Overall, the drive must be considered a success. A number of specific strikes essentially failed, including the big one with the Little Steel companies (Turrini 1997). Nevertheless, the union never really lost its momentum. The defeat at the hands of Little Steel and the recession of 1937–38 were deleterious with respect to the SWOC's efforts to organize the industry. Nevertheless, membership remained strong, as many smaller strikes and disputes were won, all the way through to World War II, reflecting the long-term success of the union. By that time, local unions at all the major steel companies, including those of Little Steel, were recognized and had successfully negotiated contracts (Northrup 1944; Rees 1997; Munley 1998).

From the standpoint of split labor market theory, the trends in this case point toward a convergence in the labor market. The wage differential between black and white steelworkers, although still significant, became less extreme. White workers were less advantaged as the work force became deskilled and as industrial unionism replaced craft unionism. There were still barriers to black opportunities and to racial harmony, but a strong black leadership emerged out of the rank and file, providing a coherent sense of purpose to channel increasing black militancy. Growing militancy among black and white workers converged on a rough class consciousness.

Employers again applied racial divide and conquer techniques. In addition, they responded to the workers' activism with violent repression (supported by state actors), which actually served to galvanize workers. There remained a certain amount of worker racism throughout the region, but in the steel industry during the late thirties, the most characteristic trend was toward racial tolerance and accord.

Constitutional validation of the Wagner Act reduced the paternalistic hold that company unions had on blacks. And unlike the AA, the SWOC, including white leaders and rank and filers, was enthusiastically inclusive of black workers. Following the "UMW formula," they solicited and used black organizers successfully in the recruitment of black rank and file workers (Dickerson 1986 pp. 144–47). The outcome in this case was an unprecedented level of interracial labor solidarity.

THE UNITED AUTO WORKERS DRIVE OF 1937–38

The story of interracial labor dynamics in the auto industry primarily took place in one location, the massive Ford River Rouge plant in Dearborn, Michigan, a suburb of Detroit. One of "the Big Three," Ford employed approximately ninety thousand workers, eleven thousand of whom were black (Bailer 1943, p. 416). In 1937, the Rouge plant employed 84,096 workers (see Table 6.4). More than one-half of all black auto workers were employed at Rouge.

In addition to being unique in its racial composition, Rouge also had an unusual skill distribution. Black auto workers were represented in every operation of the plant and basically paid the same as whites in comparable positions. In 1939, the average annual income of white auto workers was $1,291; for blacks it was $1,092. According to Bailer (1943, p. 419), this gap represented the smallest race differential of any manufacturing industry (with the single exception of the leather industry). This unusual equity is partly explained by the fact that black employees at Rouge were concentrated in well-paying but dangerous and arduous jobs, such as foundry work (Meier and Rudwick 1979; Peterson 1979). In 1939, 38 percent of foundry workers at Rouge were black (Bailer 1943, p. 418).

The most substantial difference in resources between white and black auto workers was in the opportunity for alternative employment. Outside Rouge, black auto workers only had access to lower paying jobs scattered about in various places. General Motors employed 2,500 blacks (out of 100,000 employees); Chrysler employed 2,000 blacks (out of 50,000 total). Even the Ford Motor Company (FMC) hired very few blacks (about 1,175) elsewhere (Meier and Rudwick 1979). In addition, black labor employed at places other than Rouge were typically not utilized in production, especially skilled work (Bailer 1943).

Table 6.4
Distribution of Black Employees in the Ford Rouge Plant, October 1937

	Production			Non-Production			Total		
	All	Black	% Black	All	Black	% Black	All	Black	% Black
Foundry	8,980	4,199	46.76	3,274	460	14.05	12,254	4,659	38.02
Foundry Machine Shop	3,524	609	17.28	428	7	1.64	3,952	616	15.59
Motor Building	11,723	580	4.95	2,854	174	6.10	14,577	754	5.17
"B" Building	5,671	243	4.29	3,797	321	8.45	9,468	564	5.96
Spring and Upset Building	3,842	500	13.01	1,642	74	4.51	5,484	574	10.47
Pressed Steel Building	4,754	375	7.89	2,292	180	7.85	7,046	555	7.88
Rolling Mill & Open Hearth	5,510	889	16.13	2,683	293	10.92	8,193	1,182	14.43
Tool Rooms	—	—	—	5,131	51	0.99	5,131	51	0.99
Construction	—	—	—	3,515	232	6.60	3,515	232	6.60
Misc.	—	—	—	—	—	—	14,476	638	4.41
Total	44,004	7,395	16.81	25,616	1,792	6.99	84,096	9,825	11.68

Source: Bailer 1943, p. 418

The exclusion or subjugation of black workers at auto plants other than the Rouge has been attributed to the hostility of white workers (Bailer 1943; Northrup 1944). However, Ford established an interracial work force in the early twenties when there was an abundance of jobs and little threat of unionization (Lichtenstein and Meyer 1989, p. 63). Thus, neither the economics of a short labor market queue nor the politics of attempting to racially divide attempted unionization (which was done later) explains Ford's nondiscriminatory hiring.[7] The difference between Ford versus GM and Chrysler suggests that employers bear a good deal of the responsibility for interracial work relations. Gartman suggests that "[c]apitalists merely reflected the general racism of American society, believing that blacks were incapable of performing any but menial labor" (1986, p. 250). In addition, the exclusion of blacks generated loyalty among white auto workers, and according to Gartman, employers deliberately reminded white workers of their racial cushion as a way to blur class divisions with racial loyalties (1986, p. 250). As such, the racial dynamics at Ford—a paternalistic relationship between the employer and black workers—were extraordinary for the industry.

The rare opportunities afforded black auto workers at Rouge had profound effects on their attitudes toward Ford. In fact, the relationship between Henry Ford and the black community in Detroit was one of the crucial factors in this story (see Korstad and Lichtenstein 1988; Stepan-Norris and Zeitlin 1996; Brueggemann 2000). Henry Ford established a secure relationship with a number of prominent black leaders, including influential clergy. By the mid-thirties, he was the largest employer of black labor in Detroit. Most black employees of Ford had been there for some time. Any black worker who was seeking employment was almost forced to go through one of Ford's contacts in the black community. Consequently, Ford had a significant degree of control among Detroit's black elite, particularly among churches. There was an aura about Henry Ford in the black community. He was considered more than a paternal benefactor—almost a hero. In the context of a white racist community and few other alternatives, this devotion was not at all unfounded. Thus, when labor disputes arose in the late thirties, black leaders and rank and filers alike were very reluctant to oppose Ford (Meier and Rudwick 1979).

The 1937–38 recession, which led to increased unemployment, also enhanced loyalty to Ford among blacks (Northrup 1970, p. 60). Horace Sheffield, black UAW organizer remarked, "Of course, this made the conflict even sharper as far as the various ethnic groups were concerned because you not only had to fight Ford, you had to fight these groups in the community. . . . The thing that had the greatest impact, really, was Ford shelling out the hard dollars. I mean really the tremendous amount of money that he gave these folks. Now clearly, it affected, this (black community) leadership . . ." (quoted in Stepan-Norris and Zeitlin 1996, p. 52).

The United Auto Workers was established in August 1935. Like SWOC, the UAW was formed right in the midst of the conflicts that ensued between the AFL and the CIO after the latter organization formed in October 1935. In May 1936, the UAW decisively rejected the AFL. The influence of AFL leaders would, however, linger for years to come. In fact, this initial conflict portended difficult internal struggles that would plague the UAW leadership for some time (see Lichtenstein 1995; Stepan-Norris 1997b). Nevertheless, the late thirties was an active and charged time for the new auto union.

When open class struggles erupted in the thirties, as the union movement picked up momentum at GM and Chrysler, black auto workers were essentially neutral (Meier and Rudwick 1979). The UAW waged a series of "sit-down" strikes, the strategy being to occupy the buildings housing the means of production. In sit-down strikes, a neutral stance was relatively more favorable to the interests of employers than in conventional strikes, in which case neutrality favored the union.

Throughout its early years, the UAW had done little to foster any special allegiance from black workers, which contributed to tensions when the UAW held a strike on Chrysler in 1939. The company tried to start a back-to-work movement among black workers and recruit new black strikebreakers. Out of the two thousand black workers employed by Chrysler (Bailer 1943), only 187 crossed the picket line in the strike on Chrysler (Gartman 1986, p. 252). This small group did so on the basis of economic need and indifference toward the union, Bailer suggests, not because they believed the company was concerned with their interests (1943). It was not enough to resume production. So the strategy of the company for breaking the strike became to incite interracial violence and then call for intervention from the National Guard (Meier and Rudwick 1979, p. 68; Gartman 1986, p. 252). This, however, backfired as prominent black leaders and the union leadership recognized the dangers and cooperated to defuse the situation. The company was then unable to garner any kind of support from the black community and the strike held. The UAW unionized Chrysler soon thereafter.

The wave of dramatic and successful sit-down strikes against the General Motors Company had invigorated labor throughout the industry. Then successful union activism against the Chrysler Company had left Ford the only company of the Big Three that was nonunion. Furthermore, by the late thirties, the average wage at Rouge was five cents less per hour than that of the entire industry, and ten cents less than that at Chrysler or GM. In short, the UAW leadership was bent on organizing Ford, and the rank and file there was increasingly conscious of its conditions and impatient for change (Howe and Widick 1949).

The UAW drive at Rouge began in May 1937 when several UAW leaders, including Walter Reuther and Richard Frankensteen, went to the Rouge to distribute literature. FMC Servicemen attacked the unionists, in what became known as the Battle of the Overpass (Bernstein 1970, pp. 570–71). They also attacked the journalists at the scene. Several photographs survived the skirmish, however, and these accompanied stories in local papers the following day. The pictures represented the first public documentation of the repression that the Service Department practiced regularly at the Rouge and damaged the public image of Ford (Pflug 1971, pp. 79–80). To Ford's advantage, however, black employees were utilized by the Service Department in the attack. This engendered the hostility of white rank and file unionists toward many black employees (Bailer 1943, p. 422).

A few months later, the UAW returned, this time with one thousand workers prepared for a confrontation with Ford Service men. There was no violence. Instead, the FMC solicited the support of the Dearborn City Council, which promptly passed an ordinance outlawing the distribution of literature in congested areas, such as the gate where the unionists were congregated. Over the next few months, numerous unionists were arrested (though never tried) for such distribution (Howe and Widick 1949, pp. 96–97). The tolerance of local police with respect to the Service Department's violent practices and the city's prohibition of the union's distribution of literature signified tacit state support of the company's repression. UAW organizer Stanley Nowak characterized this cooperation in no uncertain terms:

> The Ford Motor Company . . . actually controlled the municipalities: Dearborn, all of Lincoln Park . . . Ecorse; River

Rouge . . . all of the municipalities down the river. Because that's where the Ford workers lived. They controlled it— well, they had all kinds of municipal acts against distributing leaflets, against organizing meetings, and in Dearborn particularly. So to get in front of the Rouge plant, nearby where workers were going to work, it was impossible. You'd be arrested for the violation of a city ordinance, in the early days. (They later broke up that violation.) But at first . . . it was absolutely impossible to get anywhere. . . . Like a military camp. . . . Like a fortress. (quoted in Stepan-Norris and Zeitlin 1996, pp. 64–65)

The drive continued into 1938 without any real degree of success. Declining employment, due to the recession of 1937–38, weakened the union. However, UAW successes at GM and Chrysler illustrate that other factors were at work at Ford (Bernstein 1970). Meier and Rudwick indicate that the intelligence network and violent repression maintained by the Ford Service Department was most effective (1979). As Bernstein notes, "Ford Service engaged in systematic intimidation" (1970, p. 740). This department worked carefully with its black contacts at Ford to keep the black rank and file in line. Throughout this drive, the vast majority of black workers never wavered in their support for Ford. Local black leaders were constantly excoriating the evils of the union. And, of course, white unionists identified black employees, and the black community overall with Ford. The company's racial divide and conquer tactics were thoroughly effective (Meier and Rudwick 1979).

The union leadership espoused racial equality from its inception. In 1937, both John L. Lewis and Homer Martin (president of the UAW) proclaimed an inclusive stance in letters to Roy Wilkins, the assistant secretary of the NAACP.[8] The union took concrete steps to facilitate the recruitment of black auto workers. Stepan-Norris and Zeitlin (1996; see also Goldfield 1993; Stepan-Norris 1997a) attribute such policies, at least partially, to the leftist leanings of important UAW officials and their influence in the union. These efforts included educational programs designed to enlighten white workers about racial issues and the use of black organizers (Foner 1974, pp. 221–23; Meier and Rudwick 1979, p. 34). An informal group of black and white unionists began meeting to specifically address racial issues in organizing at the Rouge. These regular meetings of the "Negro Committee," as the group became known, constituted significant initial steps toward dealing with white racism and recruiting blacks (Brueggemann 2000). The union leadership received the support of many national black leaders including Wilkins and A. Philip Randolph (President of the Brotherhood of Sleeping Car Porters) (Foner 1974, pp. 221–23; Korstad and Lichtenstein 1988, p. 744).

The white rank and file, however, was hostile toward the black community in general and Ford employees in particular. Interestingly, black and white Ford workers worked alongside one another for years in accord. This did not, however, mitigate the resentment that developed during the 1937–38 drive. At most auto plants, there was a caste system in place wherein the few black workers employed were confined to particular spheres, typically entailing unskilled, arduous, or dangerous work. Although blacks were concentrated in dangerous work at Rouge, the occupational distribution there was more open and cannot be considered a caste system (Northrup 1944).

The problem for the UAW at the Rouge was convincing black workers of its sincere objective of improving conditions for black auto workers in and beyond Rouge. It was, after all, outside the Rouge in unionized plants where conditions for blacks were worse—where a caste system was in effect. There were not many black union leaders at the time. These factors, combined with the increasing racial hostility of the white rank and file at the Rouge, did not engender the trust of black workers there. The union leadership was aware of this problem and the need to address racism among the union's members. There were, however, more immediately pressing problems for union leaders.

From its establishment, the UAW leadership was rife with intense and destructive factionalism (Nelson 1998). The unrepresentative and inept AFL leadership of organized auto workers before the establishment of the UAW-CIO had contributed to the emergence of a radical wing (which had several subfactions itself). During all the early years of the UAW, various factions were jockeying for control (Howe and Widick 1949; Stepan-Norris and Zeitlin 1996). These groups included AFL hangers-on, who dominated in the first couple years, progressive industrial unionists associated with the CIO, socialists, and communists (Bernstein 1970; Goldfield 1993; Stepan-Norris and Zeitlin 1996; Stepan-Norris 1997b). A number of factors shaped this struggle, including the influence of state and federal government and local business. Moreover, it was compounded by ambitions for personal power, as well as particular personalities (see Howe and Widick 1949, p. 71). Of these, the CIO associates and the communists were the factions most dedicated to racial inclusion.

There were two central consequences of this factionalism. Most importantly for the drive, the leadership was disorganized. The instability of the UAW leadership made for a shaky connection with the national CIO. John L. Lewis tried to mediate in several circumstances, typically creating flimsily balanced coalitions that would subsequently fall apart. The internal strife diminished the focus and efficacy of the drive on Ford (see Meier and Rudwick 1979).

The second result of this struggle, which is related to the first, was the impact on the recruitment of black workers. The AFL leadership had not invested in organizing black workers and was regarded as racist. The recognition of the need to appeal to black auto workers motivated the new union leadership to establish the "Negro Committee." However, this organization got caught in the factional crossfire. Born out of one faction, coopted by another, and then attacked by the former one, the Negro Committee was disabled and left powerless (Meier and Rudwick 1979, p. 47; Stepan-Norris and Zeitlin 1996, pp. 145–46). With this development, any kind of institutionalized effort to recruit black auto workers disintegrated. Although black employees at Ford only comprised about 12 percent of the work force, they constituted a crucial component in the balance of power between the union and the company.

Though differentials existed, there was not a decisive gap between black and white workers in terms of wages or skills. Blacks were included in every operation at the Rouge and paid wages that were similar to those of their white counterparts. They were paid less than most white workers in other plants, but mostly because the latter contexts involved union-negotiated contracts.

The most important differences were the paternalistic relationship between Ford and the black community, and the lack of equal opportunities for alternative work. Alternate opportunities were extremely limited for black auto workers, especially during the recession of 1937–38 (Northrup 1970, p. 60). This served as the basis for a solid alignment with Ford. Moreover, his paternalistic relationship profoundly shaped the expectations of black auto workers. Indeed, it affected the attitudes of the entire black community and thus the race relations of Detroit. These attitudes of loyalty and complacency constitute motives that differed dramatically from those of white auto workers. Ford fully capitalized on this rapport, throwing in divide and conquer tactics—getting black Ford employees identified with the company in an attack on pickets—that proved sufficient to prevent any solidarity across racial lines.

The most conspicuous racism emanated from white labor. Despite years of racial accord in the workplace, the white rank and file was overtly intolerant. The union leadership, though concerned with the interests of both white and black workers, was ineffective in persuading black workers or black leaders of a sincere concern with addressing their interests (at the Rouge or elsewhere) or including them at all.

As the Wagner Act had been declared constitutional in 1937, the broader political context was more favorable for labor than it had ever been. Ironically, perhaps, the black community had strong leadership in Detroit. The National Negro Congress was fairly strong, supportive of the CIO, and the first to get behind the UAW (Foner 1974, pp. 221–23). The Urban League, associated with conservative business interests, was also fairly strong. The most prominent black organization by far, however, was the NAACP, which in 1937 sided with Ford (Meier and Rudwick 1979, pp. 34–107). Thus, strong political organization among the black community was not equivalent to worker consciousness. In 1937, between a sometimes racist, conflicted union and a strong, paternalistic employer, the reasonable ally for the black community was Ford. Although the dominant trend from 1934 was economic recovery, the "Roosevelt recession" occurred in 1937–38 and some two million workers became unemployed. The slack labor market may have exacerbated racial competition and the risks workers were willing to take in general.

Despite strong leadership and small differentials in skill or wages, there was evidence in this case of a split labor market. The differences in resources, specifically opportunities for alternative work, were integrally related to Ford's control of the black workforce. White rank and file racism further alienated black workers. Union factionalism contributed to a poorly run drive, the perception of inefficacy, and the absence of any organized effort to recruit black workers. The outcome was a failed drive; Ford remained nonunion. No significant degree of interracial solidarity was realized. In fact, intense racial antagonism grew out of the drive.

THE UNITED AUTO WORKERS DRIVE OF 1940–41

> [The UAW] set up a drive, about sometime in 1940, where they concentrated on the black community. I got involved in it. . . . We set up an office on Milford in the black community and it was a matter of ringing doorbells and really talking to folks in the plant. That sort of thing. Yeah, and as a matter of fact, I am, at the time of the strike, why I was president of the Detroit NAACP Youth Council. The senior branch opposed the organization of Ford and we in the Youth Council favored it. . . . (UAW official Horace Sheffield quoted in Stepan-Norris and Zeitlin 1996, p. 103)

In 1940, many of the important conditions that shaped the UAW drive of the late thirties were still present. The occupational distribution and wage structure at Rouge were virtually the same. Most Ford employees at the Rouge had been there for some time. Employment rose substantially in 1939, and continued to expand thereafter through the war. Nevertheless, while improved, the options of black auto workers at the Rouge for equally good alternative employment remained minimal.[9] There were, however, some crucial changes in the plant and in the union.

Despite the persistence of racism at other plants, such as Chrysler and Briggs, the expectations of black Ford workers of their employer changed in the late thirties and early forties.[10] Although upgrading of black workers at the Rouge had been much more prevalent than at other plants, it was still not on par with the mobility of white employees.[11] Blacks remained concentrated in dirty and dangerous foundry work. By the early forties, they began to question the company's role in this inequity more and more. Several other important developments contributed to this changing consciousness.

The union was increasingly strong. Success in various organizing drives throughout the industry in the late thirties inspired auto workers. Ford was a glaring exception. By the end of 1939, the Wagner Act started to have a number of important concrete implications. It gave workers the right to vote on their own representation in collective bargaining processes, and effectively curtailed the company union system. The National Labor Relations Board created by the Wagner Act started making decisions in labor disputes, several of these in the auto industry. Most were very favorable to the UAW (Stieber 1962, pp. 6–8; Meier and Rudwick 1979). Despite that auto workers were choosing the UAW to represent their interests, Ford continued to reject the union's legitimacy. In addition, clear signs of recovery from the 1937–38 recession were evident. Employment was back up to a level comparable to 1936 (Darby 1976).

Inside the UAW, factionalism among the leadership became acute in 1938. In 1939, a compromise candidate, R. J. Thomas, was chosen president of the UAW. His seven-year tenure would be rife with conflict. The first few years, however, were characterized by relative comity. This temporary accord was facilitated by several important NLRB decisions that helped Thomas consolidate and legitimize his authority (Stieber 1962, pp. 7–9; Howe and Widick 1949).

Throughout the early forties, the union had made a number of efforts to recruit black members, and perhaps of equal importance in this case, to solicit the support of the broader black community. Articles and flyers were published with explicit attention to the interests of black auto workers and to the culpability of Ford over unequal conditions based on racial background. Emulating the success in coal and steel, the UAW also began to institutionalize inclusiveness. Union locals explicitly adopted the miners' formula of including a black candidate on the election slate for top offices (Foner 1974, p. 253; Korstad and Lichtenstein 1988, p. 794).

A revitalized drive began at Rouge during the fall of 1940. The CIO and UAW devoted huge resources toward the effort (Northrup 1944). This included tactics, funding, and personnel. Michael Widman, a CIO official and ex-UMW organizer, was sent to lead the drive. He utilized black and white organizers for recruitment. Several political developments aided the union effort too. Early during the campaign, the Ford Company lost an NLRB ruling that mandated the reinstatement of several union workers who had been dismissed (Northrup 1944, p. 99). In fact, there was an NLRB report that implicated Ford in the practice of a number of unfair labor policies (Howe and Widick 1949, p. 97). In October 1940 a justice of the peace (and subsequently a circuit judge) declared the city ordinance banning the distribution of literature in crowded places unconstitutional (Northrup 1944, p. 99). As the drive picked up momentum, Ford's "Service Department" resorted to beating a number of unionists and union sympathizers. Over the months the organizing drive became an open fight (Howe and Widick 1949; Meier and Rudwick 1979).

A number of black community leaders came out in support of the union in 1940 (Howe and Widick 1949; Meier and Rudwick 1979). These included local and national officers of the National Negro Congress and of the NAACP. Even some local leaders of the traditionally conservative Urban League got behind the drive. But, Ford generally retained support in the black community, earned through his own brand of racial inclusion. The quote from UAW official Horace Sheffield that prefaced this section reflects both the UAW's concerted effort at racial inclusion and the lingering reticence of senior NAACP officials, accustomed to Ford beneficence. In time though, the union successfully engendered the support of local NAACP leaders who carried a great deal of clout in the city's black community. By the spring of 1941, the UAW had hired seven full-time black organizers. The appeal to and mobilization of the city's black elite was a crucial new strategy on the union's part (Meier and Rudwick 1979).

The drive moved into high gear when an unplanned strike began on April 1, 1941. Rank and file workers stopped work in the rolling-mill plant, and the Rouge was totally shut down by nightfall (Howe and Widick 1949, pp. 100–101; Lichtenstein 1995, p. 178). On April 2, the union formally announced a strike. There were numerous skirmishes between union pickets and Ford workers, mostly Servicemen and black employees. The company sent groups of workers out a number of times to attack the picket lines. After the first attack thirty-six picketers were injured and treated at the union's hospital (1949, p. 103). But the picketers, including a number of blacks, repelled each of the attacks. It is important to note that during the melee Dearborn police—whom Meier and Rudwick (1979, p. 90) characterize as anti-union—stood by passively and watched the Ford employees attack the pickets (Howe and Widick 1949, pp. 103–105). The company was also able to "obtain an injunction ordering the pickets to clear the roads leading to the Rouge plant" (Howe and Widick 1949, p. 104). Still the strike held.

The loyal Ford employees were mostly black, numbering between 1,500 and 2,500 (Foner 1974, p. 254; Meier and Rudwick 1979, p. 87). Everyone knew that the skirmishes could easily escalate into full-blown race riots, which the union claimed was Ford's strategy. A race riot would force intervention by state troopers, which could break the strike

(Meier and Rudwick 1979, p. 87–107).[12] The blacks remaining in the Rouge plant comprised a few strikebreakers who had been imported, some workers particularly loyal to Ford, and many who were still skeptical and indeed fearful of the union.

In an important effort to deflate the racial tensions, Walter White, president of the national NAACP, issued a press release on April 4 explaining that huge numbers of white Ford workers had not joined the union.[13] It was not just black employees. Later, on April 22, White would telegram the governor to explain the strategy of the Ford Company to incite racial violence so as to necessitate the use of state police to break the strike.[14]

The tide turned against Ford. Enraged over the possibility of a race riot, many black workers and leaders questioned the company's policies and motives for the first time. Significant numbers of black autoworkers shifted support to the union, although probably not the "overwhelming majority" claimed in union press releases.[15] The vast majority viewed the choice between an increasingly effective and seemingly sincere union, and the paternalistic albeit infamous employer, a vexing dilemma. When the strike began, the majority of blacks were passive, neither picketing nor attacking pickets. The key to union victory, according to Meier and Rudwick, was that the union had "won the hesitant neutrality" of most all black Ford employees (1979, p. 102).

Two important developments resulted from the strike. First, the pickets held. The union withstood the repression of the company, and this was crucial to the increasing perception of efficacy the union enjoyed. The second result was that Ford's violent, racially charged tactics were perceptible to all watching, including the leadership of black Detroit. Several important black leaders who had previously been loyal to Ford or neutral soon publicly endorsed the union (Meier and Rudwick 1979, p. 94). The staunchest defenders of Ford in the black community remained silent, unable to any longer explain away Ford's violent and racialized tactics.

The strategy of the company, guided by the Service Department, galvanized the opposition. Of the blacks remaining in the plant, many trickled out during the ten-day strike. The pickets never faltered. On April 10, 1941, the Ford Motor Company struck a compromise with the United Auto Workers. The following May, the UAW won an NLRB election at Rouge by an enormous margin. Soon thereafter, the company agreed to huge concessions, including "a union shop, dues checkoff, grievance machinery, seniority, time and a half for overtime, premium pay for night workers and two hours' pay employees called in but not given work" (Howe and Widick 1949, p. 105). Race relations were powerfully altered as a result of the drive and strike. The black community and the UAW forged a new relationship that changed the balance of power in labor issues of Detroit (Nelson 1998).

The outcome in this case was an enormously successful drive that resulted in a significant degree of interracial labor solidarity and ultimately a successful strike. The key to the converging interests of black and white workers here was twofold. First, changing political opportunities for the union created new possibilities for the empowerment of workers, black and white alike. This was accompanied by changing expectations of black workers. The resulting accord facilitated the continuing convergence of resources, motives, and interests (Brueggemann 2000).

In terms of split labor market theory, this case presents some interesting questions. With an increasingly tight labor market in the early forties, competition among auto workers was not terribly intense. Black workers, however, still had limited opportunities for alternative work and strong loyalties to Ford. Within Rouge, the skill and wage differentials were only slight, particularly compared to other plants and industries. In short, the racial differences in the early 1940s were virtually the same as those of the late 1930s, despite an improvement in the economy. There was one crucial development though. The expectations of black workers increasingly resembled those of the white workers as paternalism broke down. They questioned company policies that encompassed racial divisions and accepted the union's inclusive efforts.

A number of factors contributed to the union's efficacy. These include indirect support from the federal government. Although local government was tacitly supportive of Ford as it tolerated violent anti-union tactics, the governor did not comply with the company's strategy, which afforded the union the opportunity to diffuse the potential for racial conflict. A cohesive leadership linked to the CIO was also important (Lichtenstein 1995). UAW leaders persuaded a number of black leaders and some black workers of the union's sincere interest in addressing the interests of the black rank and file. They built this interest into the organization according to the "formula" of hiring black recruiters and placing black officers (Korstad and Lichtenstein 1988). The related perception of efficacy and sincerity was critical to the drive's success.

As a result of several factors, Ford was increasingly vulnerable. The NLRB decisions contributed to a growing sense of confidence of workers everywhere, magnifying worker consciousness. These decisions affected the company more directly by restricting several Ford policies. Increasingly assailable, the company reverted to more extreme and racially charged tactics, which backfired. Ford alienated old allies, the black elite, and thereby the black rank and file. The union, of course, facilitated the circumstances that led to such folly.

CONCLUSION

The formula worked (Lichtenstein 2002). A black vice president, officers, and organizers, along with community outreach and consistent appeals to black workers overcame a generation of racial hostility. The formula was a credible commitment on the part of the union as an organization, independent in some sense of the individual members who might retain racist beliefs in their personal lives. There is some evidence in the three cases of solidarity that workers of different racial groups interacted more in the context of a strong interracial union. It is unlikely, however, that most white workers in the interwar years overcame their personal racism, or that blacks transcended their resentment in any formulaic manner. Instead, for a time, they put racism aside.[16]

Once they set aside racist impulses and fears, workers recognized their mutual material and political interests. The key is that the union leadership embraced common class interests by way of an institutionalized racial policy. To be sure, class solidarity was far from perfect and interracial antagonism surfaced in subsequent decades in all three industries. Yet, for organizing black workers into white unions, the formula worked. It worked so well that the CIO thought it was the solution to racial division everywhere (Lichtenstein 2002, p. 84). Unfortunately for the union movement, they were wrong.

CHAPTER 7

Operation Dixie—Paternalism and Employer Discrimination in Southern Textiles, 1946–1953

God Bless the CIO.

— Black Birmingham worker

Our people down here . . . are like children, and we have to take care of them.

— A white textile owner

It is not the economics of communism that frightens the white southerner; it is the racialism of communism that frightens him.

— A southern labor organizer

In 1946, the CIO launched its most ambitious organizing campaign to date—"Operation Dixie." "Everything" was the basis for organizing, declared director Van A. Bittner. Every industry in every southern state was fair game, although organizers would concentrate on "textile workers everywhere" and lumber and oil workers in a few selected states. The strategy was simply to contact as many workers as possible and to facilitate biracial, industrial unionism (Marshall 1967, pp. 254–56). Bittner, a steelworker, began the drive aided by six assistant directors from the communications, textile, auto, and steel unions. They established a

155

Southern Organizing Committee (SOC) to advise the national leaders and appointed twelve state directors. More than one-million dollars were put into the campaign, a remarkable sum for the time. Several hundred organizers were sent South.[1]

Contemporary observers saw "Operation Dixie," as the logical extension of unionization to a region that was ripe for it. Supporters imbued the drive with high hopes. The campaign followed on the heels of the heady days of great success of industrial unionism in the northern auto and steel factories—and in coal in the South—which organizers thought could be followed by a similar pattern in textiles. Moreover, the campaign began at the precise moment the South began to integrate itself more fully into the national social mainstream following World War II. Having been a partner in fighting international fascism, the South was presumably moving toward the long-heralded "New South" of heightened racial tolerance and industrial development. Unions would follow.

In short, at the national and regional levels, conditions seemed conducive to success. Yet the campaign failed miserably. Given recent CIO successes, high regional hopes, and theoretically pro-union conditions, what accounts for the failure of the campaign? Operation Dixie is an enigma in terms of the major theoretical foci of this work. This case appears to contradict the assumption of split labor market and other theories that employers do not actively discriminate. As in prior cases, employers should hire cheaper minority labor in a constant quest to cut costs and to maintain high profit margins. Employer discrimination is not "rational" in this theoretical sense. Yet the overwhelming evidence from the history of southern textiles points to employers actively discriminating against black workers. In the 1940s, no more than 2 to 5 percent of the operative positions in textiles was black.[2] How may we account for this anomaly? Theory and evidence based on our previous cases suggest that minority workers would be more likely to strikebreak and dominant workers would be more pro-union. While minority labor might have more to gain from union membership, they were typically more desperate for jobs and were traditionally less trusting of unions. Blacks were used as strikebreakers in northern industries (reported in chapters 5 and 6) and in many non-textile southern industries (Hurst 1972; Robinson and Bell 1978; Zingraff and Schulman 1984; Newman 1978). Operation Dixie, however, exhibited a reverse pattern. Blacks militantly supported the drive, while white textile operatives, the main target of the drive, were strongly antiunion. Explaining the anomalies of union organization requires us to examine the distinctive aspects of the South's historical development. After some background, we return to the union drive, giving special attention to the city of Kannapolis, North Carolina, as a prototypical example of Operation Dixie.

SOUTHERN "FOLK": PATERNALISM AND SEGREGATION

As late as 1940, the South remained the most predominantly rural region in the United States.[3] As the major economic category in the region, agriculture formed a pocket of traditional social relations in the industrializing economy (Mann 1990). Industrialization in the South was heavily concentrated in one of the oldest of industries—textiles. Although less industrialized than the North overall, the South was the center of the nation's textile industry. From 1939 to 1946, southern textiles as a percentage of the total U.S. textile industry increased from 41.2 to 45.1 percent. Textile workers also constituted the highest percentage of nonagricultural southern laborers (dropping slightly from 30.7 percent in 1939 to 26 percent in 1946). The next closest industry percentages were in food, from 5.5 to 12.3 percent, and in lumber, steady at 13.2 percent over the same period.[4]

The "textile manufacturing" mode of industrialization, as Boyte (1972) calls it, tends to leave intact traditional social relations (Blauner 1972). Widespread class consciousness that bound workers from different communities was therefore more complicated than in industries concentrated in other regions (Roscigno and Danaher 2004). Textile mill villages, which were often company towns, were built upon the plantation model (Billings 1979; Marshall 1967). As such, the biracial caste paternalism of plantation agriculture was recast as a uniracial class paternalism of the textile industry. Since textiles were central to the development of the South's postbellum economic life, and to its political and social character, the traditionalism of these social relationships persisted in the postbellum period (Zieger 1991; Wright 1986). As the textile industry grew, the demand for capital investment was more than could be met by a single industrialist. Southern textile owners sought other local sources of capital, and hired commission agents in the North to locate capital sources in return for stocks or for the mill agency contract. This kept control over operations in their hands.

Commission houses had an interest in maximizing production as sales commissions were based on sales volume. As Wood notes, this "exacerbated tendencies toward overproduction and low prices" (1986, p. 37). The result was less autonomy and economic benefits to southern workers, strengthening paternalism.

As envisioned by "New South" leaders, postbellum industrialization was designed to avoid the class pitfalls of northern and British models of economic growth. Class-based worker discontent found up North threatened industrial anarchy. Fear of "northern" style industrialization fostered disdain for union movements, which to the white southern mind presented the possibility of a direct frontal assault upon the southern community itself. Attacking the burgeoning northern industrial economy also served to reaffirm the region's virtue and honor lost at the end of the Civil War (Carlton 1982, p. 85).

Racial exclusivity, labeled "Anglo-Saxon" virtue, contributed to the maintenance of southern "folk" community (Carlton 1982, pp. 83, 89–90). Paternalism was immutably fused with racism in the mill towns, which provided a distinctively southern social bulwark against any threats to the "folk" solidarity. For white workers, and perhaps for the industrialists, black exclusion was an issue of "moral economy" (Stokes 1977, pp. 204–208; McLaurin 1971, pp. 61–65). Consequently, sustaining either class or race-based progressive movements in the South was quite difficult. To link class and interracial solidarity, as did Operation Dixie, was even more risky.

White textile workers were recruited from agriculture, mainly from failed farmers. Mill work was thus often associated with low esteem, poor education, economic insecurity, and social isolation. A "cotton family" community and culture was created within mill towns, in which, as a local minister noted, there was a "distinctive social line . . . there was quite a dividing line socially" between the textile community and the other inhabitants (quoted in Newman 1978, pp. 204–205). Textile work represented a step down the social ladder. Many started the step as putative sojourners, hoping to earn enough to regain the farm, but most never did.

Moreover, textile paternalism included the mill owner's provision of land and structures—mills, houses, stores, churches (Griffith 1988; McLaurin 1971; Zingraff and Schulman 1984). Paternalism was the major basis for cultural continuity among white workers who were "a cultural group, heirs to a folkish culture" (Newby 1989, p. 5). Despite the loss of autonomy, some ex-farmers may have initially found mill work more interesting than farm life, but the novelty of factory work would soon wear off, giving way to routinization. Deprivation occasioned by marginal social backgrounds predisposed these former farmers to a sort of desperation that precluded assertive challenges to mill owners. The result is that the structural limitations imposed by white paternalism produced a social quid pro quo: the guarantee of minimum care by owners only in the absence of unionization (Zingraff and Schulman 1984; Newman 1978).

For most blacks, textile employment would represent economic advancement, not the downward mobility experienced by many whites (see also Brueggemann 2002). When large numbers of blacks finally did enter the textile industry as operatives twenty years after Operation Dixie, it was, relative to their past status, a step up. Segregated along socioeconomic-economic lines, most southern blacks lived in agricultural communities where they toiled as tenant farmers or as sharecroppers. While an undisputedly oppressive system, blacks nevertheless developed a certain autonomy within it. Because of the social significance of race, white landlords were less involved in the "family matters" of black tenants and did not attempt to impose the same moral code on black families that they did upon white ones (Newman 1978, p. 219). The black church was a particularly independent institution, which served to generate cohesiveness, not so much through theological dogma, but from the social network created through collective bonding (Davis, Gardner, and Gardner 1941). Politically, blacks, of course, had severe restrictions on their rights and behavior. White textile workers experienced a less onerous and less demeaning control, but they nevertheless lived with tight restrictions and paternalistic oversight both in the workplace and textile towns. This stood in marked contrast to the immediate, personal interests shown by masters toward slaves on the plantation. Ironically, the paternalistic relationship of antebellum slavery was, in the postbellum period, more typical of white mill worker conditions than of those of the black community. Mill owners kept a watchful eye on white workers.

Southern textile workers had briefly unionized in large numbers around World War I (1916 to 1921). They exhibited widespread militancy during strike waves between 1929 and 1933. The largest mobilization of labor in the region up to that point, the General Strike of 1934, revealed unprecedented militant potentialities. However, the utter failure of that effort and the related devastation of numerous mill communities contributed to enduring caution about the promise of unions (Roscigno and Danaher 2004). The relative attitudes of workers toward employers and unions during decades to come were rooted in this conflict. Fear compounded the deeply embedded traditionalism in constraining class-based solidarity.

Thus, while southern mill workers subsequently reacted militantly against employers for the stretch-outs and wage-cuts, they were not in favor of unionization (Bernstein 1970; Zieger 1991). It is important then, to separate labor militancy itself from worker pro-unionization attitude and action. Despite these sporadic episodes, southern laborers failed to institutionalize an organizational base upon which to oppose mill owners effectively. A lethal combination of the political power of textile industrialists and state repression defeated both an AFL drive in 1929–37, and a CIO drive in 1937 (Wood 1986). Strikes or work stoppages before Operation Dixie augured poorly for the organizing drive. From 1927 to 1936, textile strikes in no single southern state exceeded ninety-five conflicts (e.g., Alabama had 36; South Carolina had 91; Tennessee had 32; North Carolina had 95), while in northern states the quantity was much higher (e.g., New York had 617; New Jersey had 155).[5] The 1947 Taft-Hartley Law had differential effects as well. All understood that it was an "antilabor" piece of legislation that made organizing more difficult (Martin 1980). Yet it disproportionately hurt southern workers, as northern workers were more likely to already be protected by a union (Wood 1986). Perhaps, as Boyte (1972, p. 43) contends, for all the familial richness of life in the southern Piedmont areas, continually absent were the autonomous social conditions necessary for textile workers to "establish independence."

The perception and strategic use of fear took different forms during these early drives. A drive in the 1930s by the communist-influenced National Textile Workers Union, for instance, was doomed by racism and red-baiting. "Do you want your sisters or daughters to marry a Negro?" queried the Gastonia, North Carolina, paper (Quoted in Rowan 1970, p. 59).

WHEN EMPLOYERS DISCRIMINATE

Black employment in southern textiles had actually been going *down* since the nineteenth century. From 1890 through 1930, the percentage of blacks who worked in operative positions in the southern textile industry was quite low, declining from about 17 percent in 1890 to near 2 percent in 1930. By way of comparison, the percentage of black workers in the southern iron and steel industry in 1890 and 1930 was about 52 percent and 82 percent, respectively (Wright 1986, pp. 180–98). Racial distinctions followed industry lines, more than geographic ones. White cotton mills sat close to black tobacco mills in Danville, Virginia, and in Durham, North Carolina. The 98 percent white Avondale cotton mill was in Birmingham, the same town where two-thirds of the iron and steel workers were black (Wright 1986, p. 178).

Textile owners forfeited the chance to take advantage of the South's cheapest labor source (Cobb 1982). Prior to the war, the forfeit may have been slight because of an abundance of white labor, not just male heads of households, but whole farm families (McHugh 1988). From 1920 to 1930, the white population increased in most of the South, while the black population decreased, and there was no significant increase in foreign population (Rowan 1970, p. 57).

Black employment in textiles, as elsewhere, increased during the war years and continued to climb, although still not in *operative* jobs. Between 1940 and 1960, blacks rose from close to 5 percent of Alabama textile employees to a southern state high of near 6.5. Georgia saw a smaller increase, going from about 5.5 to just over 6 percent. In North Carolina, the 1940 percent was near 3, in 1960, closer to 4. Blacks in South Carolina textiles made up around 4.4 percent in 1940, and about 5 percent in 1960. Tennessee's percentages were only 2.5 in 1940, and just 3 twenty years later (Rowan 1970, p. 62).

In 1948, CIO plant surveys in North Carolina still found only a few blacks in the textile mills targeted by Dixie organizers. For instance, only twenty of the three hundred employees of the Regal Cotton Mill in Wake Forest were black, and none of the 350 employees of the Alpine Cotton Mill in Morganton was black.[6] When blacks were hired, they mainly held janitorial or other marginal jobs outside the plant (Rowan 1970, p. 66; Wright 1986, p. 188). These anomalous situations were *not* the result of racially restrictive laws. Company policies regarding race were almost entirely unregulated by law in southern states.[7] No state laws (except South Carolina's) required segregation in the textile mill as they did for schools and transportation. Employers themselves continued to enforce segregation in the workplace. In Alabama, no textile firms desegregated until the 1960s. Industrialists saw segregation patterns as "natural," dictated by "racial norms" among white workers, but also by the (self-fulfilling) difference in "observable skills" of black and white workers (Wright 1986).

The spread of a distinctive southern labor market created "horizontal segregation" for low-skill workers (Wright 1986, p.183). In the textile industry, although blacks were largely excluded, the base wage for white labor was closely linked to the black wage scale in agriculture. Wright notes that "mill owners were able to get white labor at a black wage" and thus "industrialization and competitive profit-seeking were perfectly consistent with continued segregation by race" (1986, p.183). This drift toward wage convergence is the "grain of truth" in the notion that white cotton mill wages were kept down by the threat of replacement by black workers. Mill owners voiced such a threat only rarely, and, given the racism of white workers toward such a move the few threats that were made lacked credibility.[8] Their credibility rose when the CIO sought to raise wages. Employers could claim with some resonance in the community that integration would be forced upon them by the union (and the communists, Yankees, federal government, and other outsiders).

The U.S. Labor Department concluded in 1947, shortly after Operation Dixie began, that while the obstacles "retarding" unionization were found in other regions, they were of more recent origin in the South. The Labor Department concluded:

1. Comparatively recent industrialization in the region had not allowed former agricultural workers sufficient time to become "disciplined" to urban industrial behavior patterns that typically lead to unionization.

2. An oversupply of labor had placed workers in "exposed" conditions where it was difficult to risk organizing.

3. Historically, company towns—the mill villages—had been "highly important in textile industries," slowing the unionization process.

4. Geographic isolation of workers due to the dispersion of industries in outlying areas rather than in cities prevented worker solidarity.

5. Racial prejudice had been used to slow unionization.[9]

Operation Dixie would have to challenge two persistent southern themes: racism and paternalism. To be successful, the union would have to confront, and remove, both the cultural salience of racism and the structural bulwark of paternalism.

ORGANIZING THE UNORGANIZED

The campaign to "organize the unorganized,"[10] grew out of the CIO's move in the forties to consolidate its gains to meet the threat of a new national political conservatism. The Political Action Committee (PAC), the CIO's political arm, had been established in 1943 (Foster 1975, pp. 3–4). It was designed to foster labor's interests through writing, conferences, and more direct political party coalitions.

Operation Dixie was firmly grounded in the political ideology of interracial industrial unionism espoused by the PAC. The link between labor's political arm and the street level was provided by two men, George Mitchell and Stetson Kennedy. Mitchell served as the first southern director of PAC, while Kennedy, a writer, chronicled the fight between "progress and reaction" in the South.[11] His 1946 book, *Southern Exposure*, revealed regional injustices. In it, and elsewhere, Kennedy observed that black and white workers had at least one thing in common: the same enemies.[12]

White economic and political leaders, whom Kennedy called the "slaveocracy," stood in the way of reform for both blacks and labor. He tied the fate of blacks to the union movement. In an early draft of *Southern Exposure*, he wrote that freedom of expression was secure in the South "provided (1) your skin is white, (2) you do not have a foreign accent, (3) you are not a union organizer . . . you do not address an interracial audience," nor advocate "equal rights for Negroes." Throughout the South, he continued, "you cannot speak for labor unions without running the risk of being tarred and feathered (if you are white) or lynched (if you are black)."[13]

Kennedy was associated with a small band of white and black southern progressives, members of a self-styled Radical Gospel. Most members believed, as did Stetson Kennedy, the most prolific writer among them, that a sort of "native fascism" permeated the South, ruled by a "slaveocracy" elite of large farmers, businessmen, and industrialists. Perhaps more important, they argued, southern workers had passively accepted a nineteenth-century, antebellum, paternalistic ideology, refurbished by this elite in the twentieth century, which was antithetical to southern labor's interests. On two critical points, most of the reformers agreed, workers had been blindly misled. White workers had uncritically adopted the elite's antiunion attitude, and they had accommodated themselves to the racial division between workers. Such "political illiteracy" engendered by the "slaveocracy," left little chance southern workers would easily develop class consciousness, much less any degree of interracial solidarity.

CIO's INTERRACIAL CLASS SOLIDARITY

From the organizers' and Radical Gospel's viewpoint, unionization was one means of mobilization that might reduce the racial split in the labor market. The reformers agreed that blacks "must be emancipated economically and politically" before they could be "emancipated socially." Blacks must "first join democratic labor unions and beat a democratic path to the polls," (Kennedy 1946, p. 349). Meanwhile, white workers should "arm themselves with a ballot in one hand and a union card in another."[14] As one organizer wrote after a union meeting:

> I had the feeling that, if it were not for the racial bias and underdeveloped political intelligence, most of these men would be good unionists. But because of the bias they are ripe for trouble—and they will make trouble if necessary.[15]

The CIO-PAC gave the Radical Gospel one of its main chances to fuse racial tolerance with unionization. Of course, the CIO did not pursue interracial organizing just for reasons of ideology. Ideology was important, however. The communist influence in the CIO stressed an egalitarian, classless ideal. Most of those in the Radical Gospel, who would have eschewed the atheism and strict party line dogma of the communists, saw racial equality as a desirable end, whether achieved through labor unionizing or other means in society as a whole.[16]

There were practical considerations as well in supporting interracial unionization. First, the CIO had black support in the North, and in some southern non-textile unions such as mining. Moreover, blacks had been used as strikebreakers to help defeat earlier attempts at unionization (see chapters 5 and 6). Fostering interracial unionizing would therefore project the CIO's egalitarian ideals to workers, build on its past interracial successes, and prevent recurrence of black strikebreaking.

Goldfield (1987) criticizes the CIO for not pursuing interracial solidarity more aggressively. However, Operation Dixie pulled few punches in its racial egalitarianism (Griffith 1988; Hill 1965; Kennedy Papers). Racial inclusion must be interpreted in context relative to time and place. From today's vantage point, the CIO may not have been sufficiently progressive (Hill 1996). But its efforts were far more inclusive compared to any other movement in the South's history before or during the campaign (Griffith 1988; Marshall 1965, 1967). To insist that the CIO was not racially progressive enough is to engage in "presentism"—imposing today's values into a historical context very different from our own. In those times, given the cultural salience of race and the bifurcated nature of the textile work force, for the drive to have been even more racially inclusive would have undermined the movement in other ways. That Operation Dixie was not racially progressive enough is not the main reason for its failure.

The CIO, in this sense, was quite advanced in its interracial ideology, seldom shying away from taking national and local stands clearly in support of racial equality. Along with many speeches to the same effect, CIO officials stressed at the beginning of the campaign the importance of racial inclusiveness. A 1946 memo from CIO Organizing Committee National Director Van A. Bittner to all those involved in Operation Dixie made the issue clear and straightforward: "There is no question of race or national origin in our campaign of organization," he wrote. "We are organizing all workers in industry because they are God's human beings. This Christian precept of mankind is fundamental with CIO."[17]

Philip Murray, president of the CIO, wrote in the journal *Labor Reports* that "[t]he man who nourishes in his heart prejudice . . . because of differences in race, color or creed is a really sick man. . . . Our organization considers racial . . . prejudice part and parcel of the whole system of discriminatory practices" that labor unions organized to oppose.[18] Campaign pamphlets stressed unionism as a "civil right" in the same way racial equality should be.[19] A steady stream of cartoon drawings from the national CIO office illustrated that racism by workers against each other hurt the interests of all workers.[20] An equally steady stream of pamphlets yoked together union solidarity with racial equality. As one CIO pamphlet ended, using the words of Ben Franklin: "We must all hang together, else we shall all hang separately."[21]

The CIO even created a "Committee to Abolish Discrimination" to branch outside its organizing campaign and be involved in the national civil rights scene. The committee officially endorsed President Truman's civil rights proposals. It also supported the CIO's general counsel's (Arthur Goldberg) brief to the U.S. Supreme Court urging the holding that any racial segregation by any governmental body was unconstitutional.[22]

Minutes of the CIO's annual conferences, such as the one in 1951, provide clear indications that Operation Dixie organizers at the local level also displayed the same vehemence concerning racial equality. They were aware that race was a provocative subject, but maintained the necessity of interracial organizing in the Dixie campaign.[23] To be sure, racial prejudice among white workers continued to prove an obstacle to unity.[24] Organizers and reformers knew that the division of CIO unions along racial lines could only damage the general interests of southern labor. A 1946 directive warned organizers to be prepared for company literature that stressed as one of its central few themes "Negroes will become Foremen."[25] A racially divided rank and file could hardly present a united political front behind PAC. Such concern was reinforced by reports from organizers in the field. In some ways, one organizer suggested, his lot was an easier one. "They used to kill you for organizing a union," he reported to Kennedy, "and now they just knock your teeth out." On the racial issue, however, there had been little progress. "If we could just get the white workers to start hating the boss the way they had the blacks, we'd have it made."[26]

Because of its stress upon integration, the CIO had a much more favorable image in the black community than did the AFL. The AFL had to deny charges by blacks of discrimination within its ranks, justifying its many segregated locals as "frequently required by law," or arguing that such racial segregation was "desired by Negro workers themselves" (Marshall 1967, p. 249). In contrast, CIO leaders tried to conduct integrated meetings at union halls, sometimes scrambling the chairs to avoid racially separate rows and columns. White workers often imposed a racially segregated order back upon the chairs before the meetings began.[27] Other organization sessions became gatherings presided over by blacks. As Philip Murray put it, the campaign invoked the "freedom of southern workers from economic and political bondage" and advanced the hope of purging from the South "all types of racial and other forms of discrimination" (Marshall 1967, p. 258).

Racial issues permeated the organizing drive. Kennedy, in his regular "Dixie Drive" labor news column, warned white workers that industry leaders were making desperate efforts to turn workers' "just grievances against them into unjust gripes against some minority." Racial prejudice presented a strong threat to the southern labor movement, he wrote, and could best be dealt with by focusing on common black-white worker interests. "A strong union movement," one free from racial discrimination," would eventually lead to success in the drive.[28]

Given the history of negative white worker reaction to the proposed hiring of blacks in southern textile mills, the "black" threat came not from strikebreakers but from the very act of unionization. Operation Dixie raised the haunting specter of joining an interracial union. This alone was enough to cause trepidation among white workers. However, textile companies could, and did, compound that threat. The companies suggested that if white workers joined the Textile Workers Union of America (TWUA), they would have to *belong* to a union that was biracial. The companies further threatened that under "outside" union pressure, blacks would be brought into the textile mills to work alongside, or even "become Foremen" over, whites.[29]

Many of the South's textile mills were in the Piedmont, an area where comparatively fewer blacks lived. Presumably, this might have meant that white textile workers had less rational reason to be racist than if they had worked in areas with higher black population densities. But population concentration of a subordinate group is not required for levels of racism to be high (Van den Berghe 1967). Racism was a cultural trait of the region that permeated across distance and time (Williamson 1986).

Racism in the mills was of course not created by textile owners when the drive began. White workers had for generations been imbued with, and had contributed to, the region's hegemonic racial philosophy. This ideology was not simply developed by white elites and foisted upon white workers (DuBois 1935). In any case, the belief in the sanctity of the racial organization of southern society obviously worked against the CIO. To be for the union was to be against the South, defined of course along strict racial lines (Griffith 1988). Lower-class whites who were against Dixie engaged in such overt violence as shooting a "little wooden church full of holes" during an interracial organizing meeting. Upper-class textile company representatives race-baited by telling workers they had seen CIO organizers talking to blacks: "I saw him shaking hands with '_____' (a black) right down there by the county courthouse" (Griffith 1988, p. 80).

Neither lower nor upper-class whites held a monopoly on the use of racism to thwart the drive. Lower-class whites received help against blacks entering the workplace from the Klan, which used overt and covert means to accomplish its goal. The Klan headlined its newspaper, *The Fiery Cross*, with the words: "THE CIO WANTS BLACKS AND WHITES ON SAME LEVEL" (which was basically true). It also claimed the CIO was a communist organization masquerading as a labor union (which was not). During the drive, more new Klan locals, or Klaverns, organized in the textile areas than did CIO locals. Indeed, in South Carolina, the Klan was strongest in the western textile areas of the state (Chalmers 1965, p. 320).

Newspapers quoted southern businessmen as saying that if the Klan wanted to run the CIO out of the South, they were for the organization, and knew "plenty of good men" who felt the same. Textile industrialists may have looked kindly on such Klan intimidation of blacks and Dixie organizers as when Klansmen raided a South Carolina National Youth Administration Office, assaulted blacks, and left behind the sign: NIGGERS, YOUR PLACE IS IN THE COTTON PATCH (Chalmers 1965, p. 321).

Race affected the southern political sphere as well. By the late forties, threats of racial integration were used as a tactic to help defeat several Senate, House, and other statewide candidates, including Claude Pepper, Frank Graham, and Ellis Arnall. Most strikingly, the integration threats were associated with a reduction in union votes for these candidates as compared to previous years. The southern PAC director felt that exploitation of the race issue not only divided the labor movement, but "seriously impaired the political efforts of PAC" (Powell 1978).

RACIAL SOLIDARITY AND CLASS CONSCIOUSNESS

Racism soon proved to be a serious impediment to the campaign (Kennedy 1946; Peters 1994). When observers of the southern social scene such as Stetson Kennedy wrote about contemporary developments, they always pointed out the continued symbiotic link between a regional economic elite and the perpetuation of racism. For Kennedy, the "slaveocrats" were twentieth-century aristocrats who denied the South "economic, political and racial democracy" (1946, p. 48). An ironic result of this domination was the development of a white southern worker who was an "inarticulate radical, lacking in class consciousness." Reformers must not, he warned, make the common mistake of "injecting totally lacking class consciousness" into the minds of southern workers. "In other words," Kennedy wrote, "I hate to adopt, even as a last resort, the common NYC technique of interpreting the southerner as a natural Marxist." Since "Marxists are seldom seen by proletarians" in the South, he added, "it would be a trifle incongruous to fit one in the picture."[30]

Meshing racism with "white" class paternalism in the textile mills kept vibrant among white southern workers a dominant "racial" consciousness. Textile workers often expressed great dismay over the prospect of joining a union to which blacks belonged. In Tennessee, Georgia, North Carolina, and South Carolina, white workers expressed their reluctance, or direct refusal, to join integrated unions. Operation Dixie organizers' reports from 1947 through 1951 in these states continually note the problems posed to the drive by worker racism. Workers refused to come to integrated union meetings, sat in separate sections of union halls, told organizers that they "didn't go for working with colored people," or that they feared working with black foremen.[31] One organizer invited both black and white workers to a meeting to establish a local committee to form the basis for a union drive. At the meeting, he noted, "The white people left when they saw the Negroes and I lost my committee."[32] "We are not here in this CIO movement to say that white should marry colored," lamented organizer Frank Bender in the same 1951 minutes of the meeting. "We just want to make it so that we may move up the ladder together." Besides these four deep southern states, it was also clear to Virginia organizers that racism could be an antiunion tool used against Operation Dixie.[33]

Even before Operation Dixie, little firm evidence exists of any deep-seated interracial solidarity in the textile mills (Hall et al. 1987). Whites were more closely enmeshed in preserving their status in the mills. There were ideological effects of paternalism as well. Others have noted the negative relationship between southern industrial paternalism and white worker class consciousness (Zingraff and Schulman 1984; Newman 1978). Clearly, worker fear, and its normative flip side, deference—two traits commonly associated with industrial paternalism—operated during the Operation Dixie campaign.[34] Leading organizers were especially struck with textile workers' seeming lack of common cause with the campaign. There was "no accounting for the lack of intelligence on the part of some workers," Van A. Bittner wrote in 1948.[35] South Carolina organizers noted that textile workers were "too close to the bosses to think of a union.[36] Textile workers in Tennessee told organizers they "could not understand why people wanted a union."[37] Organizers wrote of meeting "bitterly anti-union workers" in South Carolina[38] or of being told by a male worker to "go to hell, that he didn't want to have anything to do with unions." Unions "were trouble makers," according to a female worker, and "there was no use in talking to her, because there was nothing I could say that would change her mind."[39]

A comparison of textiles to other industries—both in and outside the South—shows that in *nonpaternalistic* industries, unionization was more likely to succeed (Peters 1994). Racist class paternalism in the textile mills helped to enhance the primacy of racial solidarity over that of class solidarity among workers. Race-based paternalism between white workers and white owners presented a particular problem to interracial unionizing. Textile workers—whether "rational" or not—felt a racial solidarity with employers against unionization. White quiescence, or deference to textile owner authority, cannot be separated from the desire of both workers and owners to avoid integration. Based on experience, industrialists knew that white workers would react negatively, even violently, to the introduction of black workers alongside them in the textile mills; this was in fact the basis for the first instances of textile worker militancy (Wright 1986; Carlton 1982). Things had changed little in this regard by the time of Operation Dixie. White textile workers still held a disdain for working with blacks, or for the prospect of sharing union membership with them. Textile owners were quite aware of this, and the national representative for the TWUA believed the Klan worked along with companies to defeat interracial textile unionization.[40]

Ironically, among black workers, a subordinated *racial* group, we see *class* militancy in support of Operation Dixie. Southern blacks, including rural blacks, tended to possess more "class conflict consciousness" than did white workers. Paternalism meant "white" paternalism, a textile structure in which blacks were not a part (Zingraff and Schulman 1984, p. 133). As noted, sharecropping and tenant farming, while exploitative, allowed blacks more autonomy and was therefore more conducive to a "conflict ideology" (Newman 1978).

Effectively then, black workers responded much more positively to industrial unionism than did white workers. Organizers noticed that blacks were "highly politicized." Beneath an exterior of social deference lay a quick propensity to support transforming movements such as Operation Dixie. One organizer remembered that "blacks were very susceptible to unions. All the way through they were." A labor lawyer at the time noted that "many, if not all the people who looked to the CIO for help were black." In North Carolina, an organizer noted that "[b]lacks were right with ya! They were smarter than the whites, where the union was concerned. They had more to gain. And they knew that." Blacks "responded more to organization at the time than the white people did. They sure did." As a communications organizer in Texas saw it, "the only time you could do very much with low income people was when a large group of them were black" (Griffith 1988, p. 72). By 1950, it had become clear to many organizers that blacks realized and could therefore say that the "CIO is the best labor organization for the Negro."[41]

Consequently, textile organizers found great difficulties in convincing white operatives of the advantages of organizing a union. The few blacks in textiles, and the large number of blacks outside textiles, however, had little trouble seeing common cause with the CIO. In 1945, blacks in the Sumter furniture industry, and in the Charleston and Winston-Salem tobacco industry, for example, were "more readily organized" than their white counterparts, according to CIO regional director reports.[42] Similarly, in the larger industries outside textiles, such as food workers for Ralston Purina in Charlotte (where black workers outnumbered whites by three to one), blacks displayed more class solidarity. "The whites have never been in the union," North Carolina CIO Director Franz E. Daniel wrote in 1952, but the "Negro workers are a pretty good bunch and the unquestioned leader of this group."[43] In the Tennessee Wax Paper industry in 1949, organizer B. C. Glover found that as far as white workers were concerned, the campaign was "not making very fast progress," but the "colored people are ready and waiting on the whites."[44]

Unions in woodworking, food, tobacco, and mining industries in the South were growing by "four or five times as much" as in the past, according to social activist Lucy Randolph Mason. Mason noted the same pattern of black militancy in Mississippi and Arkansas, despite strong repressive measures against unionization by local authorities. Blacks turned to the CIO with great enthusiasm, using the exuberance of their culture—church and union songs and prayers—to such an intense degree that Mason called it a "primitive church pattern."[45] Similar to the slave songs that linked together freedom from slavery with spiritual rebirth (Stuckey 1971), the church songs, and union campaign slogans of Operation Dixie offered both social advancement and spiritual liberation. An interracial union drive offered the hope of equal treatment through class solidarity, and perhaps entry into textile jobs.

The positive response by blacks to the Dixie drive, however, turned into a negative factor for the general mobilization potential of Operation Dixie. For beneath the surface of the organizing campaign lay an implicitly understood realization of Dixie organizers. This was, again, more a subtle awareness than an explicit formulation: that if blacks outside textiles exhibited more class consciousness than did whites, racial ideology might preempt class solidarity. Whites, who comprised some 90 percent of the textile workers targeted in the campaign, had become intertwined in their work and community environment in an institutionalized system of racist class paternalism. Even though employers' exploitation and domination were a familiar part of such dynamics, workers in these settings were generally more resistant to unionization than in other industries.

PATERNALISM AND REPRESSION

Repression was especially severe in the South. Allan S. Haywood, CIO vice president and director of organization, noted the success of "southern reactionary Democratic congressmen" in blocking progressive legislation at the beginning of Operation Dixie. He, like other supporters, nevertheless maintained that the CIO could be successful in the South, both organizationally and politically.[46]

As labor's political arm, the PAC might have influenced politicians toward a more moderate position. However, as one PAC publicist put it: "It was not possible to support only ideal candidates. The choice was sometimes between the none-too-good and the outright labor-baiting isolationist" (quoted in Lichtenstein 1982, p. 174). In other words, southern labor failed politically to influence change, largely because of white worker preoccupation with race, and the lack of voting opportunities for blacks (Norrell 1991). White political solidarity was most clearly demonstrated by the "Dixiecrat" revolt from the Democratic Party over the party's strong civil rights plank in the 1948 presidential campaign.

Several leading southern Democrats walked out of the party's convention, and ran a third-party ticket that year (Grantham 1988).

Conditions for Operation Dixie organizers were even worse at the city level. Local political and business authorities and law enforcement agencies often worked in concert against the campaign. A common example was found in Thomasville, Georgia, where police broke up organizing meetings held in city parks. The Thomasville city manager refused CIO permit requests not only because they were pro-union gatherings, but also because of their interracial nature. The city manager said he was not going to have "racial tension in Thomasville" as had occurred in South Carolina.[47] Not surprisingly, similar incidents occurred throughout the late forties and early fifties. The North Carolina Highway Patrol sent nine cars out to break up a picket line in 1952.[48] Police interfered with organizing efforts in Fayetteville, North Carolina (where the chief said "I don't like the CIO").[49] Local arrests of organizers (some of which became Justice Department cases involving violations of freedom of speech issues) occurred in Virginia, North Carolina, and other southern states.[50] The FBI investigated collusion between the city police force and the Russell Mills in Alexander City, Alabama, to "beat up organizers, deprive workers of their civil liberties, run staff members out of town, etc."[51]

The Dixie campaign was also met with vigilante violence. A Charleston, South Carolina, organizer was pushed in his car off the road and warned to "stop fooling around in Charleston." A Tullahoma, Georgia organizer distributing leaflets was almost run over.[52] Mob violence against TWUA organizers often revealed the close connection between racism and antiunion sentiment, including collusion between the Klan and the textile companies.[53]

With few exceptions, southern newspapers were also highly critical of the campaign. Worst were fringe papers, such as *The Independent*, published in Anderson, South Carolina, which railed against "Negroes, Jews and labor."[54] Even the moderate leading newspapers failed to offer support.[55]

These overt reactions were merely the surface manifestation of a more deep-seated, regional reaction to Operation Dixie. Griffith (1988) argues that the negative reaction by the South's social status quo was largely due to a critical mistake made by the CIO in the misalignment of strategy to region. The CIO goal of class conscious, interracial industrial unionism developed in the North was ill-fitted to the "reality of social relations" in the region: the impenetrability of a racial and class hierarchy (Griffith 1988, p. 46).

Deeply interwoven into the fabric of southern society, paternalism was integral to both textile company and local political repressive moves against Operation Dixie. Repression in this context carries more than its typical meaning of the superior resources of an upper-class and state apparatus. Since white textile workers were closely tied to the southern folk community, (however objectively disadvantaged they may appear to us today) repression included the social norms of everyday life as well. Paternalism acted as a velvet glove, gingerly, but surely, maintaining relations of domination and subordination (Jackman 1994).

Opposition from the textile companies started with persuasive techniques appealing to the white textile worker's "place" in the textile community, and how that position would be threatened by unionization. Company opposition was thus couched in a paternalistic "concern" for the interests of the worker, either their "social" position in the textile community as a member of a unique racial "family," or their more direct practical interest that would allegedly be hurt by unionization. The company's antiunion plan usually began with an order for *Militant Truth*, an antilabor pamphlet aimed at yoking interracial unionism to communism, atheism, and anti-southernism. On the eve of union elections, the pamphlet appeared mysteriously in workers' mailboxes. The *Militant Truth* had a particular disdain for the CIO, calling it the "alien-Communist-controlled CIO." Its masthead carried an open Bible superimposed on a cross and the legend "The Word Of God" on one side. On the other side was an American flag and the legend, "Constitutional Americanism." As E. Paul Harding, Operation Dixie's public relations director wrote to radio columnist Drew Pearson, "A combination of Winrod, Bible-Belt Fundamentalism, flag-waving, and Red-and-labor-baiting make *Militant Truth* an irresistible potion for impressionable Southerners."[56]

The Truitt Manufacturing Company in Greensboro was more direct about the union threat to paternalism. Voting for the union, Truitt suggested in an October 30, 1946, letter to employees, would have meant the end of "close, personal relations" between company officials and workers, "not because we want to change," but because the union would block the company's efforts to solve personal problems of employees. "If you come to see us with a personal problem . . . we will be forced to say, 'Sorry, you will have to send a union representative. They won't let us deal with you personally.' "[57]

Southern employers differed little from their northern counter-parts in claiming that unions were only interested in dues or that they would cost jobs. However, their emphasis on the overlapping concerns of workers and their own did distinguish southern paternalistic employers. In a typical instance, the manager of Alpine Mills in Morgantown, North Carolina wrote in March 1947 that he could "help you more without the Union than I can with it."[58] The management of Perfection Spinning Yarns, Belmont, North Carolina, followed a similar line. Employers and employees had "worked together for a long time," the manager wrote in March 1951. "I believe that you have faith in the willingness of your company to do all it can for you and to continue to do so, to get you the same wage increases" and other job benefits. The CIO had "nothing to contribute . . . but trouble."[59]

Southern racist paternalism did not exist in a social vacuum. Several related factors in the region (e.g., religion, politics, the press, anticommunism, and conservative unionism) contributed to the influence of paternalism in the lives of textile workers. Each of these was more directly interjected into, and more proximate in, the lives of southern textile workers, than in those of workers in other southern industries. Each also enhanced the resiliency of racist textile paternalism's resistance to interracial unionization.

PATERNALISM AND RELIGION

Religion was another key component in the social life of southern "folk," and was particularly central to the culture of the mill village. While the use of religion to slow unionization could be found in other industries throughout the South,[60] the paternalism of the textile village provided an extraordinary level of "sacred" resistance to the "secular" Operation Dixie campaign. The antiunion element of religion worked on two different levels. There was a general one in which Christianity was pitted against unionization. A more specific level operated in the mill village, where workers followed the lead of southern pastors.

The general level was perhaps the most effective one, for it established an overall pattern in which the churches throughout mill villages in the region worked against the CIO. David Burgess, a CIO-PAC employee, testified before a Senate Labor Subcommittee in 1950 that it was the nature and scope of textile paternalism that accounted for the religious opposition to the Dixie campaign. Textile owners owned houses and streets in the villages, dominated the politics and law of the village, and often donated the land on which the church was built. Consequently, the "average minister of mill towns is hardly free to preach the gospel unafraid." Not surprisingly, Burgess noted, the minister is often "the captive of his benefactor; and consequently, when the workers begin to organize, he remains judiciously silent or attacks the CIO loudly and hysterically as the 'Mark of the Beast.' "[61]

Most mill village pastors preached a mutual exclusivity between belonging to a CIO union and being a Christian. "No CIO member could go to heaven," residents of Easley, South Carolina, were told by the superintendent of the Sunday School at Glenwood Baptist Church. "It's either Christ or the CIO," the Baptist minister of the church at the Pacific Mills in Lyman, South Carolina, said from the pulpit. "You can be a Christian or a CIO man, but you can't be both."

While the CIO and the Radical Gospel group mounted organized efforts to counteract the negative impact of southern religion, they were largely ineffective. As the CIO officially resolved during a PAC Convention in Virginia near the end of Operation Dixie, "deep prejudice" against organized labor had been "carried through" religion as well as through the region's other structures.[62] It was no social coincidence, of course, that the churches, like the workplace and the textile community, were racially segregated.

ANTICOMMUNISM

Red-baiting was another postwar means of continuing the "siege" reaction, as well as to protect textiles from the threat of unionization. Nativist, racist, and anti-Semitic publications emerged during the postwar period, which often asserted a link between communism and the Dixie campaign. In a common example, one newspaper editor wrote that "[i]t is generally assumed that the CIO is shot through with communism, and I do not like communism." He added that he did not like to "get orders from Washington, much less from Moscow" (Marshall 1967, pp. 262–63). In addition, pamphlets such *Communist Infiltration into Operation Dixie*, by Joseph Kamp, floated around textile mills close to union election time.[63] While the CIO found it difficult to secure ad time on radio stations, the antiunion message that the campaign was "unpatriotic and disloyal" was constantly getting through the airwaves.[64] The one senator organizers viewed as a friend, Senator Frank Graham of North Carolina, was forced to issue pamphlets that attempted to explain the "communist charges" to his constituents.[65]

The CIO issued leaflets, flyers, and pamphlets that sought to answer the charges. Union dues were not being sent to Korea to aid the communists, a leaflet entitled "The Big Lie" argued in 1950.[66] "Red-baiting hysteria must be wiped out inside the union and out," a CIO pamphlet stressed. Employers, it continued, do not care about the political opinion of workers and union leaders. "To a boss, he who fights is a Communist. We will outlaw all red-baiting as a boss's weapon."[67] "RIP OFF THEIR MASKS, AND UNDERNEATH YOU FIND DECEIVERS," titled another pamphlet aimed at criticizing the unfair use of First Amendment press freedoms by publishers of antiunion pieces such as the *Militant Truth*.[68]

The TWUA was aware it would face such charges and warned organizers beforehand to be prepared to deal with claims that "Unions are run by Communists."[69] The purging of some CIO unions of communist influence in the late forties, as the South Carolina director of the campaign noted, was probably a wise move.[70] The red "taint" nevertheless remained strong no matter what the CIO did. As one organizer reported in 1946, employees were told that the CIO is "a Russian organization originated in Russia."[71] At times, textile workers themselves revealed the importance of the communist charge. A foreman in Tennessee used the charge to spark a fistfight with an organizer,[72] while Tennessee workers told another organizer that "anyone who patronizes a union is a communist."[73] Workers in a South Carolina mill told an organizer that they believed a union leader had received a leave of absence from her job to attend a "Commie School."[74] As the cold war began, red-baiting became a seemingly insurmountable obstacle. As Brownie Lee Jones, Director of the Southern School For Workers, Inc. in Richmond, wrote in 1948, "Sometimes I really wish I could be a communist—if you won't red bait then you are just automatically assumed to be—when will people learn what a communist is—or is not?"[75]

In Mississippi, the National Labor Relations Board scheduled an election for December 3, 1946, at the Grenada Industries Company, makers of women's hosiery. The November before, the *Grenada Daily Sentinel* editorialized that CIO organizers had circulated among the "well satisfied" employees of the plant. If the workers voted for a CIO union, the newspaper continued, they would "favor surrendering their rights to the CIO." The editor continued:

Communist-influenced national laws set up the machinery under which such elections are called, providing that a majority of voters in an industry may transgress the individual rights of all employees, and make the individual who prefers to keep his rights as such, subservient to the CIO.

This charge linking racial equality with communism was a common one. It presaged by two decades a similar claim that would also resonate with many southerners during the Civil Rights Movement.

CONSERVATIVE UNIONISM

Textile industrialists and southern politicians were aided in their anticommunist campaign by the AFL, which had also launched a postwar organizing drive in the South. In contrast to the CIO, the AFL emphasized "cooperation" with southern employers and sympathy with the historic struggle of the South to overcome its destitution since Reconstruction (Marshall 1967). There had always been substantial tension between the CIO and the AFL. Now, however, deeper animosities simmered. William Green and George Meany, both AFL leaders, began to speak of "communist domination" of the CIO. Green warned, perhaps preaching to the converted, that industrialists should "[g]row and cooperate with us or fight for your life against Communist forces" (Marshall 1967, pp. 246–53).

Most strikingly, the AFL's opposition to the CIO was couched in a tone and language strongly reminiscent of the employers and other opponents. For example, the CIO's TWUA rival union in the AFL, the United Textile Workers of America (UTWA) ran a public relations campaign that depicted the TWUA as "nonlocal," and the UTWA as a "loyal, dependable, 100% American organization."[76] George Googe, southern representative for the AFL, blamed a recent cost of living increase on a subversive "handful of CIO leaders" and upon agitation that had led to strikes. Even the Georgia Farm Bureau entered the fray, with the president of that organization calling the CIO the "spearhead of Communism."[77]

Clearly, rivalry between the CIO and the AFL hurt the campaign.[78] In the mills, CIO organizers found the AFL competition disquieting. One Tennessee organizer, meeting workers at the plant gate, was drowned out by AFL representatives. Another found himself discussing AFL "propaganda" left inside a Memphis mill and read by workers.[79] It appears the AFL was permitted more access to the mills than the CIO. As one observer wrote, a Tennessee company "permitted AFL members to circulate all through the mills to fight the CIO."[80]

KANNAPOLIS: AN OPERATION DIXIE PROTOTYPE

The prototype for the Operation Dixie campaign is perhaps best illustrated in Kannapolis, North Carolina. All of the social "bulwarks" faced by CIO organizers were illustrated at Cannon Mills in Kannapolis. Moreover, this case illustrates the importance of understanding textile industrialization as an integral part of the South's postbellum social "folk" residue. Kannapolis gave vent to many of the cultural, economic, and political continuities of the Old South.

Kannapolis housed the largest mill village in America, not just the South, set in an unincorporated city of fifty thousand. Charles Cannon was the owner of the twenty mills centered around Kannapolis. He was not only the mill village economic and social master, but its political ruler as well (Griffith 1988, p. 46). As in other mill villages, conservative one-party dominance was merely the statewide counterpart to the local control exercised by mill owners. Given the ideological and practical affinity of the southern Democratic Party with figures such as Cannon, there was little likelihood that organizers could count on state government for assistance. Nor could they depend on local authorities, who at Kannapolis, as elsewhere during the campaign, tended to use the law as a tool to arrest or intimidate organizers, and otherwise slow the campaign.[81] Similarly, the local press, *The Daily Independent*, took a strong editorial stance against the campaign. Copies of the *Militant Truth* received "considerable" circulation to mill workers' homes, and were noted by organizers inside the mills as well.[82]

Worker racial prejudice was available to be tapped, organizers wrote. One way to exploit the racial issue was to raise the possibility that under TWUA contracts "white workers could be forced to work under a Negro overseer."[83] Since race segregation had been the pattern of development of the "New South's" textile industrialization, the cultural salience of racism remained operative at Kannapolis.

Most of the South's textile mills were smaller in scale, and farther spread apart geographically, than the Cannon Mills. The many textile mills in geographic proximity might lead one to predict the development of class solidarity through worker *and* community concentration. However, there remained at Kannapolis the persistence of southern "community" characteristics. This was particularly true in respect to racist paternalism, which presented perhaps the strongest block to interracial industrial organizing. Despite owning a large industrial empire with many plants, Charles Cannon, or "Uncle Charlie" as he was known to his workers, maintained an active, direct personal presence, influence, and power base in his textile mills. A CIO organizer wrote,

> Everybody loved him. He was their daddy. The father, the grandfather, the great-grand-father, all lived here. And everybody looked to Uncle Charlie Cannon. He was Santy Claus. He was good to my daddy. He was good to my granddaddy. He give us a job, give us a place to live. They'd say, "I gotta be faithful to him. Long as he likes me, he'll take care of me." (quoted in Griffith 1988, p. 50)

Ruth A. Gettinger, the public relations director of the North Carolina CIO campaign, proclaimed that the "only issue is freedom from Cannon domination." Cannon workers themselves did not view the situation in the same way. "Cannon is very popular," she informed the Atlanta office in 1946, "both in the community and with his workers."[84] Cannon's popularity was not solely based on "felt" solidarity, for he skillfully blended the work and community environment in a way that deepened workers' ties to him. First, he pursued a policy—followed in many textile mills in the South after 1915—of employing more than one family member. This created, one organizer wrote, "a high family income on relatively low wages," and of course family dependence on Cannon for economic survival as well. Cannon also spent time visiting workers, and developed effective programs for "local pride, political influence and fringe culture."[85]

So influential and pervasive was this carefully cultivated sense of shared effort and interests between workers and owners that it seemed to obscure the importance of another potential challenge to the effects of paternalism. Many textile workers in other areas were sharply separated, both physically and socially, from the non-village environment. Kannapolis workers, however, "can and do read," owned automobiles and radios, and had contact with the outside world. Apparently, however, contact with the outside world was not a significant enough force in itself to lead to challenges to class paternalism. As CIO staffers wrote, Kannapolis workers nevertheless remained "insulated" from outside ideas, and exhibited a "pattern of rationalization built around the prestige of Charles Cannon . . ." Consequently, the CIO staff concluded, the worker's "mental attitude" was the same as if they had been physically and socially isolated in the average mill village (Griffith 1988, p. 53).

As far as most organizers saw it, Cannon workers were in a separate world. The reception they received from workers for their organizing efforts was even worse than expected. "All situations are a little cold," wrote organizer D. L. Culver in 1946, "Kannapolis is very unresponsive." Cannon workers "do not understand . . . nor are they willing to make a very consistent effort in the interest of organiza-tion."[86] The reception in one plant was "very cold," Culver wrote the CIO's regional director. The national director wrote in a monthly re-port that "sentiment for unionism is not too good in Cannon. . . ."[87]

Worker reluctance to unionize may at least be partly explained by rational considerations of the coercive underbelly of loyalty. Organizers noted that some workers were afraid of losing job security, or that women were afraid of not finding other work outside the mill. Some workers were "afraid of being fired and losing their houses" if they took part in a union movement.[88] Moreover, most textile workers would not, or could not, envision a better life inside the confines of the village with a union contract, or imagine any sort of life outside those confines.

Organizers realized that such obstacles presented incredible hurdles to overcome. D. L. Culver wrote a multipage document of suggestions, calling for strategic legal action against local intimidations by the sheriff, the reversal of city and state laws that denied the CIO the use of public address systems, and access to the radio airwaves. He further called for "basic education" to teach workers "what a union contract does or can mean."[89] Cannon organizers put out a series of leaflets designed to answer the charges made by antiunion forces. These were largely prac-tical: wages would increase with a union contract; it is legal to unionize; working conditions would improve.[90]

Criticizing "Uncle Charlie" was to be avoided. Yet the economic plight of workers could not be separated from the organizational own-ership and control of the mill village. Pointing out inequities alone could not guarantee an effective strategy. It was not so much that mill workers were entirely ignorant of their social subordination, but that they had accommodated themselves to holding a subservient position in what had been a traditionally hierarchical structure. For many, it seems, the "payoff" for holding this position—housing, income, a uniracial work place, and no black bosses—was enough to offset the subordination. Compared to the alternatives in southern society and measured against the cultural salience of racism, this makes some sense. As such, these white workers were "pragmatic" in their acceptance of social inequality, rather than "normative," as Lockwood (1966) has argued in other settings. Or more precisely, they were pragmatic given the prevailing norms.

White quiescence also followed another southern motif of out-ward politeness. Workers may have perpetuated a social "ruse" of feign-ing agreement with the system, and their position in it, much like their antebellum counterpart in paternalism, black slaves. As Genovese (1965) and others note, slaves carefully cultivated a covert form of resistance to slavery that allowed them subtle control over the workplace and the pace of their tasks. While there is little empirical evidence of such feigning in the Dixie campaign, white textile workers may have done the same—overtly docile, covertly resistant. Griffith argues that "[t]he workers wanted help" (1988, p. 61). Nevertheless, unionization would have taken them far beyond social "parrying" toward outright confron-tation with the industrial "plantation owner" on whom they depended for so much. They had been willing to display militancy over attempts to introduce blacks into the workforce. The 1934 general strike also revealed the militant potential of southern workers when employers degraded working conditions, that is, when their loyalty was not re-turned. They were not so willing to exhibit the same restiveness for the promised improvements from an *interracial union movement*.

CIO organizers accepted that white workers did not respond to pleas based just on "rational" considerations. Griffith puts it: "[O]ne cannot want for people what circumstances do not encourage them to want for themselves" (1988, p. 171). Organizers finally concluded that, "the desire to improve present material conditions is almost non–existent. It may possibly be cultivated, but this would require a long period of time" and education (Griffith 1988, p. 53).

In the end, neither time, nor anything else, was enough. After seven weeks of effort, any optimism had faded away. The CIO main-tained a meager presence in Cannon for the duration of Operation Dixie. Workers at Kannapolis, however, like the majority of textile workers in the South, were not brought to a National Labor Relations Board election (Griffith 1988, p. 57).

CONCLUSION

By 1947, organizer Bittner announced "real progress" had been made in the campaign. Yet the 324 new locals created in six southern states were far fewer than what organizers had hoped for at the beginning of Operation Dixie. By the next year, as the flow of money from affiliates dried up so did the drive (Foster 1975; Garrison 1976). An *Atlanta Journal* columnist pointed out in April 1948 that Operation Dixie simply was not meeting expectations. "It's going to be a long hard pull," one organizer predicted. "It's not going to be as easy as one of the boys thought," another organizer said. By the campaign's end, organizers ruefully compiled new membership lists in the four figures per state. The hope had been for increases of from seventy-five to one hundred thousand per state.[91]

Though it is impossible to determine to what extent, some CIO directors reportedly pulled out of organizing rather than risk defeat. In October 1946, the North Carolina director suggested stopping the campaign at one plant before taking "a licking." The following December, the campaign's regional director wrote the Tennessee director suggesting that a similar course of action be taken at the Peerless Woolen Mills.[92]

The CIO had more success in *non-textile* drives. In the state with the most complete remaining set of records, North Carolina, organizing committee files show that in 1946, the CIO won forty-four elections and lost twelve. In 1947, the CIO won thirty-five, and lost seven elections. The 1948 election records reveal that twenty-four elections were won and fifteen were lost. In 1949, the CIO won thirteen, but lost six elections. In 1950, election wins totaled three, and losses four. Note the decline in the number of elections as the drive fizzled. In all union elections for the three-year period 1948–50, the CIO received 6,910 votes, while a total of 9,995 workers voted against the CIO. From 1946 to 1950, the CIO received 18,625 votes; 15,167 workers voted against the CIO.[93]

When comparing textile organizing to other Operation Dixie organizing drives, we may get a more complete picture. Unions in the steel and wood industries proved relatively successful. In Alabama, steel and wood far surpassed textiles in organizing, even at the beginning of the campaign.[94] Near the end of the campaign in 1950 and 1951, while in all the southern states the TWUA had won only ten petitions, the United Steel Workers had won twenty-nine, and the International Wood-workers had won twenty.[95]

The paucity of TWUA victories belies the fact that the campaign concentrated on textiles. For, as the Alabama state director of TWUA wrote George Baldanzi in 1946, the relative slowness of the drive in textiles represents a different pattern than that of the "victories" in wood, steel, and auto industries.[96] Though available records do not allow for systematic comparisons among southern states by industry, the research department of the New York headquarters of TWUA provides useful information of textile union vote outcomes. In its report on North Carolina TWUA elections won and lost from June 1, 1946, through February 2, 1949, the research department noted that a total of thirty-nine elections had been held. Of those, only fourteen were TWUA victories, and some of those were by slim margins. At the Safie Company in 1947, for example, 494 workers voted for the union, and 445 voted against it.[97]

The North Carolina experience was apparently a typical one. In the early part of the campaign, from May through December 1946, the TWUA took part in forty-seven elections in nine southern states. The CIO won twenty-one and lost twenty-six (Griffith 1988, p. 57). Similarly, TWUA memos point out a small improvement in the percentage of southern textile workers covered by TWUA contracts during the length of the campaign. From April 1946 to August 1949, only 19 percent of all southern textile workers were in shops covered by a union contract. From September 1949 to April 1950, that figure had risen to 28 percent, and for the year 1951 reached 33 percent.[98]

Despite the improvement, however, at most only one-third of workers in the target "bellwether" industry had chosen to vote for the TWUA by the end of the campaign. Since the campaign's success, as we have seen, rode heavily upon success in this dominant southern industry, Operation Dixie itself was clearly in for a fall. By the late forties, the communist question resurfaced, becoming freighted with intensifying cold war politics. By 1953, the Southern Organizing Committee was officially terminated, for all practical purposes ending Operation Dixie (Marshall 1967, pp. 256–63). From 1946–48, the TWUA spent $400,000 and gained only fifteen thousand new members. In terms of bargaining elections, TWUA lost sixty-three of 111 votes held in the late forties. Indeed, the pattern of Operation Dixie was one of retrenchment rather than progress. Fewer union contracts existed at the end of the campaign than in 1948. TWUA had organized 20 percent of the South's textile workers before 1948. Two years later, the figure had dropped to 14 percent (Marshall 1967, p. 261).

Some simply placed the blame on white southern workers themselves. From the organizers' and reformers' point of view, white southerners formed a group of laborers that was

> [p]robably the most politically illiterate of any industrialized nation in the world. It doesn't regard itself as a class of workers. It hasn't any concept of politics other than personality and various superficial things. And, in effect, it hasn't the slightest idea what its own interests are, and has been brought around to supporting the interests of those people who are exploiting them.[99]

Though Operation Dixie was officially closed in 1953, it was clear several years earlier that the movement had failed. Offices were gradually phased out during the late 1940s. By 1949, southern membership in the CIO was no greater than the four hundred thousand total that had existed on the day the Atlanta office of Operation Dixie opened in 1946. The TWUA president remarked that textile workers were "worse off today in the South than we have been" (Griffith 1988, pp. 161–62).

The CIO had also underestimated the strength of the AFL and the importance of employer attitudes as factors negatively affecting unionization. For many workers, its racial and political program made the AFL a more acceptable alternative. Some employers even took measures to enable AFL versus CIO union representation (Marshall 1967, pp. 266–68). Thus, despite some CIO gains in the auto, rubber, and communications industries, most southern workers who were union members belonged to the AFL. While the AFL increased its share of the South's total union membership from 1939–53 from 56 to 62 percent, the CIO's share declined from 23 to 20 percent during the same period (Marshall 1967, p. 269).

Operation Dixie was a "colossal failure" (Billington 1975, p. 274). After spending $4 million on textiles, and $11 million in the overall effort, the CIO could only count a handful of new members. From the beginning of the drive at the end of World War II, until 1951, near the end of the drive, union membership among textile workers had declined by 10 percent.

THE RATIONALITY OF PATERNALISM

Southern industrial paternalism retained sufficient cultural residue of the Old South that loyalty on the part of workers cannot be portrayed as a purely rational choice. It was rooted in a "felt" racial solidarity. But this solidarity was linked to a deferential relationship between workers and owners. And this power relationship was shaped in special ways through previous struggles as well, most notably the success of employers in the Great Strike of 1934.

In any case, southern paternalism certainly did serve the rational interests of textile owners. "Kept" workers could be expected to perform with little disgruntlement, particularly since most first generation sojourners probably viewed their mill village as a "second chance" in their economic existence. Housing, loans, security, and other paternal benefits of loyalty cost employers, but the benefits also totalized the costs of resistance.

A number of factors, distinctively southern in character, thus shaped this story. Among the most important was paternalism. Racist class paternalism thus provided a social bulwark against the interracial, class-based agenda of Operation Dixie. Textile owners could consider racial preferences in hiring because the southern labor market had already developed "horizontal segregation" (Wright 1986, p. 183) that did not split wages as dramatically as one might expect given Jim Crow segregation. Since antebellum textile industrialization had been built upon the goal of maintaining the white "folk," the industry was perpetually segregated by race. Seeing segregation patterns as "natural," dictated by "racial norms," industrialists shared the view of white workers that black exclusion was an issue of "moral economy" (Stokes 1977, pp. 204–208; see also McLaurin 1971).

Dominant workers—white textile workers—considered their job and social status interests to be more closely bound with their community interests, as opposed to an interracial, class-based union movement such as Operation Dixie. We may understand this as the result of a covert "deal" between textile employers and workers: no blacks in return for no unions. The deal would not have worked without the prior salience of race in southern culture. The credibility of employers' force demonstrating in 1934 remained vivid and therefore contributed to the deal as well. White workers' job interests thus included the maintenance of racial exclusivity through racist class paternalism in the textile mills. Interracial class militancy in support of Operation Dixie would have threatened both their presumed normative interests in racial superiority, and their structurally conditioned interests incident to paternalism.

Southern blacks found their exclusion from the dominant industry to mirror their exclusion from southern society in general. They had little stake in supporting the system that had historically disadvantaged them. Separated as a race, they saw class solidarity in support of Operation Dixie as a mechanism to achieve economic and social progress. The irony is that blacks were excluded from the industry that was the main target of the union drive. This was the one place where their class militancy might have made a significant difference.

After Operation Dixie failed, the growth of industrial unionization in America largely came to a halt. Its failure left absent the union basis for social progress in the South. Absent too was the strong leadership of organized labor in southern desegregation and in the Civil Rights Movement in the 1950s. Ultimately, textile segregation collapsed (to the extent it has) not because burgeoning salience of class solidarity between races, but rather in the context of a confluence of factors including market pressures, the modernizing pressures of an industrializing society. Perhaps most importantly, segregation in the South and by extension in the textile industry, was defeated by the Civil Rights Movement organized in large part by the church and the autonomous institutions of the black community.[100] Some unions, notably the UAW, supported the Civil Rights Movement from the beginning, but none led and the AFL-CIO lagged well behind in support. As a result, civil rights and labor movements diverged from their common class interests.[101]

CHAPTER 8

Conclusions—Organizing Solidarity

Even union shocked by victory.

— *Atlanta Journal-Constitution*, June 26, 1999

Textile workers in Kannapolis, North Carolina, voted by slim margin for representation by the Union of Needletrades, Industrial and Textile Employees (UNITE). After failing during Operation Dixie in the 1940s, and again in 1974, 1984, 1990, and 1997, Kannapolis seemed a lost cause. Bruce Raynor, UNITE secretary-treasurer, remarked that while past drives were "brutal and vicious" and that he had been "mocked and screamed at for being a white man married to a black woman," this one was "relatively peaceful" (quoted in *AJ-C* 1999, p. B1). While a genuine victory, this recent development is probably less significant than the fact that it took fifty years to achieve. It is the connection between earlier union organizing efforts and today's labor movement that drew us to take up this study.

With that in mind, we have pursued three primary objectives in this work. First, we have sought to learn more about the history of each case. The narrative chapters offer individual case studies of race, labor, and collective action. Explaining the contingencies of these pivotal cases is important for understanding the larger historical trends in race and labor relations. Second, we sought to further develop racial competition theory by examining split labor markets in a comparative sense.

Previous research in this area has tended to focus on single instances, thus obscuring anomalous cases that provide fruitful ground for theory building and for delineating scope conditions. A third and less explicit goal has been to draw strategic guidance and inspiration from history to inform emancipatory projects of the future. While the history and theory outlined here are significant in and of themselves, we think there is every reason to believe that power relationships will continue to be shaped through racial competition and class solidarity. The choices key actors make in such circumstances may be informed by the lessons of this analysis. Below we offer summaries of the historical findings and theoretical lessons. We conclude with a brief remark on the political and moral implications of this study.

HISTORICAL OUTCOMES

The history described here reveals a range of complex circumstances in which interracial labor organizing takes place. In American history, it is a rare moment when interracial organizing is successful. The nine cases presented here show that many factors inhibit the formation of inter-racial labor movements. The most general findings in this analysis are that recent migration and racialized paternalism have a negative effect on the proclivity of workers to cohere around class interests. Other factors are important in specific cases, but migration and paternalism (either their presence or absence) mattered in all these cases.

Racial competition among workers inhibited all the organizing drives, but to differing degrees. Cases where dominant workers sup-ported the union while minority workers engaged in widespread strikebreaking have the most serious implications for race relations and for the labor movement. Here we find the highest potential for racial violence. Cases characterized by dominant worker support for the union but minority antipathy include the Comstock miners of 1869, the 1919 steel strike, the United Mine Workers' drive of the late 1920s, and the Amalgamated Association's drive of 1934. During the 1919 steel strike, interracial solidarity held in the cities of Cleveland and Wheeling, but the overwhelming pattern of race relations was one of high levels of minority strikebreaking. In all these particular cases, working-class fragmentation and racial violence undermined union success. Aside from the Amalgamated Association, recent mi-nority migrants played a significant role in the development of strikebreaking. This was clearest with the strikes in the Comstock mines and the 1919 steel strike.

While racial antagonism and racist ideologies are less evident where patterns of strikebreaking are not specifically linked to race, these cases have dramatic implications for the potential success of organized labor. The United Auto Workers' drive of 1937–38 is a good example of how employers can undermine working-class mobilization. In this context, the company cultivated paternalism among minority workers. Ford's skillful use of divide and conquer tactics paid off by successfully forestalling unionization. The Ford case provides an important contrast with the white racist paternalism that undermined Operation Dixie. Ironically, in both cases employers institutionalized an ideology of black inferiority—in the Ford case, management claimed that black workers needed paternalism, and in the South, paternalistic employers claimed that blacks did not belong within their "family" of employees.

Perhaps the most interesting outcome is found in the CIO's attempt to organize southern workers in Operation Dixie. In this situation, the usual constellation of class and racial alliances expected by theory were inverted when employers cultivated paternalistic relationships with the dominant racial group in the labor force. Minority workers were more amenable to unionization while dominant workers shunned union participation to demonstrate loyalty and protect their privileged positions. Black workers comprised a large minority labor force in most of those few successful CIO industrial unions that organized non-textile southern industries (Kimeldorf and Resenburger 1987, p. 78). Blacks finally entered southern textiles in large numbers in the 1960s (Zingraff and Schulman 1984, p. 113), and not surprisingly, collective action by black workers began within a decade of their being integrated into the industry (Newman 1978, p. 204). This inversion of patterns that characterized our earlier cases, which have now largely become the norm, underscores how class and racial relations in the labor market are skewed by migration and by paternalism.

Bear in mind, however, that the case of Operation Dixie is special. It is our only case that examines split labor market dynamics in the South, where the cultural salience of race is distinctly different from other regions. Much sociological theorizing on industrialization, as Blumer (1990) noted, has assumed linear trends in unionization with industrialization. Neoclassical theory, as well as some split labor market theorists, also assumes a declining salience of race relative to class relations (Wilson

1978). The organizers in Operation Dixie shared something like both of these assumptions. The results, however, demonstrate the important influence preexisting social contexts have on organizing campaigns. While white racist paternalism was the most important distinction in comparative terms, we also described several other characteristics of southern textile employment that help explain the anomalies of this case. Whatever argument may be made about the genesis of racism—that it existed before slavery, or was a convenient justification for economic exploitation—during the time of Operation Dixie it was culturally salient and shaped white workers' understanding of their material interests.

In general, unions failed when they faced either recent minority migrants or racist paternalism. Racist paternalism, in effect, substitutes for recent migration in creating a stark racial difference in interests and motives. As paternalism is an institutional source of racial division in the company, as opposed to differences due to individual market circumstances, employers cannot escape at least some responsibility for fomenting racism. When minorities are the focus of employer paternalism, existing incentives to break strikes and eschew union participation are reinforced.

What did it take to realize interracial solidarity? Historically high levels of interracial solidarity were realized in the United Mine Worker's drive of 1933, the Steel Workers' Organizing Committee drive of 1937–38, and the United Auto Workers' drive of 1940–41. This does not mean that in instances where solidarity was realized that white and black rank and filers necessarily interacted beyond their work and union contexts, or even that interpersonal racism was eradicated. It means that both blacks and whites joined the union in substantial numbers and that the union held together with some degree of stability compared to those cases with racially divisive outcomes. These three cases reveal the conditions that are best for an organizing drive and also indicate what a union must do to take advantage of those conditions. In keeping with the theoretical postulates, a common core finding is that unions achieved interracial solidarity when they organized a largely local minority workforce lacking paternalistic connections to employers. Where these conditions hold, minority and dominant workers are similar in their support for unionization.

Beyond these commonalities, we find particular patterns that were important in American labor history, and continue to be important in similar situations. Strong unions could overcome repression, weaker ones only succeeded without it. Although it is unclear that it was a critical determinant, successful unions also enjoyed favorable political legislation, in each instance legislation that the labor movement helped bring about. All three cases of realized interracial labor solidarity took place in contexts that were politically favorable to labor. This was most directly linked to the New Deal and its role in the general liberalization of the country (Korstad and Lichtenstein 1988). The role of federal legislation is distinct from local state support in the practice of repression, which was present in all of the cases with the exception of the UMW drive of 1933.

Most importantly, organizers learned from their failures, and from the successful innovations of others. Utilizing the "formula" was a tactical innovation in industrial unionism that signified a turning point in the labor movement. Such tactics counteracted the appeals from employers to black workers to be strikebreakers and they alleviated the tension linked to cross-cutting solidarities (i.e., racial identities) among workers. Industrial and market forces were not sufficient. The success of those unions that did institutionalize inclusion underscores the importance of this tactical innovation.

THEORETICAL ARGUMENTS

The patterns found in these nine cases have important bearing on the theoretical questions with which we began. Split labor market theory has provided a useful model for analyzing racial and ethnic antagonism. At the very least, its successful application to a wide variety of cases demonstrates the utility of the approach. However, we have maintained throughout that the theory is deficient in several key areas. The history of interracial solidarity has not been explored in previous racial competition literature, despite the (admittedly rare) cases of biracial organizing prior to the Civil Rights Movement. Such cases do not invalidate the theory. Rather, they suggest that we should expand the theory to account for the factors that promote solidarity in the face of split labor market conditions.

The varied outcomes of the case histories offered here illuminate this void. (See the appendix for a more systematic and formal comparison of these cases.) Rather than assume strikebreaking as an aberrant condition and solidarity a passive condition, we postulated that both result from how market and organizational attributes structure the options and interests of workers and unions. The split labor market factors in particular reveal the connections between social structural contexts, such as racial differences in resources and motivations, and the individual strategies and choices of the relevant actors in the context of both positive and negative outcomes. The specific cases and the comparison offered in the previous section demonstrate the contingency of sequenced actions that led to the various outcomes. Each of the cases involves distinctive circumstances peculiar to a specific series of actions as well as analytical factors implicated in broader patterns of labor history.

The broader explanations yield generalizable principles, some closely aligned with split labor market theory and others associated with alternative perspectives. The general principles should apply widely, and should serve as a starting point in subsequent research. For explaining minority strikebreaking, the core explanation includes minority migration and racialized employer paternalism. This theoretical argument assumes employer preference for the lowest wage labor, and it applies where this premise is operative. This set of results, therefore, affirms the original propositions of split labor market theory. The caveat is that cases of paternalistic relations fall outside the scope of the market assumptions, which points to the salience of institutional factors.

Where employers pursued paternalism, a Marxist divide and conquer theory may provide a better explanation (Roemer 1979; Reich 1981). Paternalistic relations between an employer and one racial group of workers resulted in the estrangement of that segment from another racial group. As such, paternalism may alter and even invert the expected alliances and interests in a split labor market situation. The case of Operation Dixie demonstrates that when employers cultivate racist paternalism among the dominant workers, these workers are likely to align with employers rather than with an integrated union. If paternalism is directed at the minority workers, the typical racial split in motivations and interests predicted by the theory becomes more deeply entrenched (even without recent migration). Ford's paternalistic relations with Detroit's black community in the thirties, for instance, strengthened the propensity for minority workers to strikebreak. This was a conscious divide and conquer employer tactic. Paternalism is thus the key factor in adjudicating between dominant worker racism spawned by market competition and employer racism that divides the working class. In cases where market-driven competition contributes to strife among workers, employers may be passive. In racialized paternalistic relationships, in contrast, they are active in fostering the strife.

As a general rule, we should expect disproportionate minority strikebreaking with recent migrants or with paternalistic employers. Our cases strongly support this conclusion. How confident can we be that our conclusions about the other determinants (such as unfavorable political conditions) are broadly generalizable? This depends on comparisons to cases that we don't have but assume do not exist. If contrary cases exist, then our conclusions only apply to our cases. Historically, this seems unlikely.

Evidence from the National Miner's Union (NMU) in 1931 suggests that a high commitment to interracial solidarity could overcome unfavorable political conditions. Like other radical unions, however, success was temporary. Such cases may not be fully comparable to those considered here, or at least, they require additional qualifiers. Another avenue for further research would be the UMW's interracial organizing in the nineteenth century, although its success is debated (Gutman 1976; Hill 1988; Letwin 1998). The UMW's failure in the 1920s to recruit black migrants to the northern coal fields might be considered an aberration. Whether aberrant or not, the racial strife of the 1920s and the NMU example led to the "UMW formula" of promoting black union organizers. The success of that formula led in turn to the institutionalization of racial inclusion throughout much of the CIO.

In our analyses of class solidarity, we find that paternalism, minority migration, union strength, and consequent minority strikebreaking are the minimum necessary conditions for explaining different levels of worker solidarity among these nine cases. These factors offer a basic logic of interracial solidarity that is generalizable to similar cases.

Certainly other factors may be important as well. For example, in the case histories several factors did play an important role in specific instances of local organizing, even if they do not emerge as necessary causal determinants at the level of case comparison. Repression, for instance, affected most of the drives and defeated some locals. In moving from local to national levels, however, we lack sufficient cases without repression to make definitive comparisons. And one could think of other factors. (See the expanded model in our appendix.)

Subsequent research might seek cases with combinations of factors different from those studied here. A good starting point would be to look for labor organizing drives where employers tried paternalism with recent minority migrants. Another is where unions had state support in facing racist paternalism. If found, these cases could adjudicate between necessary and contributing causes.

The resilience of minority migration as necessary in all comparisons, despite considering alternate determinants, supports the general importance of split labor market theory for understanding interracial solidarity and conflict. For theory building, the narrative histories of union drives underscore the importance of political and ideological contexts for understanding market and organizational processes. That the pattern of race relations depended heavily on the context of employer-employee relations suggests that the prior articulation of the theory places undue emphasis on economic factors. This point has been made before (Burawoy 1981; Boswell 1986). Here we also consider how political and ideological contexts affect the costs and benefits of union compliance. This incorporates politics and ideology into the theory without violating its basic premises. It also allows for the consideration of other contexts in subsequent research, an endeavor we encourage. While the core propositions of split labor market theory applied to the costs and benefits of organizing in every case, the amount of cost or benefit changed in each context.

SOME IMPLICATIONS

In a society such as ours—one rooted in a deeply racist past and one that generates ongoing inequalities in the present—interracial solidarity is an uncommon and fragile phenomenon. This study shows that it only develops when institutional, political, and labor market conditions are all aligned to promote cooperation across racial lines. Once obtained, solidarity is easily disrupted and can be difficult to restore. For this reason, we must pay special attention to the historical patterns that underlie those uncommon instances of that success.

The union organizing drives we studied involved overt and widespread racism that was far worse than what is faced by any movement today. Most of the campaigns collapsed under the weight of problematic racial dynamics. However, a few managed to overcome racism and prevail. It is unlikely that most white workers completely repudiated their personal prejudices, or that blacks transcended their resentment. Rather, workers set aside racist impulses and fears as they pursued their mutual material and political interests. Although the solidarity was far from perfect and interracial antagonism surfaced in subsequent decades in all three industries, the results of this analysis illuminate when and how union leadership was efficacious in securing common class interests by way of institutionalized racial policy. Their success in the face of the American dilemma surely provides enduring lessons.

One implication of the "formula" is that inclusion should be institutionalized in visible ways. This lesson is instructive for social movements in general, and will only become more salient in the context of increasingly globalized political economy. Evolving, global capitalism will continue to generate new technologies (see Noble 1984; Brueggemann and Brown 2003), more fluid patterns of migration (Massey and Taylor 2004), and a broader range of middle classes or multiple class locations (Wright 1985). Such complexity combined with the absence of militant traditions (Roscigno and Hodson 2004) will make the strategic pursuit of solidarity challenging indeed. A revitalized and global labor movement must grapple with how such lessons of institutionalized inclusion relate to global class struggle (see Boswell and Stevis 2000; Cornfield and McGammon 2003).

Another less obvious point is that even the most inclusive unions may fail among groups with a short-term orientation to their place of employment or a long-term paternalistic relationship with their employer. Highly visible racial inclusiveness itself can also be a hazard to organizing where the dominant group has the impression that organizing will lower their wages or job opportunities to minority levels. The volatile risks of using racially conscious policies to achieve racial integration resound in the current debate about affirmative action. White workers balk at the impression that they are the exploiters. Unscrupulous politicians exploit this impression for short-term political advantage, as southern pols did in the 1940s and '50s.

Unions and other social movement organizers face a moral and strategic dilemma. As the history examined here reveals, minority engagement in collective action can be necessary for realizing long-term goals for broader groups. Racially conscious inclusion policies are therefore needed to secure minority support. They may, however, undercut dominant support where the policies are perceived to undermine majority interests. Opposition to affirmative action policies can be reduced by including class along with race and gender.[1] Widespread support develops even when disproportionately poor minorities garner a greater gain. That is, the interests of particular groups, women or minorities for instance, may benefit without others' resistance when policies are organized around broad agendas. Likewise, where the miners' formula worked, it was clear that the goal was one of class solidarity that would benefit all workers, even if minorities' gains were greater.

Appendix—Qualitative Comparative Analyses of Strikebreaking and Solidarity

In the preceding chapters, we have described cases where dominant unions faced racial competition by blatantly, and successfully, discriminating against minorities, where they were defeated by the history of discrimination (including their own), where they successfully overcame discrimination, and where they were defeated despite their overcoming discrimination. These diverse outcomes reflect the causal complexity that underlies most social phenomena. The cases reveal much about the intersection of race and class within the U.S. labor movement, and each narrative could be interpreted separately. In this appendix, however, we focus on the commonalities across cases, rather than their historical specificities, shifting our emphasis toward theory construction. Starting with the deductive propositions derived from split labor market theory (see chapter 2), we expect the prime solvent of class solidarity to be minority strikebreaking by recent migrants. Anomalous and contradictory findings, however, will require us to expand the theory inductively, incorporating additional factors to resolve them.

In the sections that follow, we first use formal analytical methods to develop a model of minority strikebreaking. We then repeat the process to examine the more complex determinants of varying degrees of working-class solidarity, which is partially a function of the presence or absence of minority strikebreaking. Analytical comparison of historical cases is, we think, of great use in constructing social theories, but we realize that the methods themselves are not always of great interest. Ironically, analytical methods are designed to make obvious the logic and assumptions behind the process of comparison, and thus to the extent the methods succeed, what might otherwise be seen as insightful interpretation can appear rather obvious. This appendix includes our detailed tables, tracks the logic of the formal comparisons that undergird the conclusions we present in chapter 8, and applies Qualitative Comparative Analysis (QCA). We invite interested readers to proceed through the steps of the comparative analyses, to which we now turn.

A COMPARATIVE ANALYSIS

Despite the differences in outcomes and the variety of causal determinants referred to in previous chapters, our cases are similar in important respects. First, the same cast of actors is found in all instances: unions involved in organizing drives and strikes, employers who resist the union, state authorities of varying stripes, and a labor force of individual workers that includes a large number of minorities. In all cases, union organizers were forced to confront racial labor cost differences, although the impact of racial differences varied with the extent of recent migration. Racist ideology was ubiquitous, but how unions dealt with racist members and how employers used racism differed substantially. Class conflicts forced both dominant and minority workers to consider the costs and benefits associated with class-based collective action versus individual strikebreaking. As discussed in chapter 2, an individual's interest in long-term versus short-term goals and the strength of intergroup compliance norms affect one's estimates of the costs and benefits.

In chapter 2, we presented a game-theoretic simulation of four possible levels of working-class solidarity, and Figure 2.2 presented our theoretical expectations for the fate of organizing drives under conditions of a racially split labor market. To briefly recapitulate, the tradeoff between long-term and short-term benefits is central in split labor market theory: recent migrant minorities will more likely pursue short-term economic gains and will not invest in the long-term benefits that accrue to union members. Weak unions will find it difficult to overcome racial antagonism and to recruit minority members, and they will be more likely to attempt to preserve wage differentials through exclusion or caste systems. Strong unions, on the other hand, have the confidence and resources that come with recent victories and can risk pursuing solidarity for its long-term benefits. Interracial solidarity is most likely where the union is strong and minority workers are local.

Minority union antipathy and strikebreaking undermines solidarity in all other situations.

Note that there is an implied temporal relationship between minority strikebreaking and overall levels of worker solidarity: the latter is partially a function of minority decisions about whether to strikebreak. For these reasons, we empirically separate these two outcomes in the analyses that follow. Additionally, Figure 2.2 linked worker solidarity levels to race relations. Long-term solidarity was predicated on the development of a biracial class coalition, although logically, long-term union compliance could obtain among dominant workers even where minority workers are strikebreaking if the latter group is proportionately small. The point is that high compliance is not necessarily dependent on interracial solidarity. While the theory implies an association between minority strikebreaking and overall levels of worker solidarity, the split labor market approach focuses on the choices of racial segments of labor rather than the success of labor organizing initiative. Here, we endeavor to elucidate that association.

The following analyses seek to achieve causal explanation at two levels. First, we focus on minority strikebreaking as a dependent condition to test propositions from split labor market (and other) theories. Then, we use minority strikebreaking as an independent condition to derive more general explanations of overall class solidarity.

Below, we empirically evaluate the four game-theoretic outcomes previously presented in Figure 2.2 to assess the usefulness of the abstract model. For our analysis, we cull data from the previous chapters. Specifically, we focus on the Comstock miners strike in 1869 (chapter 4), the AFL-led Great Steel Strike of 1919 (chapter 5), six New Deal–era organizing drives spanning coal mining, steel, and the auto industry (chapter 6), and the CIO's "Operation Dixie" campaign in the southern textile mills from 1946–52 (chapter 7).

An appropriate first test of the theory is our narrative interpretations of the nine cases. These narratives tell us that split labor market conditions underlie most (but not all) instances of minority strikebreaking. Interracial solidarity rarely occurred in the presence of split labor markets, although where there were exceptions, the narrative interpretations pointed toward the important intervening factors. How valid are our interpretations? What determinants are necessary or only contributing? What combinations are sufficient to explain minority strikebreaking and solidarity? What are the actual and implied scope conditions of our general theory? To answer these questions, we turn to formal methods of comparative history.

QUALITATIVE COMPARATIVE ANALYSIS

Comparative methodology builds on the case study approach but allows analysts to systematically compare similarities and differences across cases to reveal common causal determinants. Important historical events usually depend upon a conjuncture of causes operating within a specific context.[1] Moreover, various causal combinations may produce the same outcome (Ragin 1987, pp. 25–27). By using formal methods to sift through the causal and empirical complexity, we can parcel out the concepts and propositions of general significance.

One of the most important advances in analytic methodology is the development of Qualitative Comparative Analysis (QCA) (Ragin 1987; Ragin, Mayer, and Drass 1984).[2] QCA uses Boolean algebra to systematically compare outcomes and causes in case studies. We apply QCA to examine the deductive theoretical propositions derived from our game-theoretic model in chapter 2. QCA has two steps. The first step involves the creation of a "truth table" that lists the causal combinations associated with actual cases and any additional combinations that are theoretically possible but not present in the data. A truth table can be thought of as a formal representation of the theory that maps abstract propositions onto empirical observations and their outcomes. The total number of possible combinations for a truth table equals 2^X, where X is the number of causes (Ragin 1987, p. 87). A table (or theory) with two causal determinants, for instance, implies four possible combinations; three determinants produce eight combinations, and four determinants yield 16 combinations.[3] The array of theoretical possibilities is dichotomously coded (where "1" and "0" represent the presence and absence of causes, respectively) and then matched to actual cases and their outcomes. Truth tables force researchers to make explicit their theoretical presumptions, allowing others to question the validity of a given model and the conclusions derived from an analysis.

In the second step, QCA employs Boolean algorithms to logically reduce the various causal combinations to their simplest form. The result is a symbolic equation where uppercase letters designate the presence of a condition and lowercase letters designate its absence. A plus sign (+) represents the logical operator "OR," while multiplication indicates the logical "AND" (Ragin 1987, p. 89–92). QCA is a logical method, not a quantitative one. On the truth table, 1 + 1 does not equal 2. Rather, 1 + 1 symbolizes that the presence of either of the two conditions causes the outcome in question. The results show, if the number and variety of cases permit, what causes are necessary and/or sufficient for a particular outcome.[4]

QCA ANALYSIS OF STRIKEBREAKING AND SOLIDARITY

We coded cases according to the definitions given for each factor in Table A.1; codes for each case are presented in Table A.2. Of course, union locals and minority communities differed, organizing conditions changed over time, and organizers were not always consistent. The binary coding required us to back away from the detail found in the narrative interpretations and focus instead on the broad social conditions that had the most significant impact on the organizing drive. This was not a difficult decision for most cases, although some qualifications were necessary.

Our first truth table, Table A.3, shows the distribution of the nine cases according to split labor market determinants. The theory expects minority strikebreaking when unions are weak (U) and where minorities are recent migrants (M). The most important qualification concerns minority strikebreaking (S), which we define as cases where most minorities opposed the union (regardless of dominant worker support). In two cases, the AA drive of 1934 and UAW drive of 1937–38, union leaders called off the campaign without conducting a strike, in part because of minority antipathy toward the union and expectations that minority workers would cross the picket line. In essence, the strike was broken before it could begin. Although other factors may have contributed more significantly to the demise of the drives, there was a clear racial difference in workers' support for the union and for a possible strike (in game theory terms, minority workers "defected"). We consider these cases comparable to ones that did reach a strike, and thus code them as minority strikebreaking in the analysis.

Note that the four combinations of causal conditions are the same as the four models presented in Figure 2.2 from chapter 2 (strong/weak union with local/migrant minorities). The result, S = M + U, upholds a basic proposition of split labor market theory. Minority strikebreaking

Table A.1

Causes of Strikebreaking and Solidarity

M = Recent Minority Migrants (1 = high proportion; See chapter 3)

U = Union Strength (1 = historically weak)
    We measure strength by union victories or losses in the last 5 years.

R = Repressive Acts (1 = high repression)
    Repression is widespread arrests and attacks by police or by company
    guards with clear police acquiescence.

P = Paternalistic Employer (1 = paternalism)
    Paternalism includes company unions, housing, and other benefits
    distributed on the basis of filial loyalty.

F = Federal Legislation (1 = unfavorable to labor prior to 1933)
    Passage of the NRA coal codes in 1933 and the Wagner Act in 1935
    created a much more favorable political climate for union organizing.
    Although the Taft-Hartley Act of 1947 reversed some legislative gains,
    the political context was still far superior to that before the New Deal.

I = Institutionalized Inclusion (1 = not present)
    All the unions officially accepted minorities except the Comstock
    miners. Inclusive unions differed in that they had minority organizers
    and high ranking staff, and actively recruited minority members.
    Inclusive unions often had racist locals and some locals recruited
    minorities without institutional reforms, as in Wheeling and Cleveland
    in the 1919 steel strike. As with other factors, we code the union's
    general character.

E = Economic Recession (1 = present)
    A recession is two consecutive quarters of economic decline. Recession
    occurred in 1920, 1933, 1937, 1945–46, and 1949.

S = Minority Strikebreaking (1 = present)
    This is present when most minority workers crossed the picket line or
    otherwise did not support the union. In the AA 1934 and UAW
    1937–38 cases, union leaders called off the drive without a strike, in
    part because of minority antipathy toward the union and expectations
    that minority workers would strikebreak.

A, B, C, D = Union Solidarity Levels (1 = present)
    Based on the model presented in Figure 2.2, we identify four union
    solidarity levels, which we label as follows: A = High and Long-Term
    Solidarity; B = Low and Short-Term Solidarity; C = Moderate and
    Short-Term Solidarity; D = High but Short-Term Solidarity. For each
    case, we classify the solidarity level based on the history of the
    organizing drive and strike.

Table A.2
Case Coding, Sources, and Qualifications

Comstock Miners (1869)

M	(1)	Coolidge 1909, p. 498; Zo 1978, pp. 152–53; Chen 1980, p. 15
U	(0)	Lingenfelter 1974
R	(0)	Lingenfelter 1974
P	(0)	— not applicable —
F	(1)	Wallace et al. 1988
I	(1)	Coolidge 1909, p. 33; Zo 1978, p. 123
E	(0)	See list above
S	(1)	Chiu 1967, pp. 14–16; Saxton 1971, pp. 54–55
D	=	High but Short-Term Solidarity

Steel (1919)

M	(1)	Wilson 1978, pp. 66–70; U.S. Bureau of the Census 1922, pp. 661–65
U	(1)	Foster 1920, pp. 8–15; Brody 1965, pp. 18, 26–27, 42
R	(1)	Foster 1920, pp. 110–39; Brody 1965; Interchurch World Movement 1920
P	(0)	— not applicable —
F	(1)	Wallace et al. 1988
I	(1)	Foster 1920, pp. 205–12; Brody 1965, pp. 162–63; Spero and Harris 1969
E	(0)	See list above
S	(1)	Foster 1920, p. 207; Interchurch World Movement 1920, pp. 177–78; Brody 1965, pp. 162–63
D	=	High but Short-Term Solidarity

United Mine Workers: UMW (1927–29)

M	(1)	McAdam 1999, pp. 78–80; Nyden 1977; Greene and Woodson 1930; Lewis 1987; Spero and Harris 1969
U	(1)	Spero and Harris 1969; Nyden 1977
R	(1)	Nyden 1977; Lewis 1987, p. 115
P	(0)	Nyden 1977; Lewis 1987, p. 115
F	(1)	Wallace et al. 1988; Brody 1980; Tomlins 1985
I	(1)	Spero and Harris 1969, pp. 225–28; Nyden 1977; Lewis 1987
E	(0)	See list above
S	(1)	Spero and Harris, 1969, pp. 225–28; Nyden 1977; Lewis 1987
D	=	High but Short-Term Solidarity

United Mine Workers: UMW (1933)

M	(0)	McAdam 1999, pp. 78–80
U	(1)	Nyden 1977
R	(0)	Wilson 1978, p. 72; Johnson 1979, p. 169

continued on next page

Table A.2 *(Continued)*

United Mine Workers: UMW (1933) (continued)

P	(0)	Nyden 1977; Lewis 1987
F	(0)	Wallace et al. 1988; Fritz and Veenstra 1935, pp. 159, 183; Schlesinger 1960, p. 334
I	(0)	Foner 1974, p. 214
E	(1)	See list above
S	(0)	*Crisis* 1935 (quoted in Foner and Lewis 1981, p. 339)
A	=	High and Long-Term Solidarity

Amalgamated Association of Iron, Steel, and Tin Workers: AA (1934)

M	(0)	McAdam 1999, pp. 78–80
U	(1)	Cayton and Mitchell 1939, p. 68
R	(1)	Cayton and Mitchell 1939, pp. 132–34
P	(1)	Cayton and Mitchell 1939
F	(0)	Wallace et al. 1988; Cayton and Mitchell 1939
I	(1)	Cayton and Mitchell 1939; Lynd 1973
E	(0)	See list above
S	(1)★	Dickerson 1986
D	=	High but Short-Term Solidarity

★The organizing drive stopped short of a strike, but there was a clear racial difference in union support. Black workers showed considerably less enthusiasm for the union and few participated in the short-lived drive.

Steel Workers Organizing Committee: SWOC (1937)

M	(0)	McAdam 1999, pp. 78–80
U	(0)★	Cayton and Mitchell 1939, p. 193; Northrup 1944, p. 179
R	(1)	Cayton and Mitchell 1939, pp. 216–17; Sweeney 1956, p. 33; Progress Publishers 1977, p. 379
P	(0)	Brody 1987, p. 21
F	(0)	Schlesinger 1960, p. 425; Skocpol and Finegold 1990
I	(0)	Foner 1974, p. 224, 1983; p. 43; Dickerson 1986, p. 144
E	(1)	See list above
S	(0)	Cayton and Mitchell 1939, p. 218
A	=	High and Long-Term Solidarity

★As a new CIO organization, SWOC had no history of its own. We code it as "strong" based on the recent victories of the CIO.

United Auto Workers: UAW (1937–38)

M	(0)	McAdam 1999, pp. 78–80
U	(0)	Howe and Widick 1949; Meier and Rudwick 1979
R	(1)	Bailer 1943, p. 422; Howe and Widick 1949, pp. 96–97; Pflug 1971, pp. 79–80
P	(1)	Meier and Rudwick 1979
F	(0)	Wallace et al. 1988
I	(0)	Howe and Widick 1949, p. 71
E	(1)	See list above

continued on next page

Table A.2 *(Continued)*

United Auto Workers: UAW (1937–38) (continued)
S   (1)★   Meier and Rudwick 1979, p. 61
B   =   Low and Short-Term Solidarity

★The organizing drive stopped short of a strike, but there was a clear racial difference in union support. Black workers showed considerably less enthusiasm for the union and few participated in the short-lived drive.

United Auto Workers: UAW (1940–41)
M   (0)   McAdam 1999, pp. 78–80
U   (0)   Meier and Rudwick 1979
R   (1)   Howe and Widick 1949, p. 103; Meier and Rudwick 1979, p. 88
P   (0)   Meier and Rudwick 1979, p. 107
F   (0)   Howe and Widick 1949, p. 99; Meier and Rudwick 1979
I   (0)   Meier and Rudwick 1979
E   (0)   See list above
S   (0)   Meier and Rudwick 1979, p. 107
A   =   High and Long-Term Solidarity

CIO "Operation Dixie" (1946–52)
M   (0)   Wilson 1978, pp. 66–70; McAdam 1999, pp. 78–80
U   (0)   Preis 1964, pp. 376–77; Martin 1980, p. 1; Marshall 1967, pp. 246–69
R   (1)   Preis 1976, p. 377; Marshall 1967, p. 258
P   (0/1)★   Goldfield 1991; Wood 1986
F   (0)   Wallace et al. 1988
I   (0)   Kennedy 1946, p. 349
E   (1)   See list above
S   (0)   Zingraff and Schulman 1984; Newman 1978
C   =   Moderate and Short-Term Solidarity

★Employer paternalism excluded minorities. We code it "0" for explaining minority strike-breaking and "1" when explaining overall union solidarity.

Table A.3
Split Labor Market Determinants of Minority Strikebreaking

M	U	S	Cases
1	1	1	Steel (1919), UMW (1927–29)
1	0	1	Comstock Miners (1869)
0	1	0/1	AA (1934) = 1; *UMW (1933) = 0*
0	0	0/1	*UAW (1937–38) = 1;* SWOC (1937), UAW (1940–41), Operation Dixie (1946–52) = 0

Key: M = Recent Minority Migrants (1 = high proportion), U = Union Strength (1 = historically weak), S = Minority Strikebreaking (1 = present)
QCA Results:
S = M + U
s = mu [2 contradictions: UAW 1937–38, UMW 1933]
Diversity Index: 100%

(S) occurs where there is a high proportion of recent minority migrants (M) or a weak union (U). The analysis is inadequate, however, since minority strikebreaking also occurs under other conditions. The table shows two contradictory cases, the (italicized) UMW drive in 1933 and the UAW drive in 1937–38. Contradictory cases are specific combinations of factors with both positive and negative outcomes (Ragin 1987, p. 113). When the same combinations of causes are associated with different outcomes, the model is improperly specified. At this point, we return to the case histories to search for other causal determinants that could resolve the contradictory results. We then expand the original truth table to consider the new factors.

We are using (and advocating) a hierarchical approach to comparative historical research (Boswell and Brown 1999). General theory structures the analysis a priori by defining the theoretically relevant factors and positing causal mechanisms. The theory provides the parameters of the initial, and most parsimonious, truth table. This truth table defines the research question and identifies what cases address the question. Analysis of the table exposes empirical contradictions and contextual weaknesses in the theory. The second stage is to expand the initial table with factors from the historical narratives and from alternative theoretical perspectives. Second-stage analysis yields specific explanations for each case that include a set of all relevant contextual determinants. The costs, however, are a high level of complexity and limited generalizability, producing long equations that include symbols for all contributing factors.

The third stage is to compare tables to refine or expand the general theory inductively. One must explain any cases that were not covered by the original propositions. The models exhibiting the "best fit" with the results are the ones that fully explain the cases with the smallest number of determinants. This final analysis is thus situated between the first, parsimonious theoretical model and the second set of detailed equations. Our last model explains the variation across all the cases while sacrificing as little generality as possible. It refines the theory and delineates its scope conditions, yet it also excludes superfluous causes while retaining only the variable(s) necessary to resolve initial contradictions.

INDUCTIVE REVISIONS

The case studies suggest that the contexts within which unions organized had important effects on solidarity and strikebreaking. While not explicitly addressed by split labor market theory, several of these contributing causes are central to other theories of race or labor relations (reviewed in chapter 2). For the analyses, we operationalize five contextual determinants as follows (refer to Tables A.1 and A.2 for measures and codes).

First, *state repression* includes state sponsored or state supported efforts to break a strike or cripple an organizing drive. Repression reduces the likelihood of union success and increases the risks of solidarity, especially where a minority population is politically and economically vulnerable. Note, however, that violent repression can have unintended consequences, such as yielding sympathy for the union or delegitimating employer tactics, so that the effects of repression cannot simply be assumed. By current standards, the state was repressive in almost all of the cases. Most of the cases also involved forms of employer intimidation that now might be illegal (even if such laws are not readily enforced). The extent of repression, however, was much higher in some cases. Most overt violence was local, with police acting to "maintain order" by violently breaking up meetings and picket lines. The authorities also frequently allowed company guards to "maintain order" with impunity, which we also operationalize as repression.

A second important determinant is favorable *federal legislation*. Specifically, the NIRA, the Wagner Act, and related legislation of the New Deal era significantly increased working-class mobilization and stimulated union growth prior to World War II (see Wallace, Rubin, and Smith 1988; Roscigno and Danaher 2004). Passage of these laws would have also affected the individual and collective calculations of potential costs, benefits, and risks associated with unionization. Note that the three organizing drives that successfully developed interracial coalitions occurred during this period of reform. The federal context is "unfavorable" for cases that occurred prior to the passage of New Deal labor reforms and "favorable" for those cases that occurred after.

Third, *employer paternalism* is a mechanism for co-opting the working class and reducing the threat of unionization. Paternalistic employers, personally or through company unions, distribute housing, loans, profit-sharing schemes, job security, or other benefits on the basis of filial loyalty. What makes this system so powerful is the combination of racial dependence in the North and racist segregation in the South. Paternalism that differs by race can undermine organizing by institutionalizing racism. As such, it explains how employers can profitably discriminate. Paternalism directed at white workers obviously had different effects on strikebreaking than paternalism directed at black workers. Distinct to southern textiles was that white workers had a "deal": loyalty, diffidence, and no union for paternalistic security and no competition with minority workers. In the analysis of minority strikebreaking, we only consider paternalism that includes minorities. For analyzing overall solidarity, however, we argue that all paternalism operates to undermine union support (and using two separate factors in the analyses does not change these findings).[5]

Fourth, *economic recession* undermines organizing by increasing the number of potential strikebreakers and raising the value of current job security. As minorities suffer higher unemployment, recessions may increase minority strikebreaking. Unemployment rose during recessions in 1920, 1933, 1937, 1945–46, and 1949. Note, however, that recessions can also increase worker militancy, delegitimize employers, and raise the value of wage increases. Militancy was particularly high during the Great Depression. Unemployment's mixed consequences should be reflected in union strength, but may have separate, added effects. We expect the main impact to be a drop in union solidarity.

Finally, past failures will prompt social movement organizers to adopt tactical innovations that overcome the failure's source (McAdam 1999). As found in chapter 5, racial divisions prompted CIO organizers to *institutionalize inclusion* by hiring minority officials and organizers and actively recruiting minority members. In so doing, the union was better able to communicate with minority members, discover complaints, monitor defections, and otherwise build the trust necessary to convince them that the potential benefits of class solidarity outweigh the immediate costs. Institutionalized inclusion is distinct from our outcomes because inclusion refers to changing racial policy and hiring of minority staff, whereas interracial solidarity refers to an integrated membership. A union may have institutionalized racial policy and be unsuccessful in bringing about interracial labor solidarity, as is illustrated in the cases of the UAW in 1937–38 and of Operation Dixie. We consider those unions that espoused inclusion without providing resources or clear policies and those that were openly hostile to minorities as "exclusive."

In the case narratives, each of these factors contributed to minority strikebreaking or class solidarity to some degree, but what is minimally necessary to explain the contradictory cases? Incorporating all of the forgoing factors is likely to resolve the contradictions but also produces an unwieldy model with uncertain implications (given the large number of factors and high proportion of hypothetical cases). A second question is whether we can rule out any of the contributing determinants. This does not invalidate the original focus on recent migration and union strength. Rather, it adds an analysis of the political and ideological contexts that structured individual decision making.

We expand the truth table to include these additional causal determinants, again perform QCA, and present the results in Table A.4. Due to the cumbersome nature of large truth tables, we include only those combinations for which we actually have cases when the number of causal factors exceeds four, although our results throughout are based upon consideration of all possible combinations. The resulting equations are longer and more complex than those presented above. Since it is difficult to eliminate potential causes absent critical comparisons (see below), the individual terms comprising these equations symbolically approximate the particular histories of each case and ascribe greater weight to a larger number of possible determinants. What can we learn from the expanded table? First, Table A.4 resolves the original contradiction in Table A.3. Additionally, all cases of interracial solidarity required institutionalized inclusion, favorable legislation, a local minority population, and no paternalism toward minorities. All but one drive characterized by solidarity had strong unions with recent victories (the one exception being the resurgent UMW in 1933).[6] Minority strikebreaking showed no such uniformity, although repression and the lack of inclusion come close. Repression and an absence of institutionalized inclusion are each associated with three of the four combinations that are associated with minority strikebreaking. Recent migration and paternalism also seem to be functional substitutes; each has similar effects on the interests and motivations of minority workers.

Ragin (1987, pp. 106–109) points out that Boolean algorithms can be used to derive equations for the combinations that do and do not exist in the data (equations N and n). The equation for existing combinations (N) is derived by reducing the equation that lists all primitive terms that are actually found in the data using Boolean methods. The equation for nonexistent combinations (n) is a reduced equation for all the hypothetical combinations in the data. As such, an advantage of QCA is that it explicitly delineates analytical scope. In contrast to analyses using statistical methods, adding new factors to a QCA table will not show others to be spurious.[7] Variables do not "drop out" or fail

Table A.4

Multiple Determinants of Minority Strikebreaking

M	U	R	P	F	I	E	S	Cases
1	1	1	0	1	1	0	1	Steel (1919), UMW (1927–28)
1	0	0	0	1	1	0	1	Comstock Miners (1869)
0	1	1	1	0	1	0	1	AA (1934)
0	0	1	1	0	0	1	1	UAW (1937–38)
0	1	0	0	0	0	1	0	UMW (1933)
0	0	1	0	0	0	1	0	SWOC (1937), Operation Dixie (1946–52)
0	0	1	0	0	0	0	0	UAW (1940–41)

Key: M = Recent Minority Migrants (1 = high proportion), U = Union Strength (1 = historically weak), R = Repressive Acts (1 = high repression), P = Paternalistic Employer (1 = paternalism), F = Federal Legislation (1 = unfavorable to labor), I = Institutionalized Inclusion (1 = not present), E = Economic Recession (1 = present), S = Minority Strikebreaking (1 = present), N = Existing Combinations (n = not present in the data)

QCA Results:

S = MURpFIe + MurpFIe + muRPfiE + mURPfIe

s = muRpfi + mUrpfiE

Diversity Index: 5.5%

N = mURPfIe + MURpFIe + muRPfi + muRfiE + MurpFIe + mUrpfiE

n = Upfe + Urpf + mUpe + mURp + rie + rfe + uri + urf + mre + mur + Uie + Ure + uPe + pfI + rfI + ufI + mpI + mrI + muI + urE + Mur + Mur + Uri + Upi + UrF + uRF + UrI + uRI + uPI + URE + UPE + Mi + Mf + rP + Fi + mF + rE + MP + PF + ME + FE + IE

to achieve statistical significance once the "real" cause has been included. Causal factors can only be eliminated by adding critical cases, where the outcome and all but a single cause are the same. A critical case shows that the one different cause was unnecessary. Each added determinant can take away a possible critical case comparison, while doubling the number of hypothetical combinations, such that the seven different causal determinants create a truth table with 128 possible combinations.

Having too few critical cases is known as the problem of limited diversity (Ragin 1987, pp. 104–113). We created a simple measure of limited diversity, a "diversity index," which is the ratio of observed cases to possible combinations (Boswell and Brown 1999). The higher the index, the fewer the restrictions imposed on the analysis by limited diversity and the less the results rely on possibly flawed assumptions about missing cases. Typically, the more parsimonious the model, the less diversity is required for an examination of necessary determinants. The diversity index for the expanded Table A.4 is a very modest 5.5 percent; our equations are based upon the empirical analysis of less than 6 percent of the potential combinations of these seven independent variables, which undermines our confidence that the results are broadly applicable. Some of the missing combinations may be strictly hypothetical cases in the sense that they could not really occur because they combine incompatible elements. However, we are reluctant to base our analyses on such an assumption.[8] As is typical (and appropriate), with inductive expansions of theory, the results apply with high confidence only to situations similar to our nine particular cases.

However, as described above, we are still able to derive a model with the minimal number of determinants necessary to resolve the contradictions. This minimum represents the generalizable core of a revised theory. Despite the complexity of adding five new determinants, we can readily discern that adding only one, paternalism, resolves the contradictions. In the 1934 AA organizing drive, black workers disproportionately preferred the immediate personal benefits of company unions. A similar pattern unfolded at Ford. Despite the 1937 recession, the UAW had recently won a strike at Chrysler, and Ford seemed a viable target. Yet, even if the union had won, there was a clear racial distinction in union support due to Ford's paternalism. While these two cases also differed from those with interracial solidarity in terms of other factors, only paternalism distinguishes them both.

With the contradiction resolved, we can revise the truth table to include only recent migration and paternalism, explain the outcomes, and leave no other contradictions. We present the results in Table A.5. Either recent migration or paternalism was sufficient to split union support along racial lines ($S = Mp + mP$). Conversely, of the four cases where minorities supported the union, none included recent migrants or paternalism directed at minorities ($s = mp$). However, this does not necessarily mean that minority support produced high levels of class solidarity.

CLASS SOLIDARITY

Having derived both specific and generalizable models of strikebreaking, we now move to explaining levels of class solidarity. We have characterized the cases according to the four levels of solidarity previously discussed in chapter 2 and presented in Figure 2.2. To explain

Table A.5

Paternalism and Split Labor Market Determinants of Minority
Strikebreaking

M	P	S	Cases
1	1	—	
1	0	1	Steel (1919), Comstock Miners (1869), UMW (1927–29)
0	1	1	AA (1934), UAW (1937–38)
0	0	0	UMW (1933), SWOC (1937), UAW (1940–41), Operation Dixie (1946–52)

Key: M = Recent Minority Migrants (1 = high proportion), P = Paternalistic Employer (1 = paternalism), S = Minority Strikebreaking (1 = present), N = Existing Combinations (n = not present in the data)

QCA Results:
S = Mp + mP
s = mp

Diversity Index: 75%

N = m + p
n = MP

each level, we again start with minority migrants and union strength, but now include minority strikebreaking as a causal determinant (M/m, U/u, S/s). As demonstrated in Table A.6, this time we explain all but one contradictory case, Operation Dixie. It shares the conditions of unions that achieved minority support, but class solidarity was far lower in this case.

We again expand the analysis to consider the five other determinants in Table A.7. One finding from the expanded table is that in all four cases of initially high but short-lived compliance (D) the union had not institutionalized racial inclusion. In three of these, minorities were recent migrants. Racial differences were the most irreconcilable and racial conflict was the most intense in these cases. At the other extreme, all cases of high interracial solidarity (A) had a favorable political climate and an inclusive union. The two levels in the middle (B, C) had the combination of repression, paternalism, and recession. Otherwise, the organizing conditions were highly favorable.

Finally, we seek to extract the generalizable factors, and again, we find that adding paternalism alone resolves the contradiction in the most parsimonious fashion. Table 8.2B displays the minimal truth table and equations. As mentioned above, here we consider both forms of paternalism as one deterrent of class solidarity. What if we start with

Table A.6

Split Labor Market Determinants of Four Levels of Union Solidarity

M	U	S	A	B	C	D	Cases
1	1	1	0	0	0	1	Steel (1919), UMW (1927–29)
1	1	0	—	—	—	—	
1	0	1	0	0	0	1	Comstock Miners (1869)
1	0	0	—	—	—	—	
0	1	1	0	0	0	1	AA (1934)
0	1	0	1	0	0	0	UMW (1933)
0	0	1	0	1	0	0	UAW (1937–38)
0	0	0	1	0	1	0	SWOC (1937), UAW (1940–41) = A; Operation Dixie (1946–52) = C

Key: M = Recent Minority Migrants (1 = high proportion), U = Union Strength (1 = historically weak), S = Minority Strikebreaking (1 = present), N = Existing Combinations (n = not present in the data)

QCA Results:

A = ms   High and Long-Term Solidarity [1 contradiction, Operation Dixie (1946–52)]
B = muS   Low and Short-Term Solidarity
C = mus   Moderate and Short-Term Solidarity
D = S(M+U) High but Short-Term Solidarity

Diversity Index: 75%

N = m + S
n = Ms

paternalism and leave out union strength (MP)? The results again produce one contradiction, this time the 1937–38 UAW case. Adding union strength resolves this contradiction, returning us to the same four causes as our "best" (i.e., most parsimonious) model.

We are only comparing case studies of racially split labor markets. If our goal was explaining union support in general, then all the determinants in the expanded model might prove to be important. Instead, our purpose has been to find the core commonalities for achieving solidarity despite a racial split. Given these results, we should reconsider the original game-theoretic model of worker compliance with the union. We originally proposed that the highest levels of compliance occur where the union is strong and the minorities are predominantly local (outcome A, high and long-term solidarity characterized by a biracial class coalition). Our analyses in Table A.8 support this expectation, but only in absence of paternalism (A = mps).

Table A.7
Multiple Determinants of Four Levels of Union Solidarity

M	U	R	P	F	I	E	S	A	B	C	D	Cases
1	1	1	0	1	1	0	1	0	0	0	1	Steel (1919), UMW (1927–28)
1	0	0	0	1	1	0	1	0	0	0	1	Comstock Miners (1869)
0	1	1	1	0	1	0	1	0	0	0	1	AA (1934)
0	1	0	0	0	0	1	0	1	0	0	0	UMW (1933)
0	0	1	1	0	0	1	1	0	1	0	0	UAW (1937–38)
0	0	1	1	0	0	1	0	0	0	1	0	Operation Dixie (1946–52)
0	0	1	0	0	0	1	0	1	0	0	0	SWOC (1937)
0	0	1	0	0	0	0	0	1	0	0	0	UAW (1940–41)

Key: M = Recent Minority Migrants (1 = high proportion), U = Union Strength (1 = historically weak), R = Repressive Acts (1 = high repression), P = Paternalistic Employer (1 = paternalism), F = Federal Legislation (1 = unfavorable to labor), I = Institutionalized Inclusion (1 = not present), E = Economic Recession (1 = present), S = Minority Strikebreaking (1 = present), N = Existing Combinations (n = not present in the data)

QCA Results:
A = muRpfis + mUrpfiEs   High and Long-Term Solidarity
B = muRPfiES   Low and Short-Term Solidarity
C = muRPfiEs   Moderate and Short-Term Solidarity
D = mURPfleS + MURpFIeS + MurpFIeS   High but Short-Term Solidarity

Diversity Index: 3.1%

N = mURPfleS + MURpFIeS + muRPfis + muRPfiE + MurpFIeS + mUrpfiEs

n = Upfe + mUpe + ufeS + mueS + Urpf + mURp + uRes + uRpS + res + rie + rfe + urs + uri + urf + mre + mur + Ues + Uie + Ure + Pes + Pie + uPe + pfl + rfl + ufl + mpI + mrI + muI + urE + ieS + piS + pfS + riS + rfS + mpS + mrS + MUr + MuR + URs + URi + UPs + UPi + UrF + uRF + UrI + uRI + uRI + uPI + UiS + UrS + pES + rES + URE + UPE + UES + Ms + Mi + Mf + rP + Fs + Fi + mF + Is + rE + MP + PF + ME + FE + IE

We expected the lowest class solidarity where minority migrants confronted a weak union (formal model outcome B, biracial strikebreaking). All the drives that eventually failed ended with biracial strikebreaking, but the critical difference was the level of support generated by the union before the strike's demise. While the UAW won elsewhere in 1937, the union failed to build momentum at Ford. Ford's paternalism affected blacks disproportionately, but it also restrained white support for the union (B = muPS). These results suggest that paternalism instills an aversion to union organizing that can undermine the positive effects of a strong union and local minorities on class solidarity. Paternalism co-opted minority leadership as well as minority workers. To be sure, the 1937 recession and local police repression also played important roles. With only one case, we cannot rule these factors out as unnecessary (and should not rule them out given the history). What we

Table A.8

Paternalism and Split Labor Market Determinants of Four Levels of Union Solidarity

M	U	P	S	A	B	C	D	Cases
1	1	1	1	—	—	—	—	
1	1	1	0	—	—	—	—	
1	1	0	1	0	0	0	1	Steel (1919), UMW (1927–29)
1	1	0	0	—	—	—	—	
1	0	1	1	—	—	—	—	
1	0	1	0	—	—	—	—	
1	0	0	1	0	0	0	1	Comstock Miners (1869)
1	0	0	0	—	—	—	—	
0	1	1	1	0	0	0	1	AA (1934)
0	1	1	0	—	—	—	—	
0	1	0	1	—	—	—	—	
0	1	0	0	1	0	0	0	UMW (1933)
0	0	1	1	0	1	0	0	UAW (1937–38)
0	0	1	0	0	0	1	0	Operation Dixie (1946–52)
0	0	0	1	—	—	—	—	
0	0	0	0	1	0	0	0	SWOC (1937), UAW (1940–41)

Key: M = Recent Minority Migrants (1 = high proportion), U = Union Strength (1 = historically weak), P = Paternalistic Employer (1 = paternalism), S = Minority Strikebreaking (1 = present), N = Existing Combinations (n = not present in the data)

QCA Results:
A = mps   High and Long-Term Solidarity
B = muPS   Low and Short-Term Solidarity
C = muPs   Moderate and Short-Term Solidarity
D = S(Mp+mUP)   High but Short-Term Solidarity

Diversity Index: 43.8%

N = mus + MpS + mPS + mps + muP
n = mpS + Ms + UPs + MP

can do is identify paternalism as the factor that distinguishes Ford from comparable cases.[9]

Similarly, we have one case, Operation Dixie, where minorities disproportionately supported the union (C). Employer paternalism among white workers largely explains this pattern, which deviates from our other cases. Employer manipulation of deeply rooted cultural beliefs and workplace relations of dependency co-opted dominant labor. Operation Dixie stands in sharp relief to the other organizing drives we considered in this analysis, yet the pattern of higher minority support for unions has since become the norm (see Freeman and Medoff 1984; Lichtenstein 2002).

We end the comparative analysis with the most racially polarized outcome (D), which obtains where there is minority strikebreaking (S) with either high proportions of minority migrants and no paternalism (Mp) or low numbers of migrants, a weak union, and paternalism (mUP). In the first combination (MpS), the connection between minority migrants and minority strikebreaking clearly supports split labor market hypotheses. In the second causal conjuncture (mUPS), paternalism and weak unions provide the impetus for minority strikebreaking.

We have three sets of results regarding the causes of minority strikebreaking and three sets regarding the causes of worker solidarity. To facilitate comparison, a summary of all three sets of results are presented in Table A.9. One may think of the first column, which presents results from Tables A.3 and A.6, as the initial test of propositions from the general theory. The second column, with results from Tables A.4 and A.7, lists the inductive revisions, and the final column, which presents results form Tables A.5 and A.8, gives the final revised version of the generalizable core of the theory.

Table A.9
Summary of QCA Outcomees

Outcome	Table A.3	Table A.4	Table A.5
S	M + U	MURpFIe + MurpFIe + muRPfiE + mURPfIe	Mp + mP
s	mu★	muRPfi + mUrpfiE	mp
	Table A.6	Table A.7	Table A.8
A	ms	MuRpfis + mUrpfiEs	mps
B	muS	muRPfiES	muPS
C	mus	muRPfiEs	muPs
D	S(M + U)★	mURPfIeS + MURpFIeS + MurpFIeS	S(Mp + mUP)

Key: M = Recent Minority Migrants (1 = high proportion), U = Union Strength (1 = historically weak), R = Repressive Acts (1 = high repression), P = Paternalistic Employer (1 = paternalism), F = Federal Legislation (1 = unfavorable to labor), I = Institutionalized Inclusion (1 = not present), E = Economic Recession (1 = present), S = Minority Strikebreaking (1 = present), A = High and Long-Term Solidarity (Bi-racial Class Coalition), B = Low and Short-Term Solidarity (Bi-racial Strikebreaking), C = Moderate and Short-Term Solidarity (Dominant Workers Strikebreak/Minorities Support Union), D = High but Short-Term Solidarity (Dominant Workers Support Union/Minorities Strikebreak)

★contains a contradictory case

Notes

CHAPTER 1. INTRODUCTION

1. Some migrants and immigrants traveled to distant lands for work—in some cases repeatedly—with the intention of returning home. Those who did usually had distinct motives (e.g., earning as much money as possible in a relatively short period of time) that distinguished them from long-term resident labor.

2. These particular cases are included for historical and methodological reasons. They were central to the CIO during its formative years and provide critical contrasts across a range of important variables (to be described in subsequent chapters).

3. Lieberson (1980) finds that blacks and Chinese had similar patterns for the particular time periods of our cases, but these begin to differ sharply after WWII. The source of this divergence is the reproduction of a split labor market for blacks.

CHAPTER 2. THEORIES OF RACIAL COMPETITION AND ORGANIZING SOLIDARITY

1. See Bonacich (1976, p. 36; 1972, p. 549) and Boswell and Jorjani (1988, p. 169).

2. A group of workers may all receive the same wage, but if some of the workers are nonunion, this group has lower labor costs over the long term given their diminished propensity to strike or make demands on employers.

3. Analytical induction involves examining cases one at a time, redefining phenomena, and reformulating hypotheses with the discovery of negative cases (Cressey 1950, p. 51; Znaniecki 1934; Robinson 1951, pp. 812–13). Hicks (1994, pp. 1–14) provides a critical discussion.

4. A series of studies have shown the versatility of the theory by applying it to diverse cases, without attempting to change it. Christiansen's (1979)

analysis of Filipino exclusion between 1927 and 1934 finds that a price differential led the white labor movement to exclude lower priced labor, and that the business class opposed the exclusion movement for eliminating a cheap source of labor. Similarly, Makabe's (1981) study of Japanese immigrant sojourners to Canada before World War II finds that labor cost differences generated intense competition and racial conflict. He contrasts this with Japanese immigrants to Brazil who purchased their own land, limiting direct competition. Exclusion efforts resulted in Canada, while Japanese in Brazil practiced self-segregation. Howell (1982) examines migrant farm workers from Mexico, relating labor cost differentials to levels of national development, imperialism, and migration patterns. Howell characterizes most Mexican farm workers as sojourners and describes six different types of labor displacement (also see Boswell and Jorjani 1988, pp. 177–79).

5. While Wilson (1978) focuses on the Marxist theory of "divide and conquer," Marxist analyses have also stressed the irrational nature of segregation and racial discrimination, which over the long term should be eroded by the logic of capitalist development. Greenberg (1980, pp. 129–47) identifies this as the "growth school" argument, and considers the "divide and conquer" view to be part of a neo-Marxist framework. Other analyses have explored the effects of segmented labor markets that divide workers in terms of race and gender, thus creating "a splintered working class politics rooted in class fractions" (Gordon, Edwards, and Reich 1988, p. 214). Several additional authors that have implemented or criticized the split labor market perspective include Cummings (1977), Singleton (1978), Wallimann (1984).

6. The antecedents to Olzak's version of the ethnic competition perspective are identified in Olzak and Nagel (1986, pp. 2–3). For a comprehensive articulation of the theory, see Olzak (1992).

7. Earlier versions of the theory failed to account for period and region-specific political contexts (James 1988). In response, Olzak (1992, pp. 43–44) posits that third party and social movement political challenges (including labor movement organizations) increase ethnic collective action.

8. This is what Bowles and Gintis (1993) call "short side power," where the transaction costs of market mobility are greater for one side than for the other.

9. Understanding rationality (and its limitations) is the center of the Weberian tradition. More recently, analytical Marxists have been using rational choice mechanisms to specify materialist conceptions of social action (Elster 1985; Roemer 1979; Wright 1982). Nevertheless, rational choice models are often met with distrust in sociology. The originating focus of the discipline was to explain the constitution of preferences, as opposed to assuming them; to explain the sources of structural determinants, rather than individual choices given structural determinants, and to explain organizational dynamics rather than individual behavior (see Collins 1988).

10. While we are concerned with the conceptual overlap of these approaches, we recognize that there are important differences among the practitioners of collective behavior, resource mobilization, and political process theories.

11. McAdam (1986) points out that individuals can estimate and control costs more than risks, which depend more on the actions of others and the environment. As the probable cost of inaction or failure can be extrapolated from current conditions, determining the costs tends to be more certain than the probability of success or the amount of potential gain. We then might assume that preventing these likely costs predominate in decision making. This might explain why unions embark on strikes when they seem unlikely to win.

12. Axelrod (1984, pp. 12–16) has argued that the possibility of future interactions can facilitate mutual cooperation in prisoner's dilemma situations where the importance of the next move relative to the present move is sufficiently high. As short-term workers, sojourners discount future interactions at a higher rate than other workers, which reduces the probability of cooperation.

13. Here we provide only a brief overview of our game theoretic model. Readers interested in a more detailed and technical discussion should refer to Heckathorn (1988, 1989, 1990a, 1990b) and Brown and Boswell (1995).

14. The theoretical model can apply to any type of organizing, but we will discuss it here only in terms of a union organizing drive. Bianco, Ordeshook, and Tsebelis (1990) reveal some of the problems involved in making predictions about repeated or n-person interactions based on one-shot, two-actor game theoretic models.

15. Derivation of the equations that relate the theoretical terms of the model can be found in Heckathorn (1990a, 1990b).

16. The number of subgroups (n) is less than or equal to the number of actors (N). Where n = N, the system is perfectly heterogeneous and each worker has a unique set of parameters.

17. Unlike industrial unions, craft labor, especially when trained through apprenticeship, may be able to maintain discrimination based on monopoly over scarce skills. Thus, craft labor may have less to gain from solidarity and less to lose over the long run (although a skill monopoly does encourage deskilling).

18. See William Sewell's (1988) debate with James Coleman over ideology and rational choice, where he specifically refers to Boswell's (1986) use of split labor market theory as an example of their combination.

19. The Industrial Workers of the World (IWW) and other radical unions had long actively pursued racial equality. However, the IWW was largely crushed by state repression in 1917–20 and it did not experience lasting interracial organizing (or minority strikebreaking) on a scale comparable to the cases explored here (Dubofsky 1988).

CHAPTER 3. MIGRATION AND MARKETS—THE ORIGINS OF SPLIT LABOR MARKETS

A previous version of this chapter was published in 1988 as "Uneven Development and the Origins of Split Labor Market Discrimination: A Comparison of Black, Chinese, and Mexican Immigrant Minorities in the United States," by Terry Boswell and David Jorjani. Pp. 169–85 in *Racism, Sexism, and the World System*, edited by J. Smith, J. Collins, T. K. Hopkins, A. Muhammad. New York: Greenwood. Reproduced with permission of Greenwood Publishing Group, Inc., Westport, CT.

1. While wages were often dramatically higher in the North, the cost of living was also higher (Kennedy 1930, p. 44). The net financial gain to migrants was often less than might be expected, though nevertheless still significant. Interestingly, Marks (1989, p. 123) indicates that a significant number of blacks earned lower wages in the North.

2. Migration did decline by approximately 50 percent during the 1930s (see McAdam 1999, p. 80), so the implications for previously migrated workers were less pronounced than they had been in the 1920s.

3. Statistical discrimination is another important source of discrimination by employers (Reich 1981, pp. 104–105). Statistical discrimination occurs when average skill differences are large enough between the dominant and minority ethnic groups for the employer to use race as a proxy for identifying skill differences. Following Bonacich (1972, 1976), we hold efficiency and productivity constant in this study, and thus we do not consider cases of statistical discrimination.

4. There are, of course, other sources of racial and ethnic antagonism outside of the labor market, but our emphasis is on splits in the labor market. Also, while a split labor market is neither a necessary nor exclusive cause of ethnic antagonism, it is a sufficient cause and the primary source of antagonism within the working class in capitalist market societies.

CHAPTER 4. SOJOURNER LABOR—THE PATTERN OF DISCRIMINATION AGAINST CHINESE IMMIGRANTS, 1850–1882

A previous version of this chapter was published in 1986 as "A Split Labor Market Analysis of Discrimination Against Chinese Immigrants, 1850–1882," *American Sociological Review* 51: 352–71.

1. Cheng and Bonacich's (1984) book on Asian immigration, and especially chapter 4 by Bonacich (1984), deals with Asian labor in California and Hawaii. While this chapter oddly does not refer to split labor market dynamics, the principle elements of the theory are present and the conclusions are similar

to those reached here. Unlike her previous work, Bonacich (1984) provides an analysis of class interests, the distinction between workers and petty-commodity producers, and the role of the state. However, there is little analysis of the role of ideology, the historical pattern of discrimination, the sources of segregated labor markets, or the nationalization of the anti-Chinese movement. Present in Bonacich (1984) but not covered in this chapter is a discussion of relations in Hawaii, Chinese in the agricultural sector, and the role of the state in promoting immigration. Another split labor market analysis of Chinese immigration is a brief research note by Hilton (1979), which mainly draws from the experience of the Chinese in manufacturing. While Hilton (1979) outlines the interactions between classes and ethnic groups, his research note does not analyze the role of ideology, the state, or changes in technology or class structure.

2. Saxton (1971) provides the landmark study of the organizational history of the anti-Chinese alliance. Extensive economic data can be found in Chiu (1967). General histories can be found in Coolidge (1909), Chen (1980), and Nee and Nee (1973). Seward (1881) provides an argument against the Exclusion Act that draws mainly from Congressional testimonies (as does Coolidge). Zo (1978) and Tsai (1983) analyzed Chinese immigration from the Chinese side of the ocean, drawing on Chinese sources. Fong and Markam (1991), Gyory (1998), Rhoads (1999, 2002), and Aarim-Heriot (2003) elaborate on the historical patterns discussed here.

3. The political organization of the anti-Chinese movement and the international sources of Chinese immigration have been addressed elsewhere and cannot be included in this chapter (see Saxton 1971; Zo 1978). Information on the international pressures on state action in the United States can be found in Tsai (1983).

4. Coolies typically contracted for seven years' labor in exchange for passage and minimal wages. In principle, they were "voluntary slaves," but in practice, Chinese peasants were often kidnapped and forced to become coolies. The contracts, and thus the coolies, could be bought and sold. Yet as "voluntary slaves," coolies suffered the worst of wage labor, as employers were under no patriarchal obligations. They also suffered the worst of slave labor, as workers could not escape brutish conditions through a labor market (Coolidge 1909; Campbell 1969).

5. The Exclusion Act was renewed in 1892 and 1902; in 1904 the ten-year renewal clause was removed.

6. We did not examine the discourse of the Chinese immigrants. Information on the beliefs and attitudes of the Chinese immigrants is limited; see Zo (1978) and Tsai (1983). How the Chinese interpreted the accusations of "voluntary slavery," dealt with crossing sex stereotypes in occupations, or conceived the status of self-employment in America (merchants had low status in China, Tsai 1983, p. 17) surely affected the development of the split labor

market. Examining their discourse is beyond the scope of this work, but the analysis of split labor market dynamics should benefit from such research.

CHAPTER 5. RACIAL COMPETITION IN THE GREAT STEEL STRIKE OF 1919

1. The actual number of strikes in 1919 was 3,630. During the period 1880–1937, only five years had more strikes than 1919: 1903 (3,648), 1906 (3,655), 1916 (3,789), 1917 (4,450), and 1937 (4,740) (Griffin 1939, pp. 38–39). Dubofsky's (1995) more recent assessment of U.S. labor unrest also demonstrates that worker militancy was extremely high in 1919 relative to preceding and subsequent periods.

2. The 1919 steel strike involved between 365,000 and 367,000 workers while the strike of bituminous coal miners that commenced in November involved 435,000 workers (Whitney 1920, pp. 200–01; Peterson 1937, p. 25; Foster 1920, pp. 100–01).

3. Many scholars have noted the transitory nature of black employment and high job turnover rates for black workers during this period, particularly among recent migrants to the North (see Spero and Harris 1969, pp. 178–79; Piore 1979, pp. 158–59; Gottlieb 1978, pp. 206–08; Grossman 1989, pp. 195–97). Marks (1989, pp. 158–62) argues that, despite intentions to return to the South, return migration probably did not occur on a large scale.

4. The literature on immigration and labor is enormous. Brody's (1980) collection of essays remains an excellent and accessible source. Voss's (1993) study of the Knights of Labor has become something of a standard (see also Brueggemann and Brown 2000).

5. For a more detailed discussion of ethnic relations in the iron and steel industry, see Brody (1987, pp. 42–43; 1998, pp. 119–21, 137, 258–60) and Serene (1979, pp. 131–62).

6. Slave labor had successfully been utilized in iron production since 1842 at the Tredegar Iron Works in Richmond, Virginia. Just prior to the Civil War, slave labor was implemented in the iron mills of the Cumberland River Valley of Tennessee, as well as at various locations in South Carolina, Kentucky, Georgia, Alabama, and Missouri (Dickerson 1986, p. 8).

7. Interestingly, the Knights of Labor initially filled the vacuum left by the AA Association in the Edgar Thomson works, but was also forced out by Carnegie after two years (Ingham 1991, p. 131).

8. The merger—including the Carnegie Company, the Federal Steel Company, the American Sheet and Wire Company, the National Tube Company, the National Steel Company, the American Tin Plate Company, the American Steel Hoop Company, and the American Sheet Steel Company— created the first billion-dollar corporation in U.S. history. The American Bridge

Company and The Lake Superior Iron Mines were acquired shortly after U.S. Steel's formation (Fisher 1951, p. 22; also see Garraty 1960; Edwards 1979).

9. Gulick (1924, p. 100) reports that this practice was employed frequently by iron and steel companies even before the formation of U.S. Steel and that it afforded a means to circumvent prior union agreements. If the owners could operate more profitably by directing work to their nonunion plants, then they did so.

10. Important works on the history of the IWW include Brissenden (1919), Gambs (1932), and Dubofsky (1988). A small organization still exists; their website is at www.iww.org.

11. A dual union is "an organization which claims the right to maintain itself as a body independent, and usually rival to, another association controlling the same classes of workmen and operating within the same territory" (Robinson 1920, pp. 41–42).

12. Perhaps the most significant involvement of the IWW in the steel industry occurred when the largely immigrant and unskilled workforce of the Pressed Steel Car Company of McKees Rocks went on strike on July 15, 1909 (Dubofsky 1988, pp. 198–209). By the time the steel workers attempted to deal with these divisions by organizing an industry-wide strike in 1919, the IWW was already in decline. Dubofsky (1988, pp. 443–44) reports that "although the federal trials and deportations did not force the IWW out of existence, the whole basis of its existence changed." The organization was increasingly crippled by loss of leadership and legal expenses, and much of its energy in the immediate postwar years was devoted to "the defense of civil liberties" rather than "winning higher wages, shorter hours, or a new and better world."

13. For example, in Homestead, Steelton, Gary, and Clairton, many steel officials held public office (Brody 1998, p. 123). In addition, the mayor of Duquesne was the brother of the president of a McKeesport steel plant and actively engaged in a campaign of union suppression. The beating, imprisonment, firing, eviction, and intimidation of union members and organizers before and during the strike was commonplace in the towns of the Monongahela Valley. In some cases, labor organizers were murdered (see Powers 1972, pp. 21–29; Foster 1920; Interchurch World Movement 1920, pp 197–243; *New York Times* 9/19/19, 2:1).

14. Documentation of specific instances where blacks were imported as strikebreakers can be found in the following editions of the *New York Times*: 10/3/19, 10/10/19, 10/14/19.

15. See Spero and Harris (1969, pp. 178–79); Piore (1979, pp. 158–59); Gottlieb (1978, pp. 206–08).

16. This conclusion is supported more generally at the national level by Murray's (1951) analysis of communism and the steel strike.

CHAPTER 6. THE FORMULA—INTERRACIAL
SOLIDARITY IN THE COAL, STEEL, AND AUTO UNIONS,
1927–1941

1. See Bernstein (1970); Milton (1982); Korstad and Lichtenstein (1988); Goldfield (1993); and Nelson (1996).

2. Brueggemann and Boswell (1998) have compared these cases using Event Structure Analysis (ESA) to help determine the necessary and/or sufficient sources of interracial solidarity. We used the results of this analysis to aid in constructing the narratives in this chapter.

3. The conventional emphasis in the research literature on conflict and competition among racial segments of labor is certainly warranted by historical patterns. However, these successful cases highlight the theoretical lacunae linked to the possibilities of solidarity.

4. See also Green (1980, p. 50); Seltzer (1985, pp. 17–18); Long (1989, p. 80); Trotter (1990).

5. Cayton and Mitchell write: "There is no doubt that the national officers were disinclined to make a sincere effort to include Negroes in all of the union locals. This attitude was perhaps shared by some of the officers of locals but one can say that on the whole the officers and members of the new lodges realized the necessity for organizing Negroes into the white lodges and forced the national officers to modify their position" (1939, p. 189).

6. This is true even though the skill levels were somewhat artificial, a practice maintained by employers for control (Stone 1975).

7. Ford did not hire women, however, except as clerical workers.

8. John L. Lewis to Roy Wilkins, March 19, 1937, NAACP Records, Library of Congress; Homer Martin to Roy Wilkins, NAACP Records, April 11, 1937, Library of Congress.

9. Correspondence between the local NAACP and Walter White of the UAW substantiates this claim, see J. J. McClendon to Walter White, May 12, 1941, NAACP records, Library of Congress.

10. Gloster B. Current of Detroit NAACP to Walter White, September 16, 1941, NAACP Records, Library of Congress; Press Release from NAACP, September 5, 1941, NAACP Records, Library of Congress.

11. For their part, white workers were critical of Ford, despite their relatively favorable distribution in the better jobs compared to blacks.

12. Telegram from Walter White to Governor Van Wagoner, April 22, 1941, NAACP Records, Library of Congress.

13. Press Release Walter White of NAACP, April 4, 1941, NAACP Records, Library of Congress.

14. Telegram Walter White to Governor Van Wagoner, April 22, 1941, NAACP Records, Library of Congress.

15. Press Release, April 2, 1941, UAW, NAACP Records, Library of Congress.

16. For discussion and critiques of racism within the CIO, see Foner (1974); Nyden (1977); Meier and Rudwick (1979); Lewis (1987); Goldfield (1993, 1994, 1998); Gerstle (1993); Korstad (1993); Boyle (1995); Hill (1988, 1996, 1998, 1999); and Lichtenstein (1999).

CHAPTER 7. OPERATION DIXIE—PATERNALISM AND EMPLOYER DISCRIMINATION IN SOUTHERN TEXTILES, 1946–1953

1. See Preis (1964, pp. 376–77), Martin (1980, p. 1) and Marshall (1967, pp. 246–69).

2. There is some controversy over the extent to which blacks were used as operatives in the southern textile industry. While most scholars suggest the dominance of whites in operative positions, others disagree. Frederickson (1991) notes that blacks were usually a small portion of the mill working population, and episodically, worked as fill-ins or replacements for white workers. But she acknowledges that, most often, blacks were in janitorial or maintenance work. The *pattern* of white dominance in operative positions, therefore, may still be seen as a reasonable position.

3. U.S. Bureau of Census, 1940, *Population*.

4. U.S. Bureau of Labor Statistics (hereinafter cited as BLS), *Bulletin* 1947, pp. 3–31.

5. BLS, *Bulletin 651,* 1937, pp. 94–122.

6. Reports of Preliminary Plant Surveys, North Carolina CIO, 1948, Reel 8, Series 412, Operation Dixie: The CIO Organizing Committee Papers, 1946–1953, hereinafter cited as Dixie Papers.

7. The two exceptions were a 1913 North Carolina statute requiring separate toilets in manufacturing plants, and a 1915 South Carolina law requiring segregation in cotton textiles.

8. On mill owner credibility, see Carlton (1982, pp. 249–52, 267–70); Marshall (1967, p. 81); Wright 1986, pp. 189–90).

9. BLS, *Bulletin 898,* 1947, p. 174.

10. Oral interview of Kennedy by Ralph Peters, March 1983, hereinafter cited as OI.

11. Letter to Author, Ralph Peters, in 1986, hereinafter cited as LTA.

12. Georgia Politics, Reel 2, 1935–48, Schomberg Center for Research in Black Culture, hereinafter cited as Schomberg Center.

13. Freedom of Expression, Four Freedoms Down South, 1946, Box 1537/11, *Kennedy Papers*, Special Collections Department, Georgia State University.

14. Description, *Kennedy Papers.*

15. u.d. manuscript, Reel 2, Schomberg Center.

16. OI.

17. Statement by Bittner, September 10, 1946, Reel 26, Series 51, Dixie Papers.

18. *Labor Reports* reprint, u.d., Reel 73, Series 46, Dixie Papers.

19. "Know Your Rights," u.d., Reel 17, Series 21, Dixie Papers.

20. Reel 17, Series 21; Reel 18, Series 5, Dixie Papers.

21. Reel 17, Series 21, Dixie Papers.

22. Report of Anti-Discrimination Committee, u.d., Reel 70, Series 40; Memo from Arthur Goldberg to CIO Directors and Counsels, April 24, 1950; Reel 17, Series 23, Dixie Papers.

23. Lloyd P. Vaughn to E. Paul Harding, July 30, 1951, Reel 21, Series 154, Dixie Papers.

24. u.d. editorial, 1514/8, *Kennedy Papers.*

25. CIO Directive, North Carolina, 1946, Reel 3, Series 382, Dixie Papers.

26. OI; LTA, 10/10/85; u.d. news article, 1518/65, *Kennedy Papers.*

27. OI.

28. u.d. press release, 1524/38, *Kennedy Papers.*

29. CIO Directive, 1946, Reel 3, Series 382, Dixie Papers.

30. Kennedy to Fred Hobart, February 15, 1938, 1510, *Kennedy Papers.*

31. Reel 30, Series 151; Reel 21, Series 14; Reel 18, Series 54; Dixie Papers.

32. Statement of W. A. Richards, p. 13, *Minutes*, CIO Organizational Conference, 1951; Reel 22, Series 154, Dixie Papers.

33. Virginia CIO pamphlet, Reel 61, Series 292, Dixie Papers.

34. Reel 38, Series 310; Reel 37, Series 289; Maxwell M. Lackey to Paul Revere Christopher, June 1, 1949, Reel 37, Series 289; Warren V. Morel Organizing Report, November 26, 1949, Reel 20, Series 111; Dixie Papers.

35. Van Bittner to William Smith, January 29, 1948, Dixie Papers.

36. Reel 20, Series 143, Dixie Papers.

37. Reel 30, Series 143, Dixie Papers.

38. Reel 23, Series 173, Dixie Papers.

39. Reel 30, Series 143, Dixie Papers.

40. E. John Neal to Paul R. Christopher, October 28, 1946, Reel 42, Series 3-501; Dixie Papers.

41. Dean K. Clowes in Charleston, South Carolina, Reel 17, Series 32, Dixie Papers.

42. E. L. Sanefur to Lucy Randolph Mason, May 5, 1945, Reel 63, Series 51, Dixie Papers.

43. Franz E. Daniel to Richard S. Hamme, February 29, 1952; Reel 15, Series 691, Dixie Papers.

44. Organizing Report, March 26, 1949; Reel 30, Series 143, Dixie Papers.

45. Lucy Randolph Mason to Rev. E. T. Mollegan, May 11, 1945; Reel 63, Series 51, Dixie Papers.

46. Haygood to Ernest B. Pugh, July 23, 1945, Reel 56, Series 77, Dixie Papers.

47. Lucy Randolph Mason to Turner L. Smith, June 14, 1947, Reel 63, Series 51, Dixie Papers.

48. Franz E. Daniel to John Marshall, March 26, 1952, Reel 9, Series 441, Dixie Papers.

49. North Carolina CIO memo, April 14, 1948, Reel 1, Series 193, Dixie Papers.

50. Lucy Randolph Mason to A. A. Rosen, October 30, 1948, Reel 63, Series 51; William Smith to P. E. Henderson, August 16, 1946, Reel 7, Series 195, Dixie Papers.

51. Lucy Randolph Mason to George Baldanzi, October 26, 1946, Reel 1, Dixie Papers.

52. Horace Buock to Lucy Randolph Mason, June 16, 1947; Lucy Randolph Mason to Paul R. Christopher, October 21, 1947; Franz E. Daniel to Joe Donovan, March 25, 1947, Reel 38, Series 33, Dixie Papers.

53. E. John Neal to Paul Revere Christopher, October 28, 1946, Reel 42 Series 3-501, Dixie Papers.

54. Nelle Morton to Franz E. Daniel, u.d., Reel 18, Series 56, Dixie Papers.

55. Barry Bingham to Lucy Randolph Mason, September 24, 1946, Reel 63, Series 5-1, Dixie Papers.

56. E. Paul Harding, public relations director for North and South Carolina, to Drew Pearson, November 1, 1950; Reel 68, Series 54, Dixie Papers.

57. Reel 9, Series 444, Dixie Papers.

58. Reel 9, Series 452, Dixie Papers.

59. Reel 69, Series 62, Dixie Papers.

60. Lucy Randolph Mason to S. Haywood, March 28, 1945, Reel 63, Series 5:1, Dixie Papers.

61. Typescript, David Burgess, "The Role of Churches in Relation to the CIO Organizing Drive," Reel 16, Series 18; David Burgess to Franz Daniel, February 24, 1950, Reel 16, Series 18, Dixie Papers.

62. Minutes of CIO Action Conference, Roanoke, Virginia, March 18, 19, 1952, Reel 8, Series 413, Dixie Papers.

63. Paul Revere Christopher to Gary Haigler, January 25, 1947, Reel 31, Series 154, Dixie Papers.

64. Franz E. Daniel to Jerome A. Cooper, March 2, 1951, Reel 7, Series 94, Dixie Papers.

65. Jeff Johnson to William J. Smith, April 14, 1950, Reel 9, Series 448, Dixie Papers.

66. June, 1950 leaflet, Reel 3, Series 1, Dixie Papers.

67. u.d. pamphlet, Reel 15, Series 713, Dixie Papers.

68. u.d. Reel 22, Series 151, Dixie Papers.

69. u.d. Reel 9, Series 465, Dixie Papers.

70. Franz E. Daniel to Governor J. Strom Thurmond, November 7, 1949, Reel 123, Series 123, Dixie Papers.

71. T. C. Cole to Paul R. Christopher, August 31, 1946, Reel 23, Series 3, Dixie Papers.

72. William Henderson to Boyd E. Payton, September 4, 1947, Reel 56, Series 77, Dixie Papers.

73. Organizing Report, Maxwell M. Lackey, December 3, 1949, Reel 37, Series 289, Dixie Papers.

74. Organizing Report, Nicholas Fayad, August 19, 1950, Reel 18, Series 54, Dixie Papers.

75. Jones to Lucy Mason, November 2, 1948, Reel 63, Series 51, Dixie Papers.

76. UTWA leaflet, u.d., Reel 123, Series 203; E. Paul Harding to Paul R. Christopher, October 14, 1952, Reel 31, Series 158, Dixie Papers.

77. u.d. *Atlanta Journal* article, 1514/42, *Kennedy Papers*.

78. Franz E. Daniel to North Carolina CIO staff, May 19, 1952, Reel 69, Series 7-62, Dixie Papers.

79. Organizing Report, Maxwell Lackey, December 10, 1949, Reel 37, Series 289; Organizing Report, Maloney, 1948, Reel 38, Series 310, Dixie Papers.

80. Lloyd M. Chapman to Paul R. Christopher, Tennessee director of organizing, March 18, 1947, Reel 23, Series 3-76, Dixie Papers.

81. P. L. Culver to Draper Wood, September 9, 1946, Reel 11, Series 514, Dixie Papers.

82. T. H. Wingate to George Baldanzi, September 23, 1946, Reel 11, Series 521; D. L. Culver to Draper Wood, August 28, 1946, Reel 11, Series 514, Dixie Papers.

83. George Baldanzi to T. H. Wingate, October 4, 1946, Reel 11, Series 521, Dixie Papers.

84. Ruth A. Gettinger to Allan A. Swim, July 17, 1946, Reel 11, Series 515, Dixie Papers.

85. "Observations," Typescript, D. L. Culver, September 17, 1946, Reel 11, Series 514, Dixie Papers.

86. D.L. Culver to Draper Wood, August 28, 1946, Reel 11, Series 514, Dixie Papers.

87. D.L. Culver to Draper Wood, August 20, 1946, Reel 11, Series 514; Report of George Baldanzi, u.d., Reel 11, Series 514, Dixie Papers.

88. "Activities in Forming Committees," unsigned memo, u.d., Reel 11, Series 514; Organizing Report, L. L. Shepard, u.d., Reel 10, Series 1-475, Dixie Papers.

89. "Suggestions," D. L. Culver, September 17, 1946, Reel 11, Series 514, Dixie Papers.

90. Reel 10, Series 1-471, Dixie Papers.

91. *Atlanta Journal*, April 30, 1948, 1514/42, *Kennedy Papers*.

92. William Smith to Lynch, October 30, 1946, reel 7, Series 199; C. H. Gillman to Paul R. Christopher, December 10, 1946, Reel 30, Series 142, Dixie Papers.

93. North Carolina Organizing Committee memos, Reel 69, Series 7-64, Dixie Papers.

94. Edmund F. Ryan Jr. to George Baldanzi, October 26, 1946, Reel 1, Series 1, Dixie Papers.

95. Franz E. Daniel memo on International Union Petitions From 10/1/50 to 10/26/51, November 3, 1951, Reel 69, Series 7-63, Dixie Papers.

96. Edmund F. Ryan Jr. to George Baldanzi, October 26, 1946, Reel 1, Series 1, Dixie Papers.

97. Textile Workers Union of America, Research Report, New York, N.Y., 1949, Reel 9, Series 1-449, Dixie Papers.

98. TWUA Memo, u.d., Reel 9, Series 1-452, Dixie Papers. Marshall (1967, p. 262) argues the figure is an even lower 14 percent.

99. OI.

100. In addition, a conscious attempt by new southern economic leaders in the 1960s to change the region's image—a "buy the South" campaign (Wright 1986, p. 16)—buttressed by the national political climate, also helped to create conditions of compliance with federal civil rights laws.

101. The heated debate over the relative dominance of race and class in labor relations, and the extent to which organized labor in the United States engaged in racist practices, continues today. See Herbert Hill, "The Problem of Race in American Labor History," *Reviews in American History* 24, No. 2 (June 1996); Herbert Hill, "Lichtenstein's Fiction: Meany, Ruether and the Civil Rights Act," *New Politics* VII, no. 1 (New Series) (Summer 1998); Nelson Licthtenstein, "Walter Reuther in Black and White: A Rejoinder to Herbert Hill," *New Politics* 7, no. 2 (New Series) whole no. 26 (Winter 1999); and Herbert Hill, "Lichtenstein's Fictions Revisited: Race and the New Labor History," *New Politics* VII, no. 2 (New Series) (Winter 1999).

CHAPTER 8. CONCLUSIONS—ORGANIZING SOLIDARITY

1. Wilson (1987) shows how social policies such as Social Security, which benefit the population or at least the entire working class, have far more support than programs targeted at any specific group.

APPENDIX—QUALITATIVE COMPARATIVE ANALYSES OF
STRIKEBREAKING AND SOLIDARITY

1. In Ragin's (1987, p. 25) words, "[A] phenomenon or change emerges from the intersection of appropriate preconditions . . . in the absence of any one of the essential ingredients, the phenomenon—or the change—does not emerge."

2. For a critique of the assumptions underlying the use of qualitative comparative methodology, see Lieberson (1991). For a rejoinder, see Boswell and Brown (1999). For additional examples and debate, see *Journal of International Comparative Sociology* (volume 32, 1991) and Griffin and Ragin (1994).

3. If all possible combinations are not actually present in the empirical data, one of two strategies can be followed. In the first, the analyst must make logical assumptions about how to treat the hypothetical cases in terms of their outcomes. Alternatively, the hypothetical cases can be excluded from the analysis (the more commonly chosen option). If this option is followed, the causal combinations that are derived using Boolean algebra are limited in scope to the range of cases that are fully specified in the truth table. In other words, the conclusions cannot safely be assumed to hold for any hypothetical cases.

4. This differs from statistical analyses that measure whether a variable significantly improves an explanation of a phenomenon.

5. In a separate set of analyses (not presented here) we found that the use of two paternalism variables ("white paternalism" and "black paternalism") did not change our findings regarding overall class solidarity.

6. Note that the equation for "s" has been derived using the actual data where the outcomes equal zero. Had we used DeMorgan's Law (Ragin 1987, pp. 98–99) to derive the equation for "s" based on the equation for "S," the assumption would be that all the hypothetical (nonexisting) cases are zeros, since DeMorgan's Law yields an equation for everything that is not "S." Everything that is not "S" includes both the combinations for "s" as well as 121 hypothetical combinations for which outcomes are unknown. That the diversity index falls to 5.5 percent means that a high level of confidence only applies for those cases represented by available data.

7. One should think of the causes in a QCA as the prevailing conditions or context of a case, rather than as continuous variables where an increase in "X" leads to an increase in "Y."

8. Researchers often ignore missing cases, which can lead to the possibly erroneous conclusion that absent cases could never exist. To be sure, some combinations are illogical and empirically improbable (Ragin 1987, p. 109), but such questions require explicit consideration.

9. We chose the 1937 drive at Ford for comparison because blacks were not hired in significant numbers at other auto companies.

References

Aarim-Heriot, Najia. 2003. *Chinese Immigrants, African Americans, and Racial Anxiety in the United States, 1848–82.* Chicago: University of Illinois Press.

Allen, Theodore W. 1994. *Occupied America: A History of Chicanos.* New York: Harper and Row.

Asher, Robert. 1978. "Painful Memories: The Historical Consciousness of Steelworkers and the Steel Strike of 1919." *Pennsylvania History* 45: 61–86.

Atlanta Journal-Constitution. (Specific dates and articles cited in the text.)

Axelrod, Robert. 1984. *The Evolution of Cooperation.* New York: Basic Books.

———. 1986. "An Evolutionary Approach to Norms." *American Political Science Review* 80: 1097–1111.

Bailer, Lloyd H. 1943. "The Negro Automobile Worker." *Journal of Political Economy* 51: 415–28.

Banton, Michael. 1980. *Racial and Ethnic Competition.* New York: Cambridge University Press.

Barrett, James R., and David Roediger. 1997. "Inbetween Peoples: Race, Nationality and the 'New Immigrant' Working Class." *Journal of American Ethnic History* 16(3): 3–44.

Bates, Robert, Avner Creif, Margaret Levi, Jean-Laurent Rosenthal, and Barry R. Weingast. 1998. *Analytical Narratives.* Princeton: Princeton University Press.

Becker, Gary S. 1957. *The Economics of Discrimination.* Chicago: University of Chicago Press.

Belanger, Sarah, and Maurice Pinard. 1991. "Ethnic Movements and the Competition Model. Some Missing Links." *American Sociological Review* 56: 446–52.

Beney, M. Ada. 1937. "Wages, Hours, and Employment in the United States, 1914–1936." *National Industrial Conference Board Studies* No. 229.

Berg, Elliot J. 1961. "Backward Sloping Supply Functions in Dual Economies: The African Case." *Quarterly Journal of Economics* 75: 468–92.

Bernstein, Irving. 1966. *The Lean Years: A History of the American Worker, 1920–1933*. Boston: Houghton Mifflin.

———. 1970. *The Turbulent Years: A History of the American Worker, 1933–1941*. Boston: Houghton Mifflin.

———. 1985. *A Caring Society: A History of the American Worker, 1933–1941*. Boston: Houghton Mifflin.

Bianco, William T., Peter C. Ordeshook, and George Tsebelis. 1990. "Crime and Punishment: Are One-Shot, Two-Person Games Enough?" *American Political Science Review* 84: 569–86.

Billings, Dwight B. 1979. *Planters and the Making of the New South: Class, Politics, and Development in North Carolina, 1865–1900*. Chapel Hill: University of North Carolina Press.

Billington, Monroe Lee. 1975. *The Political Revolution in the Twentieth Century*. New York: Charles Scribner and Sons.

Blalock, Hubert M. 1967. *Toward a Theory of Minority Group Relations*. New York: Wiley.

Blauner, Robert. 1972. *Racial Oppression in America*. New York: Harper and Row.

Blumer, Herbert. 1990. *Industrialization as an Agent of Social Change*. Edited by David R. Maines and Thomas J. Morrione. New York: Aldine de Grutyer.

Bodnar, John. 1982. *Workers' World: Kinship, Community, and Protest in an Industrial Society, 1900–1940*. Baltimore: The Johns Hopkins University Press.

Bonacich, Edna. 1972. "A Theory of Ethnic Antagonism: The Split Labor Market." *American Sociological Review* 37: 547–59.

———. 1973. "A Theory of Middleman Minorities." *American Sociological Review* 38: 583–94.

———. 1975. "Abolition, the Extension of Slavery, and the Position of Free Blacks: A Study of Split Labor Market in the United States, 1830–1863." *American Journal of Sociology* 81: 601–28.

———. 1976. "Advanced Capitalism and Black/White Race Relations in the United States: A Split Labor Market Interpretation." *American Sociological Review* 41: 34–51.

———. 1979. "The Past, Present, and Future of Split Labor Market Theory." *Research in Race and Ethnic Relations* 1: 17–64.

———. 1984. "U.S. Capitalist Development: A Background to Asian Immigration." Pp. 79–129 in *Labor Immigration Under Capitalism*, edited by Lucie Cheng and Edna Bonacich. Berkeley: University of California Press.

Bonacich, Edna, and Lucie Cheng. 1984. "A Theoretical Orientation to International Labor Migration." Pp. 1–56 in *Labor Migration Under Capitalism*, edited by L. Cheng and E. Bonacich. Berkeley: University of California Press.

Boryczka, Raymond, and Lorin Lee Cary. 1982. *No Strength Without Union: An Illustrated History of Ohio Workers, 1803–1980*. Ohio Historical Society.

Boswell, Terry E. 1981. "State Repression and Legitimation: The Disorganization of Labor in the Arizona Copper Industry in 1971." *The Theoretical Review* 23: 13–24, 36–37.

————. 1984. "World Formation of World Mode of Production? Alternative Approaches to World-System Analysis." *Contemporary Crises* 8(4): 379–84.

————. 1986. "A Split Labor Market Interpretation of Discrimination Against Chinese Immigrants, 1850–1882." *American Sociological Review* 51: 352–71.

Boswell, Terry, and Cliff Brown. 1999. "The Scope of General Theory: Methods for Linking Deductive and Inductive Comparative History." *Sociological Methods and Research* 28(2): 154–85.

Boswell, Terry, and David Jorjani. 1988. "Uneven Development and the Origins of Split Labor Market Discrimination: A Comparison of Black, Chinese, and Mexican Immigrant Minorities in the United States." Pp. 169–85 in *Racism, Sexism, and the World System*, edited by J. Smith, J. Collins, T. K. Hopkins, A. Muhammad. New York: Greenwood.

Boswell, Terry, and Dimitri Stevis. 2001. "From National Resistance to International Labor Politics." Pp. 150–200 in *Globalization and the Politics of Resistance*, edited by Barry K. Gills. Hampshire, UK: MacMillan.

Boswell, Terry, and John Brueggemann. 2000. "Labor Market Segmentation and the Cultural Division of Labor in the Copper Mining Industry, 1880–1920." *Research in Social Movements, Conflicts and Change*. 22: 193–218.

Bowles, Samuel, and Herbert Gintis. 1993. "The Revenge of Homo Economics: Contested Exchange and the Revival of Political Economy." *The Journal of Economic Perspectives* 7(1): 83–102.

Boyer, Richard O., and Herbert Morais. 1975. *Labor's Untold Story*. New York: United Electrical, Radio, and Machine Workers of America.

Boyle, Kevin. 1995. "There are No Union Sorrows that the Union Can't Heal: The Struggle for Racial Equality in the United Automobile Workers, 1940–1965." *Labor History* 36(1): 5–23.

Boyte, Harry. 1972. "The Textile Industry: Keel of Southern Industrialization." *Radical America* 6: 4–49.

Braverman, Harry. 1974. *Labor and Monopoly Capital*. New York: Monthly Review Press.

Brecher, Jeremy. 1972. *Strike!* Boston: South End Press.

Brissenden, Paul F. 1919. *The IWW: A Study of American Syndicalism*. New York: Columbia University Press.

Brody, David. 1965. *Labor in Crisis: The Steel Strike of 1919*. Philadelphia: J.B. Lippincott.

————. 1980. *Workers in Industrial America*. New York: Oxford University Press.

————. 1987. "The Origins of Modern Steel Unionism: The SWOC Era." Pp. 13–29 in *Forging a Union of Steel*, edited by Paul F. Clark, Peter Gottlieb, and Donald Kennedy et al. Ithaca, NY: ILR Press.

————. 1998. *Steelworkers in America: The Nonunion Era, 2nd Edition.* Cambridge: Harvard University Press.

Brooks, Robert R. R. 1940. *As Steel Goes . . . Unionism in a Basic Industry.* New Haven: Yale University Press.

Brown, Cliff. 1998. *Racial Conflict and Violence in the Labor Market: Roots in the 1919 Steel Strike.* New York: Garland.

————. 2000. "The Role of Employers in Split Labor Markets: An Event-Structure Analysis of Racial Conflict and AFL Organizing, 1917–1919." *Social Forces* 79: 653–81.

Brown, Cliff, and Terry Boswell. 1995. "Strikebreaking or Solidarity in the Great Steel Strike of 1919: A Split Labor Market, Game-Theoretic, and QCA Analysis." *American Journal of Sociology* 100(6): 1479–1519.

Brown, Cliff, and John Brueggemann. 1997. "Mobilizing Interracial Solidarity: A Comparison of the 1919 and 1937 Steel Industry Labor Organizing Drives." *Mobilization* 2(1): 47–70.

Brueggemann, John. 2000. "The Power and Collapse of Paternalism: the Ford Motor Company and Black Workers, 1937–1941." *Social Problems* 47: 220–40.

————. 2002. "Racial Considerations and Social Policy in the 1930s: Economic Change and Political Opportunities." *Social Science History* 26(1): 139–79.

Brueggemann, John, and Terry Boswell. 1998. "Realizing Solidarity: Sources of Interracial Unionism During the Great Depression." *Work and Occupations* 24(4): 436–82.

Brueggemann, John, and Cliff Brown. 2000. "Strategic Labor Organizing in the Era of Industrial Transformation: A Comparative Historical Analysis of Unionization in Steel and Coal, 1870–1916." *Review of Radical Political Economics* 32(4): 541–76.

————. 2003. "The Decline of Industrial Unionism in the Meatpacking Industry: Event-Structure Analysis of Labor Unrest, 1946–87." *Work and Occupations.* 30(3): 327–61.

Burawoy, Michael. 1981. "The Capitalist State in South Africa: Marxist and Sociological Perspectives on Race and Class." Pp. 279–335 in *Political Power and Social Theory*, edited by Maurice Zeitlin, Greenwich, CT: JAI Press.

Campbell, Persia C. 1969 (1923). *Chinese Coolie Emigration to Countries Within the British Empire.* New York: Negro Universities Press.

Carlton, David L. 1982. *Mill and Town in South Carolina, 1880–1920.* Baton Rouge: Louisiana State University Press.

Carranco, Lynwood. 1978. "Chinese Expulsion from Humbolt County." Pp. 329–40 in *Anti-Chinese Violence in North America*, edited by Roger Daniels. New York: Arno.

Cayton, Horace R., and George S. Mitchell. 1939. *Black Workers and the New Unions*. Chapel Hill: The University of North Carolina Press.

Chalmers, David. M. 1965. *Hooded Americanism: The History of the Ku Klux Klan*. Garden City, NY: Doubleday.

Chase-Dunn, Christopher. 1987. "Cycles, Trends or Transformation?: The World-System Since 1945." Pp. 92–137 in *America's Changing Role in the World-System*, edited by Terry Boswell and Albert Bergesen. New York: Praeger.

———. 1992. "The Spiral of Capitalism and Socialism." Pp. 165–87 in *Research in Social Movements, Conflict and Change*, vol. 14, edited by L. F. Kreisberg. Greenwich, CT: JAI Press.

Chen, Jack. 1980. *The Chinese of America*. San Francisco: Harper and Row.

Cheng, Lucie. 1984. "Free, Indentured, Enslaved: Chinese Prostitutes in Nineteenth-Century America." Pp. 402–34 in *Labor Immigration Under Capitalism*, edited by Lucie Cheng and Edna Bonacich. Berkeley: University of California Press.

Cheng, Lucie, and Edna Bonacich, eds. 1984. *Labor Immigration Under Capitalism: Asian Workers in the United States Before World War II*. Berkeley: University of California Press.

Chiu, Ping. 1967. *Chinese Labor in California, 1850–1880: An Economic Study*. Madison: Logmark Edition, Society Press of the State Historical Society of Wisconsin for the Department of History, University of Wisconsin.

Christiansen, John B. 1979. "The Split Labor Market Theory and Filipino Exclusion: 1927–1934." *Phylon* 40: 66–74.

Christopher (Paul Revere) Papers, Special Collections Department, Georgia State University.

Clawson, Dan, and Mary Ann Clawson. 1999. "What Happened to the U.S. Labor Movement? Union Decline and Renewal." *Annual Review of Sociology* 25: 95–111.

Cobb, James C. 1982. *The Selling of the South: The Crusade for Industrial Development, 1936–1980*. Baton Rouge: Louisiana State University Press.

Cochran, Bert. 1977. *Labor and Communism*. Princeton: Princeton University Press.

Cohen, Lizabeth. 1992. *Making a New Deal*. New York: Cambridge University Press.

Coleman, McAlister. 1943. *Men and Coal*. New York: Farrar and Rinehart, Inc.

Collins, Randall. 1988. *Theoretical Sociology*. New York: Harcourt Brace Jovanovich.

Conell, Carol, and Kim Voss. 1990. "Formal Organization and the Fate of Social Movements: Craft Association and Class Alliance in the Knights of Labor." *American Sociological Review* 55: 255–69.

Coolidge, Mary. 1909. *Chinese Immigration*. New York: Holt.

Cornfield, Daniel B. 1985. "Economic Segmentation and Expression of Labor Unrest: Striking Versus Quitting in the Manufacturing Sector." *Social Science Quarterly* 66(2): 247–65.

————. 1986. "Declining Union Membership in the Post–World War II Era: The United Furniture Workers of America, 1939–1982." *American Journal of Sociology* 91(5): 1112–53.

Cornfield, Daniel B., Holly J. McCammon. 2003.1 "Reviatlizing Labor: Global Perpsectives and a Research Agenda." Volume 11 in the JAI sereis *Research in the Sociology of Work*. Amsterdam: Elsevier.

Cressey, Donald R. 1950. "Criminal Violation of Financial Trust." *American Sociological Review* 15: 738–43.

Cummings, Scott. 1977. "Racial Prejudice and Political Orientations Among Blue Collar Workers." *Social Science Quarterly* 57: 907–20.

Darby, Michael R. 1976. "Three-and-a-Half Million U.S. Employees Have Been Mislaid: Or, an Explanation of Unemployment, 1934–1941." *Journal of Political Economy* 84(1): 1–16.

Daugherty, Caroll R., Melvin G. De Hazeau, and Samuel S. Stratton. 1937. *The Economics of the Iron and Steel Industry*. New York: McGraw-Hill.

Davis, Allison, B. B. Gardner, and M. R. Gardner. 1941. *Deep South*. Chicago: University of Chicago Press.

Dickerson, Dennis C. 1986. *Out of the Crucible: Black Steelworkers in Western Pennsylvania*. Albany: State University of New York Press.

Drake, St. Clair, and Horace Cayton. 1945. *Black Metropolis*. New York: Harcourt, Brace and Company.

Draper, Alan. 1994. *Conflict of Interests: Organized Labor and the Civil Rights Movement in the South, 1954–1968*. Ithaca, NY: ILR Press.

Draper, Theodore. 1972. "Communists and Miners, 1928–1933." *Dissent* 19: 371–92.

Drass, Kriss, and Charles Ragin. 1986. *QCA: A Microcomputer Package for Qualitative Comparative Analysis of Social Data*. Center for Urban Affairs and Policy Research, Northwestern University.

Dubofsky, Melvyn. 1988. *We Shall Be All: A History of the Industrial Workers of the World*. Chicago: University of Illinois Press.

————. 1995. "Labor Unrest in the United States, 1906–90." *Review* 18: 125–35.

Dubofsky, Melvyn, and Warren Van Tine. 1977. *John L. Lewis: A Biography*. New York: Quadrangle.

DuBois, W. E. B. 1935. *Black Reconstruction in America*. New York: S. A. Russell Company.

Dunbar, Anthony P. 1981. *Against the Grain: Southern Radicals and Prophets, 1929–1959*. Charlottesville: University Press of Virginia.

Eckstein, Harry. 1975. "Case Study and Theory in Political Science." Pp. 79–137 in *Handbook of Political Science*, vol. 7, edited by F. I. Greenstein and N. Polsby. Reading, MA: Addison-Wesley.

Edelman, Murray. 1957. "The New Deal Sensitivity to Labor Interests." Pp. 157–92 in *Labor and the New Deal*, edited by Milton Derber and Edwin Young. Madison: The University of Wisconsin Press.

Edwards, Richard. 1979. *Contested Terrain*. New York: Basic Books.

Elster, Jon. 1985. *Making Sense of Marx*. New York: Cambridge University Press.

Epstein, Abraham. 1969. *The Negro Migrant in Pittsburgh*. New York: Arno.

Feldman, Herman. 1931. *Racial Factors in American Industry*. New York: Harper Brothers.

Fisher, Douglas A. 1951. *Steel Serves the Nation, 1901–51: The Fifty Year Story of United States Steel*. New York: United States Steel Corporation.

Fleming, R. W. 1957. "The Significance of the Wagner Act." Pp. 121–56 in *Labor and the New Deal*, edited by Milton Derber and Edwin Young. Madison: The University of Wisconsin Press.

Fligstein, Neil. 1981. *Going North: Migration of Blacks and Whites from the South, 1900–1950*. New York: Academic Press.

Florant, Lyonel C. 1942. "Negro Internal Migration." *American Sociological Review* 7: 782–91.

Foner, Philip S. 1964 (vol. 3); 1973 (vol. 6); 1988 (vol. 8). *History of the Labor Movement in the United States*. New York: International Publishers.

———. 1974. *Organized Labor and the Black Worker*. New York: Praeger.

Foner, Philip S., and Ronald L. Lewis, eds. 1981. *The Black Worker: A Documentary History from Colonial Times to the Present* (vol. 6). Philadelphia: Temple University Press.

Fong, Eric W., and William T. Markam. 1991. "Immigration, Ethnicity, and Conflict: The California Chinese, 1849–1882." *Sociological Inquiry* 61: 471–90.

Foster, James Caldwell. 1975. *The Union Politic: The C.I.O. Political Action Committee*. Columbia: University of Missouri Press.

Foster, William Z. 1920. *The Great Steel Strike and Its Lessons*. New York: Huebsch.

Frederickson, George M. 2002. *Racism: A Short History*. Princeton: Princeton University Press.

Frederickson, Mary. 1991. "Race, Class, and Gender: Toward a New Synthesis in Southern Textile History." Paper presented at Southern Labor Studies Conference. Atlanta.

Freeman, Richard B., and James L. Medoff. 1984. *What Do Uions Do?* New York: Basic Books.

Frisch, Paul A. 1984. "Gibraltar of Unionism: Women, Blacks, and the Anti-Chinese Movement in Butte, Montana, 1880–1900." *Southwest Economy and Society:* 3–13.

Fritz, Wilbert G., and Theodore A. Veenstra. 1935. *Regional Shifts in the Bituminous Coal Industry*. Pittsburgh: University of Pittsburgh Press.

Gadsby, M. A. 1919. "The Steel Strike." *Monthly Labor Review* 9: 79–94.

Gambs, John S. 1932. *The Decline of the IWW*. New York: Columbia University Press.

Garraty, John A. 1960. "The United States Steel Corporation Versus Labor: The Early Years." *Labor History* 1: 3–38.

Garrison, Joseph Yates. 1976. "Paul Revere Christopher: Southern Labor Leader, 1919–1975." PhD Dissertation, Georgia State University.

Gartman, David. 1986. *Auto Slavery: The Labor Process in the American Automobile Industry, 1897–1950*. London: Rutgers University Press.

Genovese, Eugene. 1965. *The Political Economy of Slavery*. New York: Random House.

Gerstle, Gary. 1993. "Working-Class Racism: Broaden the Focus." *International Labor and Working Class History* 44: 33–40.

Gibson, Otis. 1877. *Chinese in America*. San Francisco.

Goldfield, Michael. 1987. *The Decline of Organized Labor in the United States*. Chicago: University of Chicago Press.

———. 1993. "Race and the CIO: The Possibilities for Racial Egalitarianism During the 1930s and 1940s." *Industrial Labor and Working-Class History* 44: 1–32.

———. 1994. "Race and the CIO: Reply to Critics." *International Labor and Working Class History* 46: 143–60.

———. 1997. *The Color of Politics*. New York: New Press.

———. 1998. "Race and Labor Organization in the United States." Pp. 87–99 in *Rising from the Ashes?* edited by Ellen Meiksins Wood, Peter Meiksins, and Michael Yates. New York: Monthly Labor Review Press.

Goodwyn, Lawrence. 1976. *Democratic Promise: The Populist Movement in America*. New York: Oxford University Press.

Gordon, David M., Richard Edwards, and Michael Reich. 1988. *Segmented Work, Divided Workers*. New York: Cambridge University Press.

Gordon, Milton M. 1964. *Assimilation in American Life: The Role of Race, Religion, and National Origins*. New York: Oxford University Press.

———. 1978. *Human Nature, Class, and Ethnicity*. New York: Oxford University Press.

———, ed. 1981. *America as a Multicultural Society*. Philadelphia: American Academy of Political and Social Science.

Gottlieb, Peter. 1978. "Migration and Jobs: The New Black Workers in Pittsburgh, 1916–30." *Western Pennsylvania Historical Magazine* 61: 1–15.

———. 1987. *Making Their Own Way: Southern Blacks' Migration to Pittsburgh, 1916–30*. Chicago: University of Illinois Press.

Grantham, Dewey. 1988. *The Life and Death of the Solid South*. Louisville: University of Kentucky Press.

Green, James R. 1980. *The World of the Worker*. New York: Hill and Wang.

Greenberg, Stanley B. 1980. *Race and State in Capitalist Development: Comparative Perspectives.* New Haven, CT: Yale University Press.

Greene, Lorenzo J., and Carter G. Woodson. 1930. *The Negro Wage Earner.* Washington, DC: The Association for the Study of Negro Life and History, Inc.

Greenwood, Michael. 1975. "Research in Internal Migration." *Journal of Economic Literature.* XIII(2): 397–433.

Griffin, John I. 1939. *Strikes: A Study in Quantitative Economics.* New York: Columbia University Press.

Griffin, Larry J., and Charles C. Ragin. 1994. "Some Observations on Formal Methods of Qualitative Analysis." *Siological Methods and Research* 23(1): 4–21.

Griffith, Barbara. 1988. *The Crisis of American Labor: Operation Dixie and the Defeat of the C.I.O.* Philadelphia: Temple University Press.

Grossman, James R. 1989. *Land of Hope: Chicago, Black Southerners, and the Great Migration.* Chicago: University of Chicago Press.

Gulick, Charles A. 1924. *Labor Policy of the United States Steel Corporation.* New York: Columbia University Press.

Gutman, Herbert G. 1976. *Work, Culture, and Society in Industrializing America.* Vintage Books: New York.

Gyory, Andrew. 1998. *Closing the Gate: Race, Politics, and the Chinese Exclusion Act.* Chapel Hill: University of North Carolina Press.

Hall, Jacquelyn Dowd, James Leloudis, Robert Korstad, Mary Murphy, Lu Ann Jones, and Christopher B. Daly. 1987. *Like A Family: The Making of a Southern Cotton Mill World.* Chapel Hill: University of North Carolina Press.

Hall, Thomas D. 1986. "Incorporation in the World-System: Toward a Critique." *American Sociological Review* 51(3): 390–402.

Hannan, Michael T. 1979. "The Dynamics of Ethnic Boundaries in Modern States." Pp. 253–75 in *National Development and the World System*, edited by J. Meyer and M. T. Hannan. Chicago: University of Chicago Press.

Harbison, Frederick H. 1937. *Collective Bargaining in the Steel Industry: 1937.* Princeton: Princeton University Press.

Hawley, Amos. 1945. "Dispersion Versus Integration: Apropos of a Solution of Race Problems." In *Papers of the Michigan Academy of Science, Arts, and Letters.* Ann Arbor: University of Michigan Press.

Hechter, Michael. 1990. "The Attainment of Solidarity in Intentional Communities." *Rationality and Society* 2(2): 142–55.

Heckathorn, Douglas D. 1988. "Collective Sanctions and the Creation of Prisoner's Dilemma Norms." *American Journal of Sociology* 94: 535–62.

———. 1989. "Collective Action and the Second-Order Free-Rider Problem." *Rationality and Society* 1: 78–100.

———. 1990a. "Collective Sanctions and Compliance Norms: A Formal Theory of Group-Mediated Social Control." *American Sociological Review* 55: 366–84.

———. 1990b. "A Sequential Decision Model for Mixed Sanction Systems." *Policy Studies Research Group*. Working Paper #125. University of Missouri-Kansas City, Department of Sociology.

———. 1991. "Collective Sanctions and Group Heterogeneity: Cohesion and Polarization in Normative Systems." *Advances in Group Processes* 9: 41–63.

———. 1993. "Collective Action and Group Heterogeneity: Voluntary Provision versus Selective Incentives." *American Sociological Review* 58: 329–50.

Henri, Florette. 1975. *Black Migration: Movement North 1900–1920*. Garden City: Anchor.

Herring, Harriet L. 1949. *Passing of the Mill Village: Revolution in a Southern Institution*. Chapel Hill, University of North Carolina Press.

Hicks, Alexander. 1994. "Qualitative Comparative Analysis and Analytical Induction: The Case of the Programmatic Emergence of the Social Security State." *Sociological Methods and Research* 23(1): 86–113.

Hill, Arnold T. 1925. "The Negro in Industry." *American Federationist* 32: 915–20.

Hill, Herbert. 1965. "Racial Practices of Organized Labor." *New Politics* 4(2): 26–46.

———. 1968. "The Racial Practices of Organized Labor: The Contemporary Record." Pp. 286–357 in *The Negro and The American Labor Movement*, edited by Julius Jacobson. New York: Anchor.

———. 1988. "Myth-making as Labor History: Herbert Gutman and the United Mine Workers of America." *International Journal of Politics, Culture and Society* 2(2): 132–200.

———. 1996. "The Problem of Race in American Labor History." *Reviews in American History* 24(2): 189–208.

———. 1998. "Lichtenstein's Fictions: Meany, Reuther, and the Civil Rights Act." *New Politics*. 7(1): 82–107.

Hilton, Mike. 1979. "The Split Labor Market and Chinese Immigration, 1848–1882." *The Journal of Ethnic Studies* 6 (4): 99–108.

Hodson, Randy. 1995. "Cohesion or Conflict? Race, Solidarity, and Resisitance in the Workplace." *Research in the Sociology of Work* 5: 135–59.

Howard, Walter T. 2001. "The National Miners Union: Communists and Miners in the Pennsylvania Anthracite, 1928–1931." *The Pennsylvania Magazine of History and Biography* 125: 91–124.

Howe, Irving, and B. J. Widick. 1949. *The UAW and Walter Reuther*. New York: Random House.

Howell, Frances Baseden. 1982. "A Split Labor Market: Mexican Farmworkers in the Southwest." *Sociological Inquiry* 2: 132–40.

Hunter (Floyd) Papers. Special Collections Department, Emory University.

Hurst, C. E. 1972. "Race, Class, and Consciousness." *American Sociological Review* 37: 658–70.

Ingham, John N. 1991. *Making Iron and Steel: Independent Mills in Pittsburgh, 1820–1920*. Columbus: Ohio State University Press.

Interchurch World Movement. 1920. *Report on the Steel Strike of 1919*. New York: Harcourt, Brace, and Howe.

Jackman, Mary. 1994. *The Velvet Glove*. Berkeley: University of Berkeley Press.

James, David E. 1988. "The Transformation of the Southern Racial State: Class and Race Determinants of Local State Structures." *American Sociological Review* 53: 191–208.

Jensen, Vernon H. 1950. *Heritage of Conflict*. New York: Cornell University Press.

Johnson, James P. 1979. *The Politics of Soft Coal*. Chicago: University of Illinois Press.

Kelley, Robin D. G. 1990. *Hammer and Hoe*. Chapel Hill: University of North Carolina Press.

Kennedy, Louise V. 1930. *The Negro Peasant Turns Cityward: Effects of Recent Migrations to Northern Centers*. New York: Columbia University Press.

Kennedy (Stetson) Papers. Special Collections Department, Georgia State University.

Kennedy (Stetson) Collection. Schomberg Center for Research in Black Culture, New York Public Library; referred to as Schomberg Center.

Kennedy, Stetson. Letters to Author (Ralph Peters). 1/3/85; 3/15/85; 4/10/85; 10/10/85; 3/5/86; referred to as LTA.

Kennedy, Stetson. Oral Interview with Author (Ralph Peters). March 1983.

Kennedy, Stetson. 1946. *Southern Exposure*. New York: Doubleday.

Kimeldorf, Howard, William Regensburger, and Maurice Zeitlin. 1987. *Insurgent Workers: Studies of the Origins of Industrial Unionism on the East and West Coast Docks in the 1930s*. Institute of Industrial Relations: University of California.

Kiser, Edgar, and Michael Hechter. 1991. "The Role of General Theory in Comparative-Historical Sociology." *American Journal of Sociology* 97: 1–30.

———. 1998. "Rational Choice Theory and its Critics." *American Journal of Sociology* 104: 785–816.

Korstad, Robert. 1993. "The Possibilities for Racial Egalitarianism: Context Matters." *International Labor and Working Class History* 44: 41–44.

Korstad, Robert, and Nelson Lichtenstein. 1988. "Opportunities Found and Lost: Labor, Radicals, and the Early Civil Rights Movement." *Journal of American History* 75(3): 786–811.

Kusmer, Kenneth L. 1976. *A Ghetto Takes Shape: Black Cleveland, 1870–1930*. Chicago: University of Illinois.

Labor History. 2000 "Symposium on Daniel Letwin: The Challenge of Interracial Unionism." 41(1): 63–90.

Lamont, Michele. 2000. *The Dignity of Working Men*. Cambridge: Harvard University Press.

Letwin, Daniel. 1998. *The Challenge of Interracial Unionism: Alabama Coal Miners, 1878–1921*. Chapel Hill: University of North Carolina Press.

Levenstein, Harvey A. 1981. *Communism, Anti-Communism, and the CIO.* Westport, CT: Greenwood Press.

Lewis, Edward E. 1931. *The Mobility of the Negro: A Study in the American Labor Supply.* New York: Columbia University Press.

Lewis, Ronald L. 1987. *Black Coal Miners in America.* Lexington: University Press of Kentucky.

Lichtenstein, Nelson. 1982. *Labor's War at Home: The CIO in World War II.* New York: Cambridge University Press.

———. 1995. *The Most Dangerous Man in Detroit.* New York: Harper Collins.

———. 1999. "Walter Reuther in Black and White: A Rejoinder to Herbert Hill." *New Politics* 7: 133–47.

———. 2002. *State of the Union.* Princeton: Princeton University Press.

Lichtenstein, Nelson, and Stephen Meyer. 1989. *On the Line: Essays in the History of Auto Work.* Chicago: University of Illinois Press.

Lieberson, Stanley. 1961. "A Societal Theory of Race Relations." *American Sociological Review* 26: 902–10.

———. 1980. *A Piece of the Pie: Black and White Immigrants Since 1880.* Berkeley: University of California Press.

———. 1991. "Small N's and Big Conclusions: An Examination of the Reasoning in Comparative Studies Based on a Small Number of Cases." *Social Forces* 70: 307–20.

Lingenfelter, Richard E. 1974. *The Hardrock Miners.* Berkeley: University of California Press.

Locklear, William R. 1978. "The Celestials and the Angels." Pp. 229–56 in *Anti-Chinese Violence in North America,* edited by Roger Daniels. New York: Arno Press.

Lockwood, David. 1966. "Sources of Variation in Working Class Images of Society." *American Sociological Review* 14(2): 249–67.

Loewen, James W. 1971. *The Mississippi Chinese: Between Black and White.* Cambridge: Harvard University Press.

Long, Priscilla. 1989. *Where the Sun Never Shines: A History of America's Bloody Coal Industry.* New York: Paragon House.

Lynd, Staughton. 1973. *American Labor Radicalism.* New York: John Wiley and Sons.

———. 1996. *We Are All Leaders: The Alternative Unionism of the Early 1930s.* Urbana: University of Illinois Press.

Makabe, Toko. 1981. "The Theory of the Split Labor Market: A Comparison of the Japanese Experience in Brazil and Canada." *Social Forces* 59: 786–809.

Mann, Susan Archer. 1990. *Agrarian Capitalism in Theory and Practice.* Chapel Hill: University of North Carolina Press.

Marks, Carole. 1981. "Split Labor Markets and Black-White Relations, 1865–1920." *Phylon* 43: 293–308.

————. 1983. "Lines of Communication, Recruitment Mechanisms, and the Great Migration of 1916–1918." *Social Problems* 31: 73–83.

————. 1989. *Farewell—We're Good and Gone: The Great Black Migration*. Indianapolis: Indiana University Press.

Marshall, Ray. 1965. *The Negro in Organized Labor*. New York: John Wiley and Sons.

————. 1967. *Labor in the South*. Cambridge: Harvard University Press.

Martin, Katherine F., ed. 1980. *Operation Dixie: The C.I.O. Organizing Committee Papers: A Guide to the Microfilm Edition, 1946–1953*. New York: New York Times Co.

Massey, Douglas, J. Edward Taylor. 2004. *International Migration: Prospects and Policies in a Global Market*. New York: Oxford University Press.

McAdam, Doug. 1983. "Tactical Innovation and the Pace of Insurgency." *American Sociological Review* 48: 735–54.

————. 1986. "Recruitment to High-risk Activism: The Case of Freedom Summer." *American Journal of Sociology* 92: 64–90.

————. 1999. *Political Process and the Development of Black Insurgency, 1930–1970*, 2nd ed. Chicago: University of Chicago Press

McAdam, Doug, John D. McCarthy, and Mayer N. Zald. 1988. "Social Movements." Pp. 695–737 in *Handbook of Sociology*, edited by Neil J. Smelser. London: Sage Publications.

McCarthy, John D., and Meyer Zald. 1977. "Resource Mobilization and Social Movements: A Partial Theory." *American Journal of Sociology* 82: 1212–41.

McKenzie, R. D. 1928. *Oriental Exclusion*. Chicago: University of Chicago Press.

McKiven, Henry M., Jr. 1995. *Iron and Steel: Class, Race, and Community in Birmingham, Alabama, 1875–1920*. Chapel Hill: University of North Carolina Press.

McLaurin, Melton. 1971. *Paternalism and Protest: Southern Cotton Mills and Organized Labor, 1875–1905*. Westport: Greenwood Press.

————. 1978. *The Knights of Labor in the South*. Westport: Greenwood.

McHugh, Cathy L. 1988. *Mill Family: The Labor System in the Southern Cotton Textile Industry, 1880–1915*. New York: Oxford University Press.

Mei, June. 1984. "Socioeconomic Origins of Emigration: Guang Dong to California, 1850–1882." Pp. 219–47 in *Labor Immigration Under Capitalism*, edited by Lucie Cheng and Edna Bonacich. Berkeley: University of California Press.

Meier, August, and Elliot Rudwick. 1979. *Black Detroit and the Rise of the UAW*. New York: Oxford University Press.

Miller, Stuart Creighton. 1969. *The Unwelcome Immigrant: The American Image of the Chinese*. Berkeley: University of California Press.

Millett, Stephen. 1972. "Charles Ruthenberg: The Development of an American Communist, 1909–1927." *Ohio History* 81: 193–209.

Milton, David. 1982. *The Politics of US Labor.* New York: Monthly Review Press.

Mining and Scientific Press. 1860. October 1–34.

Mohl, Raymond A., and Neil Betten. 1986. *Steel City: Urban and Ethnic Pattern in Gary, Indiana, 1906–1950.* New York: Holmes and Meier.

Montgomery, David. 1979. *Workers' Control in America.* Cambridge: Cambridge University Press.

―――. 1987. *The Fall of the House of Labor: The Work Place, The State, and American Labor Activities: 1865–1925.* New York: Cambridge University Press.

Monthly Labor Review. 1937. "The Negro in Industry: Earnings of Negroes in the Iron and Steel Industry." 44.

―――. 1940. "Earnings and Hours in Bituminous-Coal Mining, 1936." 51.

Muller, Edward N., and Karl-Dieter Opp. 1986. "Rational Choice and Rebellious Collective Action." *American Political Science Review* 80(2): 471–87.

Munley, Kathleen. 1998. "Shopfloor Memories of Organizing." *Labor's Heritage* 9(4): 60–77.

Murray, Robert K. 1951. "Communism and the Great Steel Strike of 1919." *Mississippi Valley Historical Review* 38: 445–66.

―――. 1955. *Red Scare: A Study in National Hysteria, 1919–1920.* Minneapolis: University of Minnesota Press.

Myrdal, Gunnar. 1944. *An American Dilemma: The Negro Problem and Modern Democracy.* New York: Harper and Brothers.

NAACP Records. Library of Congress, Manuscript Room. (Specific dates cited in the text.)

Nee, Victor G., and Brett De Bary Nee. 1973. *Longtime California: A Documentary Study of an American Chinatown.* New York: Pantheon Books.

Nelson, Bruce. 1996. "Class, Race, and Democracy in the CIO: The 'New' Labor History Meets the 'Wages of Whiteness.'" *International Review of Social History* 41: 351–74.

―――. 1998. "Autoworkers, Electoral Politics, and the Convergence of Class and Race: Detroit, 1937–1945." Pp. 121–56 in *Organized Labor and American Politics, 1894–1994,* edited by Kevin Boyle. Albany: State University of New York Press.

―――. 2001. *Divided We Stand.* Princeton: Princeton University Press.

New York Times. (Specific dates and articles cited in the text.)

Newby, I. A. 1989. *Plain Folks in the New South: Social Change and Cultural Persistence, 1880–1915.* Baton Rouge: Louisiana State University Press.

Newman, D. M. 1978. "Work and Community Life in a Southern Textile Town." *Labor History* 19: 204–25.

Noble, David. 1984. *Forces of Production.* New York: Alfred A. Knopf.

Norrell, Robert, Jr. 1991. "Labor at the Ballot Box: Alabama Politics from the New Deal to the Dixiecrat Movement." *Journal of Southern History* LVIII(2): 201–34.

Northrup, Herbert R. 1944. *Organized Labor and the Negro*. New York: Harper and Brothers Publishers.

Northrup, Herbert R. 1970. *Negro Employment in Basic Industry*. Philadelphia: University of Pennsylvania.

Nyden, Linda. 1977. "Black Miners in Western Pennsylvania 1925–31: The National Miners Union and the United Mine Workers of America." *Science and Society* 41: 69–101.

Nyden, Philip W. 1984. *Steelworkers Rank-and-File: The Political Economy of a Union Reform Movement*. New York: Praeger.

Oliver, Pamela. 1980. "Rewards and Punishments as Selective Incentives for Collective Action: Theoretical Investigations." *American Journal of Sociology* 85: 1356–75.

Olson, Mancur. 1965. *The Logic of Collective Action*. Cambridge: Harvard University Press.

Olzak, Susan. 1992. *The Dynamics of Ethnic Competition and Conflict*. Stanford: Stanford University Press.

Olzak, Susan, and Joan Nagel, eds. 1986. *Competitive Ethnic Relations*. Orlando, FL: Academic Press.

Operation Dixie: The CIO Organizing Committee Papers, 1946–1953. Microfilm Edition. Duke University and Georgia State University: UMI; referred to as Dixie Papers.

Paul, Rodman W. 1947. *California Gold: The Beginning of Mining In the Far West*. Cambridge: Harvard University Press.

Park, Robert Ezra. 1950. *Race and Culture*. Glencoe, IL: Free Press.

Peled, Yoav, and Gershon Shafir. 1987. "Split Labor Market and the State: The Effect of Modernization on Jewish Industrial Workers in Tsarist Russia." *American Journal of Sociology* 92: 1435–60.

Perlman, Mark. 1968. "Labor in Eclipse." Pp. 103–45 in *Change and Continuity in Twentieth Century America: The 1920s*, edited by J. Braeman, R. H. Bremmer, and D. Brody. Columbus: Ohio State University Press.

Perrow, Charles. 2002. *Organizing America*. Princeton: Princeton University Press.

Peters, Thomas Ralph. 1994. "Organizing the Already Organized: The Confrontation between Class Paternalism and Union Transformation." PhD Dissertation, Emory University.

Peterson, Florence. 1937. *Strikes in the United States: 1880–1936*. Washington, DC: U.S. GPO.

Peterson, Joyce Shaw. 1979. "Black Automobile Workers in Detroit, 1910–1930." *Journal of Negro History* 64(3): 177–90.

Pflug, Warner. 1971. *The UAW in Pictures*. Detroit: Wayne State University Press.

Piore, Michael J. 1979. *Birds of Passage: Migrant Labor and Industrial Societies*. New York: Cambridge University Press.

Portes, Alejandro. 1978. "Migration and Underdevelopment." *Politics and Society* 8: 1–48.

Powell, Daniel A. 1978. "PAC TO COPE: Thirty-Two Years of Southern Labor in Politics." Pp. 244–55 in *Essays in Southern Labor History*, edited by Gary Fink and Merle E. Reed. Westport: Greenwood Press.

Powers, George. 1972. *Cradle of Steel Unionism, Monongahela Valley, Pa.* East Chicago, IN: Figueroa Printers.

Preis, Art. 1964. *Labor's Giant Step: Twenty Years of the C.I.O.* New York: Pioneer Publishers.

Progress Publishers. 1977. *Recent History of the Labor Movement in the United States: 1918–1939.* Moscow.

Przeworski, Adam. 1985. "Marxism and Rational Choice." *Politics and Society* 14(4): 379–409.

Ragin, Charles C. 1987. *The Comparative Method.* Berkeley: University of California Press.

Ragin, Charles C., Susan Mayer, and Kriss Drass. 1984. "Assessing Discrimination: A Boolean Approach." *American Sociological Review* 49: 221–34.

Rachleff, Peter. 1984. *Black Labor in the South.* Philadelphia: Temple University Press.

Rayback, Joseph T. 1966. *A History of American Labor.* New York: The Free Press.

Rees, Jonathan. 1997. "Giving with One Hand and Taking Away with the Other." *Labor's Heritage* 9(2): 48–57.

Reich, Michael. 1981. *Racial Inequality: A Political-Economic Analysis.* Princeton: Princeton University Press.

Reid, Ira De A. 1930. *Negro Membership in American Labor Unions.* New York: Alexander Press.

Rhoads, Edward J. M. 1999. "Asian Pioneers in the Eastern United States: Chinese Cutlery Workers in Beaver Falls, Pennsylvania, in the 1870s." *Journal of Asian American Studies* 2: 119–55.

———. 2002. " 'White Labor' vs. 'Coolie Labor': The 'Chinese Question' in Pennsylvania in the 1870s." *Journal of American Ethnic History* 21: 3–32.

Robertson, David Brian. 2000. *Capital, Labor, and the State.* Oxford: Rowan and Littlefield.

Robinson, Jesse S. 1920. *The Amalgamated Association of Iron, Steel, and Tin Workers.* Baltimore: Johns Hopkins University Press.

Robinson, R. V., and W. Bell. 1978. "Equality Success and Social Justice in England and the United States." *American Sociological Review* 43(2): 125–43.

Robinson, W. S. 1951. "The Logical Structure of Analytical Induction." *American Sociological Review* 16(6): 812–18.

Roediger, David R. 1991. *The Wages of Whiteness.* New York: Verso.

———. 1994. *Towards the Abolition of Whiteness.* New York: Verso.

Roemer, John. 1979. "Marxist Divide and Conquer." *Bell Journal of Economics* 10(2): 695–705.

Roscigno, Vincent J. and William F. Danaher. 2004. *The Voice of Southern Labor.* Minneapolis: University of Minnesota Press.

Roscigno, Vincent J., and Randy Hodson. 2004. "The Organizational and Social Foundations of Worker Resistance." *American Sociological Review* 69: 14–39.

Rowan, Richard L. 1970. *The Negro in the Textile Industry.* Philadelphia: University of Pennsylvania Press.

Rudwick, Elliott M. 1964. *Race Riot at East St. Louis, July 2, 1917.* Carbondale, IL: Southern Illinois University Press.

Saxton, Alexander. 1971. *The Indispensable Enemy: Labor and the Anti-Chinese Movement in California.* Berkeley: University of California Press.

———. 1990. *The Rise and Fall of the White Republic.* New York: Verso.

Scheuerman, William. 1986. "The Politics of Protest: The Great Steel Strike of 1919–20 in Lackawanna New York." *International Review of Social History* 31: 121–46.

Schlesinger, Arthur M., Jr. 1960. *The Politics of Upheaval.* Boston: Houghton Mifflin.

Scott, Emmett J. 1920. *Negro Migration During the War.* New York: Oxford University Press.

Seltzer, Curtis. 1985. *Fire in the Hole.* Lexington: The University Press of Kentucky.

Senate Committee. 1876. *Chinese Immigration: The Social, Moral, and Political Effects of Chinese Immigration, Testimony Taken before Committee of the Senate of the State of California.* Sacramento: State Printing Office.

Serene, Frank Huff. 1979. "Immigrant Steelworkers in the Monogahela Valley: Their Communities and the Development of a Labor Class Consciousness." PhD Dissertation, University of Pittsburgh.

Seward, George F. 1881. *Chinese Immigration, Its Social and Economic Aspects.* New York: Charles Scribner's Sons.

Sewell, William, Jr. 1988. "Theory of Action, Dialectic, and History: Comment on Coleman." *American Journal of Sociology* 93: 166–72.

Shen, Tso-Chien. 1942. *What "Chinese Exclusion" Really Means.* New York: China Institute In America.

Simpson, Richard L. 1981. "Labor Force Integration and Southern U.S. Textile Unionism." *Research in the Sociology of Work* 1: 381–401.

Singleton, Royce. 1978. "A Theory of Ethnic Oppression: Toward a Reintegration of Cultural and Structural Concepts in Ethnic Relations Theory." *Social Forces* 56: 1001–34.

Siu, Paul C. P. 1952. "The Sojourner." *American Journal of Sociology* 58: 34–44.

Skocpol, Theda. 1980. *States and Social Revolutions: A Comparative Analysis of France, Russia, and China.* Cambridge: Cambridge University Press.

Skocpol, Theda, and Kenneth Finegold. 1990. "Explaining New Deal Labor Policy." *American Political Science Review* 84(4): 1297–1304.

Sofchalk, Donald G. 1996. "Steel Workers Organizing Committee and the Minnesota Iron Workers, 1937–1941." *Journal of the West* 35(2): 33–41.

Spero, Sterling D., and Abram L. Harris. 1969. *The Black Worker.* New York: Kennikat Press.

Stepan-Norris, Judith. 1997a. "The Integration of Workplace and Community Relations at the Ford Rouge Plant, 1930s–1940s." *Political Power and Social Theory* 2: 3–44.

———. 1997b. "The Making of Union Democracy." *Social Forces* 70(2): 475–510.

Stepan-Norris, Judith, and Maurice Zeitlin. 1996. *Talking Union.* Chicago: University of Illinois Press.

Stieber, Jack. 1962. *Governing the UAW.* New York: John Wiley.

Stinchcombe, Arthur. 1990. *Information and Organizations.* Berkeley: University of California Press.

Stokes, Allen Heath. 1977. "Black and White Labor in the Development of the Southern Textile Industry." PhD Dissertation, University of South Carolina.

Stone, Katherine. 1975. "The Origins of Job Structures in the Steel Industry." Pp. 27–84 in *Labor Market Segmentation*, edited by Richard C. Edwards, Michael Reich, and David M. Gordon. London: D.C. Heath and Company.

Stuckey, Sterlin. 1971. "Through the Prism of Folklore: The Black Ethos in Slavery." Pp. 245–68 in. *The Debate Over Slavery; Stanley Elkins and His Critics*, edited by Ann J. Lane. Urbana: University of Illinois Press.

Stryker, Sheldon. 1959. "Social Structure and Prejudice." *Social Problems* 6: 340–54.

Sugrue, Thomas. 1996. "Segmented Work, Race-Conscious Workers: Structure, Agency, and Division in the CIO." *International Review of Social History* 41: 389–406.

Sweeney, Vincent D. 1956. *The United Steelworkers of America.* Pittsburgh: Allied Printing.

Swidler, Ann. 1986. "Culture in Action: Symbols and Strategies." *American Sociological Review* 51(2): 283–86.

Taylor, Michael. 1987. *The Possibility of Cooperation.* Cambridge: Cambridge University Press.

Tilly, Charles. 1978. *From Mobilization to Revolution.* London: Addison-Wesley.

Todd, Arthur C. 1967. *The Cornish Miner in America: The Contribution to the Mining History of the United States by Emigrant Cornish Miners—The Men Called Cousin Jacks.* Glendale, CA: Barton.

Tomlins, Christopher L. 1985. *The State and the Unions.* New York: Cambridge University Press.

Trotter, Joe William, Jr. 1990. *Coal, Class, and Color: Blacks in the New World and the Working Class in American History.* Chicago: University of Illinois Press.

Troy, Leo. 1965. "Trade Union Membership, 1897–1962." *Review of Economics and Statistics* 47(1): 93–113.

Tsai, Shih-Shan Henry. 1983. *China and the Overseas Chinese in the United States, 1868–1911.* Fayetteville, University of Arkansas Press.

Turrini. Joseph M. 1997. "The Newton Steel Strike: A Watershed in the CIO's Failure to Organize 'Little Steel.' " *Labor History* 38(2–3): 229–65.

Tuttle, William M. 1969. "Labor Conflict and Racial Violence: The Black Worker in Chicago, 1894–1919." *Labor History* 10: 408–32.

———. 1985. *Race Riot: Chicago in the Red Summer of 1919.* New York: Atheneum.

U.S. Bureau of Labor Statistics. 1936. "Handbook of Labor Statistics." Bulletin No. 616.

———. *Bulletins, 1937–1950.* U.S. Department of Labor.

———. 1937. "Strikes in the United States, 1880–1936." Bulletin No. 651.

———. 1969. "Employment and Earnings Statistics for the United States 1909–1968." Bulletin No. 1312–16.

———. 1979. "Employment and Earnings Statistics for the United States, 1909–1978." Bulletin No. 1312–11.

U.S. Bureau of the Census. 1892. "Chinese Population."

———. 1913. *Thirteenth Census of the United States.* Vols. 2–3. Washington, DC: GPO.

———. 1918. *Negro Population, 1790–1915.* Washington, DC: GPO.

———. 1922. *Fourteenth Census of the United States.* Vols. 2–3. Washington, DC: GPO.

———. 1935. *Negroes in the United States, 1920–32.* Washington, D.C.: GPO

———. 1940. *Population.* Washington, DC: GPO.

Van den Berghe, Pierre L. 1967. *Race and Racism: A Comparative Perspective.* New York: Wiley.

Vickery, William. 1977. *The Economics of Negro Migration, 1900–1960.* New York: Arno Press.

Voss, Kim. 1993. *The Making of American Exceptionalism: The Knights of Labor and Class Formation in the Nineteenth Century.* Cornell: Cornell University Press.

Wallace, Michael, Beth A. Rubin, and Brian T. Smith. 1988. "American Labor Law: Its Impact on Working-Class Militancy, 1901–1980." *Social Science History* 12: 1–29.

Wallimann, Isidor. 1984. "The Import of Foreign Workers in Switzerland: Labor-Power Reproduction Costs, Ethnic Antagonism, and the Integration of Foreign Workers into Swiss Society." *Research in Social Movements, Conflict and Change* VII: 153–75.

Weinstein, James. 1968. *The Corporate Ideal in the Liberal State, 1900–1918*. Boston: Beacon.

Whitney, Edson L. 1920. "Strikes and Lockouts in 1916, 1917, 1918, and 1919." *Monthly Labor Review* 10: 199–218.

Wilcock, Richard C. 1957. "Industrial Management's Policies Toward Unionism." Pp. 275–316 in *Labor and the New Deal*, edited by Milton Derber and Edwin Young. Madison: The University of Wisconsin Press.

Williamson, Joel A. 1986. *A Rage For Order: Black-White Relations in the South Since Emancipation*. New York: Oxford University Press.

Wilson, William Julius. 1978. *The Declining Significance of Race*. Chicago: University of Chicago Press.

————. 1987. *The Truly Disadvantaged*. Chicago: University of Chicago Press.

Wood, Philip. 1986. *Southern Capitalism: The Political Economy of North Carolina*. Durham: Duke University Press.

Wright, Erik O. 1982. *Class Structure and Income Determination*. New York: Academic Press.

————. 1985. *Classes*. London: Verso.

Wright, Gavin. 1986. *Old South, New South: Revolutions in the Southern Economy Since the Civil War*. New York: Basic Books.

Wyman, Mark. 1979. *Hard Rock Epic: Western Miners and the Industrial Revolution, 1860–1910*. Berkeley: University of California Press.

Wynne, Robert E. 1978. "American Labor Leaders and the Vancouver Anti-Oriental Riot." Pp. 172–79 in *Anti-Chinese Violence in North America*, edited by in Roger Daniels. New York: Arno Press.

Yellen, Samuel. 1974. *American Labor Struggles, 1877–1974*. New York: Monad Press.

Zieger, Robert H., ed. 1991. *Organized Labor in the Twentieth-Century South*. Knoxville: University of Tennessee Press.

Zieger, Robert H. 1995. *The CIO 1935–1955*. Chapel Hill,: University of North Carolina Press.

Zingraff, Rhonda, and Michael P. Shulman. 1984. "Social Bases of Class Consciousness: A Study of Southern Textile Workers with a Comparison by Race." *Social Forces* 31: 98–116.

Zo, Kil Young. 1978. *Chinese Emigration into the United States, 1850–1880*. New York: Arno.

Znaniecki, Florian. 1934. *The Method of Sociology*. New York: Farrar and Reinhart.

About the Authors

Terry Boswell is professor of sociology at Emory University. His scholarly interests include class and race, revolution, world development and inequality, and world-system theory. He is currently writing a book, *Globalization and Labor Unions,* with Dimitris Stevis, and working on a grant for research on world revolutions since 1496 with April Linton.

Cliff Brown is associate professor and sociology at the University of New Hampshire. His research focuses on racial conflict and labor relations in twentieth century America. He is also working on an interdisciplinary project that considers social and economic change in fisheries dependent communities of the North Atlantic.

John Brueggemann is associate dean of the faculty and associate professor of sociology at Skidmore College. His research and teaching interest include stratification, labor history, and sociology of religion. He is currently studying communism and anticommunism in the American labor movement during the cold war era, focusing on the United Electrical Workers.

Ralph Peters is professor of sociology and history at Floyd College. His interests focus on historical sociology, social theory, U.S. history, and labor history.

Index

255

types of, 45–48, 196; and unionization, 190, 192, 194–96. *See also* black
strikebreakers; immigration; sojourners; strikebreaking
miners' formula, 5, 7, 107, 153, 193–95,
197–98; and NMU, 118, 195; and
SWOC, 137, 140; and UAW, 150,
153; and UMW, 107, 118, 124–26
Mitchell, George, 163
Mitchell, John, 93
Murray, Philip, 111, 165–66

NAACP, 6–7, 121, 125, 145, 148–49,
151–52
National Civic Federation (NCF), 93
National Committee for Organizing
Iron, Steel, and Tin Workers (National
Committee), 99–101, 105–06
National Industrial Recovery Act
(NIRA), 6, 41, 121–33 *passim*
National Labor Relations Act (NLRA).
See Wagner Act
National Labor Relations Board, 149–
50, 177, 182
National Miners Union (NMU), 5, 7,
117–21, 195; and miners' formula,
118, 195
National Negro Congress, 148, 151
National Textile Workers Union
(NTWU), 160
New Deal. *See* Coal Code; Depression;
National Industrial Recovery Act;
Roosevelt, Franklin D.; Steel Code;
Wagner Act

Olson, Mancur, 29–31
Olzak, Susan, 23–25

Panhandle War, 116–17
paternalism, 26–29, 33, 209–10; and
company unions, 128, 132, 140; at
Ford Motor Company, 142, 147–48,
152–53, 191, 194; and interracial
solidarity, 190–92, 194–96; in
Kannapolis, 180–81; in mill towns,
157–59; and racism, 163, 169–72, 180;

rationality of, 186–87; and religion,
175–76; and repression, 172–75
passim; and split labor market theory,
28–29, 42–43
Pittsburgh, Pennsylvania, 81, 129; blacks,
53, 88, 96–97, 119; steel, 87–89, 96–
102 *passim*, 112, 115–16, 123, 131–35
passim
political process theory, 20, 23, 31, 33, 44

Qualitative Comparative Analysis
(QCA), 15, 200; explained, 202–03;
results summarized, 218

racial competition theory, 5–6, 13, 16,
19–20, 24, 43, 189
Ragin, Charles C., 211
Randolph, A. Philip, 146
rational choice theory, 29
Red Scare, 97, 107, 109
reserve army, 6, 11
resource mobilization theory, 20, 24, 31
Reuther, Walter, 144
Roosevelt, Franklin D., 6, 121–23, 127,
130, 132–33, 148

sanctions: and collective action, 31–32,
34; and game theory, 14–15, 35–39
passim
Sheffield, Horace, 142–43, 149, 151
Skocpol, Theda, 15
sojourners, 3n1, 23n4, 45–51, 57; blacks
as, 51, 52–55, 86, 101–06 *passim*;
Chinese as, 8, 10, 16, 49–50, 55, 61,
70, 81; European immigrants as, 55;
and game theory, 34n12; and split
labor market theory, 4, 21–22, 24,
28–33 *passim*, 41, 58; and temporary
workers, 58–59; whites as, 158, 186.
See also immigration; migration
Southern Organizing Committee
(SOC), 156, 184
split labor market theory, 3–5, 13–15,
20–24, 32–33, 38–44, 193–96; and
game theory, 33–34, 38–39; and
migration, 45, 101; and paternalism,